Robyn Moreno is a writer/editor born in San Antonio, Texas. She is a former editor at *Latina* magazine. She coauthored a fashion book, *Suave: The Latin Male* (Universe, 2001), and has written for *Woman's Day*, *In Style* and *Glamour*, among other national publications.

Michelle Herrera Mulligan is a writer originally from Chicago, Illinois. She's published articles in *Time*, *Publishers Weekly*, and *Teen People* magazines, among many others. She was an associate articles editor at *Latina* and coordinated a special issue of *Time Latin America* focusing on young Mexican leaders. She is currently working on her first novel.

They both live in Brooklyn, New York.

BORDER-LiNE
personalities

BORDER-LiNE
personalities

A New Generation
of Latinas Dish
on Sex, Sass, and
Cultural Shifting

EDITED BY

Robyn Moreno and
Michelle Herrera Mulligan

HARPER

NEW YORK · LONDON · TORONTO · SYDNEY

HARPER

Some of the names of the individuals referred to in these essays have been changed to protect their privacy.

HarperCollins books may be purchased for educational, business, or sales promotional use. For information, please write: Special Markets Department, HarperCollins Publishers Inc., 10 East 53rd Street, New York, NY 10022.

Grateful acknowledgment is made for permission to reprint from "There But for the Grace of God Go I" by Kevin Nance and August Darnell © 1979 NANCE SONGS/PERENNIAL AUGUST MUSIC.

FIRST EDITION

DESIGNED BY DANCING BEARS DESIGN

Printed on acid-free paper

Library of Congress Cataloging-in-Publication Data

Border-line personalities : a new generation of Latinas dish on sex, sass, and cultural shifting / edited by Michelle Herrera Mulligan & Robyn Moreno.—1st ed.
    p. cm.
  ISBN 0-06-058076-3 (alk. paper)
  1. Hispanic American women—Social conditions. 2. Young women—United States—Social conditions. 3. Hispanic Americans—Ethnic identity. 4. Hispanic Americans—Social conditions. 5. Intergenerational relations—United States.
  6. Hispanic American women—Biography. 7. Young women—United States—Biography. 8. United States—Ethnic relations.
  I. Herrera Mulligan, Michelle   II. Moreno, Robyn
  E184.S75B675   2004
  305.48'868073—dc22   2004046720

11 12 13 14 15   DIX/RRD   10 9 8 7

To my mother, Alicia Herrera Granados,
who taught me I have the strength to
achieve, even when I don't know it.

—Michelle Herrera Mulligan

To my mother, Yvonne Vela Guzman,
whose strength and enduring hope
has taught me that anything
is possible.

—Robyn Moreno

A borderline is a vague
and undetermined place,
created by the emotional
residue of an unnatural boundary.
It is in a constant state of transition.

—Gloria Anzaldua,
La Frontera/Borderlands

CONTENTS

FOREWORD BY JULIA ALVAREZ   xiii

INTRODUCTION BY ROBYN MORENO AND
    MICHELLE HERRERA MULLIGAN   xxiii

I. "ME AND MY FAMILY . . ."

"*A Picture of Us*" BY ROBYN MORENO   3

"*Just Us Girls*" BY MICHELLE HERRERA MULLIGAN   15

"*Esos No Sirven*" BY DAISY HERNÁNDEZ   27

"*Your Name Is Sandoval*" BY LYNDA SANDOVAL   46

"*Balancing Act*" BY LAURA TRUJILLO   61

II. "AND AFTER WE KISSED . . ."

"*On the Verge*" BY ANGIE CRUZ   75

"*The First Wife*" BY SHIRLEY VELÁSQUEZ   86

"*Straddling Desire*" BY ADRIANA LÓPEZ   99

"*Ain't Dishin'* " BY MARIA HINOJOSA   118

"*Stumbling Toward Ecstasy*" BY LETISHA MARRERO   131

CONTENTS

III. "Am I or Aren't I . . ."

"American Girl" by Lorenza Muñoz   155

"Se Habla Español" by Tanya Barrientos   167

"Elián: A Love Story" by Gigi Anders   175

"Pilgrim" by Carina Chocano   188

"You're Half Spanish, Right?" by Nancy Ayala   194

"Getting It Straight" by Carmen R. Wong   205

IV. "When I Grow Up . . ."

"Conversations with Jesus" by Carolina Buia   227

"J.'s True Hollywood Story" by Jackie Guerra   243

"I Get Up to Work" by Cecilia Ballí   257

"Chessin' " by Nelly Rosario   271

Contributors   291

Acknowledgments   297

FOREWORD

by Julia Alvarez

¿Qué Dice la Juventud?

Reading this collection of sassy, hard-hitting, and soulful essays by young Latinas returned me to my own young years. At family gatherings, Mami and Papi, los abuelos, las tías and los tíos—in short, los viejos—would all sit together at the big table or en la sala, and we, the younger members of la familia, would be off at our own table or in little groupings in the bedrooms. When los viejos got tired of each other and the same old, same old, one of them would invariably wander over and say, "¿Y qué dice la juventud?"

What does the youth have to say for itself?

This was the cue to shut our mouths, close down the gossip mill, cut eyes at each other, and smile inanely at the uncle or aunt who had asked the stupid question. "Nada, tío." "Nothing, tía." Often, the question's silliness sparked somebody's funny bone, and one or another would burst into giggles, which, like a lit fuse, would set off the whole juventud into hilarious laughter.

"It's nothing, de verdad, just that the way you ask . . ." More laughter.

"Stop that pavería!" Mami would call from the table.

Meanwhile, the questioner would eye us, looking for the

weak link who might confess. She knew something was up. But she didn't know how to get in on our intimidades. She didn't know the magic open sesame phrase that would open us up to her curiosity. She hadn't asked the right question.

Bueno. We got lucky here. It seems Robyn Moreno and Michelle Herrera Mulligan, the editors of this collection, asked the twenty Latinas represented here the right question. Or, rather, the right *questions* about being Latina in the twenty-first century. The result is a rich assortment of answers and comeback questions. And for that we should all be very glad indeed.

¿Qué dice la juventud? What was wrong with that old question? Well, for one thing, la juventud implied that the gathering of primos, primas, and amistades present could all fit under the rubric la juventud. We, young people, ranged in age from toddlers to teenagers; we were male and female; we included rich primos along with those on the up and up (like my family), and the primos from la parte de la familia que nunca echo pa'lante (whose mami was single y el papá no sirve pa' na; whose papi was alcoholic or in one case "un comunista," giving away his housepainter earnings to el partido); we were different races, the rubias y trigueñitas and the ones openly called "negrita" or "negrito" (man, how did we all get away with that!). Most of us had been raised Catholic, true, but the older ones of us were lapsed or lapsing, embracing instead that rousing, rock-and-rolling spirituality of the sixties in which La Virgencita had morphed into Lucy in the Sky with Diamonds. ¿Qué dice la juventud? Por favor, how could we all have one thing to say about anything at all under the sun!

Besides, we knew instinctively that the older folk didn't really want to hear what we had to say. In fact, every one of us girls would have been grounded until the day we were married if we had fessed up to what we were doing with and discovering about our bodies. Los viejos just wanted to hear the old verities recited back to them. Los viejos were a drag on our fast-forward into our American liberated lives. (On our part, we blindly banded them together as one homogenous policing unit, except for the wild soltera tía winking at us in the background or the enabling gallivanting tío giving us a thumbs-up.) They wanted to know they had raised us right, good girls who kept our legs together and our mouths shut; hombrecitos who never cried, machos in the making, but butter in Mami's hands, and so on. Old and young had to hunker together as a familia and comunidad, especially after we arrived in crazy gringolandia. We had to band together against them, los gringos, who wanted to kick our spic butts out!

Those days are over. Our spic butts might not be totally welcomed and our opportunity techo might still be several feet below the mainstream glass ceiling, especially if we're the darker or poorer variety of Latina, but all in all, things have changed. And though the post-sixties, disillusioned Scrooge in me doesn't want to give a resounding thumbs-up (what with another Vietnam now brewing in Iraq; didn't we learn any better?!), I'd say things have changed for the better. We—if we still want to use a plural pronoun for all the we's we have become—now are the majority minority, which means we have numbers and leverage (no wonder all the presidential candidates are brushing up on their español), and these reversals and these times challenge us to ask new questions and to revive the old ones in order to give new answers. Do we stick together, a collective we against them? Was there ever really a we, any more than there ever was la juventud to deliver to the old members of the family the news on what we were thinking?

What endeared me to this collection, among other things, is that these young Latinas are daring to ask these questions. The hard ones that we of the previous generation were afraid to ask when we were their age, not out of modesty, as was the case with our mothers (abuelas to these young women), but out of fear to be breaking ranks when there was so much ground to be won; or, simply, out of ignorance, yes, because we didn't have the vocabulary of experience. We weren't yet identified as a population so that we could begin to ask whether we wanted to be rounded up into one checked square in a census questionnaire. We hadn't grown up and raised daughters for whom these questions would come with their mother's milk (and indigestion!). These muchachas honed themselves on our stupidity and our brilliance, our ignorance and our wisdom, our activism and our disillusionment. And now it's their turn, and we hear from them about their struggles in their familias of origin and in the ones they are creating; in their love lives; in their work lives; in their inner lives. What does this legacy of being Latinas entail? How does it play out in their families, in their bedrooms, in the office, on the writing pad and computer screen, in their hearts and souls, and even on the chessboard?

These wise, funny, very smart, and passionate young women are speaking up. In fact, if I were to single out the single most important change in this new generation, it is that these mujeres are talking, and how. They're confiando and fessing up, and that feels like the strongest bond, what creates a true community, one that doesn't leave out the thorny question or answer we don't want to think about.

In fact, the range of concerns addressed in a rich variety of styles bespeaks the open and inclusive spirit of this collection (another thing that endeared me to it). The Latinas here represent different races and mixtures thereof; they come from different professions, different class backgrounds and political orientations. They embrace different traditions, exhibit spiritual and nonspiritual inclinations. Within the qualifier of "young," we also hear from Latinas of different ages, some mas maduritas and others still hot off the university and original nuclear family press. Native-born or immigrant, each Latina here is her very own mixture of hyphens: Dominican-American, Mexican-American, Colombian-American, Peruvian-American, Venezuelan-American, Nicaraguan-American, Guatemalan-American. There are even triple combinations: Colombian-Cuban-American, and Chinese (or so she thought!)-Dominican-American. Appropriately, the collection is named *Border-line Personalities*.

Yes, these mujeres are rethinking that word, "border," and redrawing the lines. They look back, as Robyn Moreno does in her honest and funny and ay! painful essay, "A Picture of Us," to try to figure out how they fit in the picture of where they came from. What do they do with the models they were given by their mamis and tías, Michelle Herrera Mulligan asks in "Just Us Girls." Laura Trujillo asks the same questions in "Balancing Act" from the point of view of a working mother. How to affirm the traditional values of familia while at the same time balancing a hectic and challenging career? She offers us a picture of modern motherhood: all the young mothers at work sitting in the mothers' lounge pumping breast milk while editing stories and proofreading spreadsheets! Daisy Hernández also makes us laugh in "Esos No Sirven" as she reels out that litany of chismes about the different flavors of Latino men, all of them worthless, and delivers a kind of comeuppance when she reveals that, in fact, she did follow Mami's advice and prefers female love. And though Lynda Sandoval might appear to agree about the worthlessness of men in her essay, "Your Name Is Sandoval," the process of portraying her alcoholic father offers new insights into what it means to be part Sandoval, part Lynda (from her mother's Scottish/Irish/Swedish heritage), and her very own whole, integrated self.

Speaking of men, bueno, these women don't hold back. (Man, oh man, where's my fan!) I'm grateful for the insights and the honesty. In "On the Verge," Angie Cruz speaks to us from a blackout in New York City, a scary post-9/11 moment that becomes a symbolic blackout in her own heart. Torn between finding comfort from an ex-lover downtown or Mami and tradition uptown in "the comfort zone of the 'hood," she understands the impulses that have been governing her life. The blackout lights up the terror and turmoil in her own heart. Shirley Velásquez's essay "The First Wife" gives us a painful and courageous depiction of the debasement she was willing to undergo in a philandering relationship. How we all sell ourselves short. Both Adriana López in "Straddling Desire" and Letisha Marrero in "Stumbling Toward Ecstasy" address that old stereotype of the Latina seductress and the companion stereotype of the good-girl sor-juanish intellectual. Where does our desire lie? How to balance recklessness and restraint, body and soul. How to embrace our bodies or, as Letisha Marrero so beautifully coins it, royal Ricanness. How also to consider silence regarding sex as a form of self-respect, a way of not selling ourselves short, as Maria Hinojosa rightly reminds us in "Ain't Dishin'."

Which, of course, leads to the big question that underlies this whole collection: "Am I or aren't I?" How do these young women understand their Latina-ness? Where do they draw the lines that define who they are? Whether they go back to where they came from as Lorenza Muñoz does in "American Girl," only to find out they don't fit in anymore, or whether they find a wall coming up between themselves and their Latina-ness because they are "Spanish challenged," as Tanya Barrientos bravely confesses in "Se Habla Español," the question remains of how they should define themselves. The voices represented here don't come up with set answers, borders that are indelibly and rigidly defined, and that, I believe, is their strength. They come to realize that like any relationship, theirs with Latina-ness is a changing landscape, a border that is fluid, like the shoreline on the beach, in and out, high tide, low tide. As Nancy Ayala wisely states in "You're Half Spanish, Right?" we are all on a lifelong journey of discovery about who we are. As we address national issues with significant others as Gigi Anders does in "Elián: A Love Story," or struggle to define our own nationality, as Carina Chocano does in "Pilgrim," the point is to address them, to stand up and deliver, and to draw that temporary border that becomes a meeting place. Indeed, Carmen Wong invites and challenges us to join in this journey of self-definition together: "I am an American, I am a Latina. With a splash of Chinese and a dash of Italian. A mishmash and hodgepodge of conundrums and contradictions. Like it. Accept it. Deal with it. I have. And I'm still trying."

These women have come into their own. And in the final section, titled "When I Grow Up . . . ," we hear the wise viejitas in them talk about the wisdom they've gained and the livelihoods they have embraced. In "Conversations with Jesus," Carolina Buia addresses that dream many of us Catholic girls grew up with of becoming saints. How many of us girls didn't want to have Santa before our names instead of Señora

or Mrs.? Where else did we encounter powerful, brave, beautiful, activist women but among the pantheon of saints? While
Carolina Buia looks to her Catholic upbringing for insight,
Jackie Guerra looks to Hollywood and the stereotypes she has
encountered as a Latina actress in "J.'s True Hollywood Story."
Often told that the door is closed, she quips: "Never say that to
someone whose last name is *Guerra*." Indeed, her persistence
won her a part on the set of *Selena*, a rousing experience she
shares with us. Cecilia Ballí, on the other hand, presents us
with a moment in her writing life that called not for the warrior
woman or writing woman but for the daughter trying to understand her mother's need for privacy. In "I Get Up to Work," she
deals with that issue all writers face: how to present the truth of
our experience while respecting the privacy of family and
friends. Nelly Rosario chooses a different arena, the three-
thousand-year-old game of chess, to talk about the lessons she
has learned in life. With flashes of heart-deepening wisdom,
she checkmated my heart.

"How expressively oppressive the oppressed can be," she
notes at one point, and I reached for my journal to write down
that memorable insight. "My worst tries, I've learned, can be
when I am trying." In chess as in life, she concludes, "you certainly don't win with the queen hiding in the back line."

And queens they are, if by queens we mean strong and
beautiful mujeres, brave enough to know themselves and
courageous enough to speak up. There they stand, twenty of
our very own, at the front lines of who they are and what they
believe in.

How did they get to be so wise and beautiful and brave so
soon?!

I am reminded of a Native American story about an old

woman who after many years of reaching up finally touches the sky. Father Sky asks, "How did you get to be so tall?" And she replies, "I am standing on a lot of shoulders."

Yes, this juventud came out of our loins and stood on our shoulders and gained from our struggles. But what I came to realize listening to their thoughtful, passionate, smart, and sassy voices is that la lucha continues, that each new generation has to reinvent not just itself but its selves, that along with that old Latin American tradition of giving testimony comes what Paulo Freire described as auto-criticism, of looking at our selves and our communities and reinvigorating them with new names, drawing new lines that are borderlines and seams of connection and lines of print in books such as this one.

INTRODUCTION

by Robyn Moreno and
Michelle Herrera Mulligan

A NOTE FROM ROBYN MORENO

Growing up in a city like San Antonio, where Mexicans are the majority, was completely normal for me. It wasn't until I went away to college in Austin, only ninety miles north, that I realized it was in fact an anomaly. My friends and I joked that Austin was where the rest of the country really began. Everything below was actually Mexico. My sense of the real word became even more complicated when I moved to New York and got a job at *Latina* magazine. There, for the first time in my life, I came into contact with Latinos I didn't even know existed: Cubans, Dominicans, Puerto Ricans, Colombians, Chileans; some were even black.

Even though some of us had little in common, all were still familiar to me. As American-born Latinas, we had a shared experience. And at the magazine, we had a shared purpose. I zealously embraced my new, broader definition of Latina. I started listening to salsa music and eating tostones, pupusas, and pernil. I enthusiastically rolled my r's on my phone message at work. Essentially, I went overboard.

After two years, I left *Latina* to work for more mainstream publications. I was excited about having a greater audience to reach, and I knew I had to be successful in a broader way. The only problem was that the more successful I became, the fewer Latinos I saw by my side. And, as often the only minority or one of a handful of minorities, to my bosses and colleagues I began to represent all Latino life. Once, during a stint as an editor at a fashion magazine, my colleagues and I were pondering celebrity models to use for a "global fashion" spread, when someone suggested Mia Maestro, an Argentine actress. My boss asked me pointedly, "Robyn, what do you think?" I was somehow the "expert" on all things Latin, from Andalucía to Venezuela. I had seen the actress once in an acclaimed movie called *Tango*, but I had fallen asleep halfway through. I said she was perfect. In my personal life, too, I found myself encountering certain stereotypes. To most of my Latina friends, I'm not Latin enough, so I play up my gringa-Latina role by not speaking Spanish; my indifference ensures that my Spanish will never improve past slightly above mediocre. To my French boyfriend and our European friends, I'm Salma Hayek–ish. One year I had a Cinco de Mayo party, and, walking around dressed like Frida Kahlo, serving quesadillas (I tried to pass them off as "gourmet" Mexican food), I felt like I was putting on a show. A role that I created myself. And a role that doesn't really fit. I'm thirty years old, on the verge of marriage, motherhood, and everything else being an adult entails. My identity seems more important than ever. What I pick up from Latino culture and what I leave behind, as well as what values I choose to pass on to my children, are important factors in creating my own cultural self. I wanted to hear about other people's struggles. This was how I began.

A NOTE FROM
MICHELLE HERRERA MULLIGAN

One day, about a year ago, my mother said to me, "You are not a Latina." That afternoon we'd been at my grandmother's house in the Little Village neighborhood of Chicago for a visit. My mother delivered the words bluntly and calmly, as if she were dealing with a wayward child. "I don't know what you are talking about," I yelled. "I was exhausted today, and I still went all the way over there! I didn't say anything!"

My head pulsed with rage as I thought of the trip to the South Side from the northwestern suburbs where my mother lives. I pictured the hour-and-a-half drive, the corn-on-the-cob vendors rolling their carts outside my grandmother's cramped apartment, the ubiquitous shops crammed with frilly first-communion dresses. "Exactly," my mother snapped. "You'll work for all those magazines, speak in Spanish when you have to, but you don't really consider yourself one of us. When we get together, you have nothing to say." I imagined my grandmother's dinner table, surrounded by women talking about babies, telenovelas, and tamale recipes. My mother was right. I was related to these women, but that day I felt no connection, outside of the familial, to any of them. I thought to myself, "If this is what being Latina means, I guess I'm not one."

The weeks that followed I was sad and dragging, my mind always wandering back to that conversation. Though I had turned my nose up at tacos and banda music in high school, in college I had learned Mexican culture meant so much more. I'd embraced my "Hispanic side," even though I lived in mid-

Missouri at the time. I'd been through the rallies, the militancy, the slow settling-down effect of accepting my roots. I'd lived in Mexico and learned Spanish, and in my postcollege years, I'd made Latino friends and worked for Latin-oriented publications. Even though I'm half white, I thought I'd bridged the gap between my mother and me. If I didn't fit into her world, where did I belong?

I turned to my brother Rick, who is pursuing a Ph.D. in clinical psychology, for answers. "We're always going to be different," he said. "We're used to navigating different worlds, and we'll never have a place that's truly our own." He was referring to the fact that our last name was Mulligan, but in our household most of the family spoke Spanish. That we grew up (way) lower middle class, yet attended high school and college with rich people. That we didn't really look racially 100 percent anything. Rick was studying in a mostly white environment and seemed to have a resigned tiredness to his voice. "We'll never totally identify with anyone." I had always relied on Rick for conventional wisdom, but in my heart I knew he was wrong. I imagined the millions of racially mixed people born in this country, the Latinos who are born every day, those that will be born in the future.

I knew there were thousands of us who can't speak Spanish or dance well to salsa music, who have never related to their parents' cultures yet still felt disconnected to the mainstream. Who still hadn't decided what culture we wanted to create, what we wanted to belong to. I knew this very thing bound us together. Somewhere, in the back of my mind, I had an idea.

As Hispanics living in the United States we have reached a pivotal moment. We will soon no longer be a minority. Our numbers continue to grow, and this country is embracing our culture in innumerable ways. The opportunities we've capitalized on and strides we've taken have permanently transformed the experiences we have as Latino Americans. Yet as we become more educated and economically successful, we find ourselves splintering into thousands of economic and cultural subgroups (suburbanite soccer moms, migrant day workers, rapidly rising executives). On top of our already multiple ethnic subgroups, it's getting harder and harder to discover a link that binds us together. Yet we are all collectively referred to by the media, and increasingly by each other, as Latinas.

But do we really all fit under the same cultural umbrella? When we started talking about this book, we began a long series of conversations, hours-long talks with colleagues, friends, and family members about what the word "Latina" means. These talks, often over drinks or late-night phone conversations, made us realize that we were not alone in our cultural confusion. "None of my friends are Latinos," they confessed in hushed tones. "I can't really relate." Many admitted to their own racial and gender stereotypes: "I would never date a Latino, I just haven't met any as educated as I am."

Women who identified themselves as proud "Latinas" devoted to their families found themselves questioning the very nature of the word. Women who were leaders in the office and independent in every way talked about their difficulties reconciling their family ties. A Mexican-American colleague described re-creating, perfectly, a single girl's apartment when her mother came to visit—despite the fact that she'd lived with her boyfriend for five years. Another discussed her secret shame that so many Latinos haven't advanced further. She's edited newspapers and magazines for more than ten years, and described having mixed feelings when a colleague asked how to tell her gardener in Spanish not to overtrim the bushes. Instead of feeling angry at the racism this implied, she was accommodating, thinking carefully about what the best way to translate would be. She commented, "It wasn't that she asked me to help her to translate that upset me later; it was that I could still be compared to him. It made me almost angry at him for still being poor, and I hated what that implied about me."

What if you earn over $50,000 a year and don't speak Spanish in the home? What if you don't even consider yourself "Latina"? We realized that with the myriad choices we face today, identity goes way beyond race, especially in our complicated reality. Now more than ever, young women living in the United States live on so many borders. Do I want kids? If I do, will I still pursue my career with the same intensity? What if I want to stay home? What if being a stay-at-home mom isn't enough for me? Do I still believe in marriage? Monogamy? Am I a spiritual person? Buddhism or Catholicism? We put the call out to Latina friends, colleagues, and acquaintances, asking for their defining stories. The contributors to this collection share their doubts about their troubled relationships, managing their hectic lives, and considering their ethnic identity. They address questions such as: "Can we really relate to Jennifer Lopez?" "Can we still pursue our dreams, live with boyfriends, embrace alternative lifestyles, and hold on to our family's values?" "What is a Latina anyway, and do I want to be one?" After reaching out to over a hundred colleagues and friends, we selected the essays that best represented the conflicts we have in defining ourselves every day. After reviewing them, we realized they appropriately represented the four defining moments in a woman's life: experiencing childhood, falling in love, finding yourself, and choosing your calling. We coaxed, cajoled, and overanalyzed with our writers until we found the kernels of truth that bore these honest confessions. After hearing these stories, we realized this book is really about conflict. We are sexually experimental, sassy, and critical of our families and our heritage. Yet we're deeply conflicted about what that says about us and who we are. The constant state of confusion, angst, and anger brought on by our mamis' values, our bosses' demands, and our personal passions inspired *Border-Line Personalities*. The title evokes the many borders we live on as Latinas: the border between our families' cultures and North American ideals; the border between our work and home lives; the border between our dreams and desires and the daily compromises we make.

In the "Me and My Family . . ." section, the writers dish on secrets and revelations about their families they've been too ashamed to say aloud. In "Esos No Sirven," reporter Daisy Hernández recalls her mother's admonition that most Latino men are worth nothing, from her own dad and uncles to the boys she wanted to date. Daisy eventually agrees with her mother that men don't work for her, and shares why she decides to choose women instead. In another compelling essay, novelist Lynda Sandoval discusses her father's alcoholism in "Your Name Is Sandoval," and how years after his death she discovered her own addictive personality. The writer's voices range from introspective to bewildered, as fashion editor Laura Trujillo displays in "Balancing Act," her contemplation about juggling three kids and a full-time career while trying to maintain a healthy marriage and define personal fulfillment.

Our second section, "And After We Kissed . . . ," describes discovering our sexuality and how we so easily lose ourselves in relationships. While writer Letisha Marrero details her numerous affairs with unsuitable men and how she eventually learned to be in a long-term relationship in "Stumbling Toward Ecstasy," editor Adriana López divulges how she came to terms with the fact that she could no longer be monogamous. Other writers explore the thorny decision of when to commit and when to be alone.

In "The First Wife," writer Shirley Velásquez recounts her seven-year relationship with a philandering man, while novelist Angie Cruz describes how she came to peace with being alone in the midst of the New York City blackout in "On the Verge." One writer, CNN's Maria Hinojosa, opted not to confess in her essay, "Ain't Dishin'." Instead, Hinojosa shares her struggle with sexual shame, and how she ultimately chose to preserve her privacy with a new kind of silence.

The writers ponder being Latina and what it means for them in our third section, "Am I or Aren't I . . . ?" In this section, they display a compelling anger, one that rages when a stranger expects something from them the minute they hear their last names. Los Angeles staff writer Lorenza Muñoz opens the section with her painful story of leaving her native country behind, along with her Olympic dreams. In Nancy Ayala's "You're Half Spanish, Right?" she writes about being embarrassed at her illegal immigrant uncle and reconciling her own Hispanic identity. Journalist Carmen Wong addresses this issue in another way when she writes about discovering her true ethnic background, which had been hidden from her since childhood. Writer Gigi Anders gives a humorous and honest account of being on both sides of the Elián Gonzalez crisis; while reporter Tania Barrientos describes coming to terms with her lack of Spanish-speaking skills. In another take, *Los Ange-*

les Times television critic Carina Chocano recalls longing for nationality in cities around the world in "Pilgrim."

Our last section, "When I Grow Up . . . ," reflects the important choices women make that define their lives. *Celebrity Justice* correspondent Carolina Buia remembers her childhood obsession with sainthood as she explores her present-day search for spirituality. In "J.'s True Hollywood Story," actress Jackie Guerra discusses the reality of being a full-figured Latina actress in Hollywood and why she still chooses that profession. Investigative reporter Cecilia Ballí muses on her career choices and how they have alienated her from her family and upbringing. "Chessin' " is Nelly Rosario's triumphant piece on discovering her strength as a woman, as told through her love for chess.

For many of our contributors this process was a revelation. In these twenty essays, they divulge decisions and aspects of their life that many had never faced before. They cried, struggled, and often threatened to drop the project altogether. For those that stuck with the writing process, it seemed to permanently change their conceptions of themselves. As editor Adriana López put it, "I've been through years of therapy and nothing's made things clearer than writing this essay." Most of all, putting this collection together made us contend with the pathology of being Latina. We realized that ultimately, it is up to us to decide that we are Latina, to individually determine what the term means. We grappled with the implications of this on our greater culture, and argued about the word's ability to entirely define us. At the end of this process, we realized that no matter how loaded, conflicted, and difficult the term may be, we are Latinas. Through heritage and by choice.

I

"Me and My Family . . ."

A PICTURE OF US

BY ROBYN MORENO

I'm not sure exactly whose idea it was to celebrate my mom's fifty-fifth birthday at Graceland. But somehow I found myself standing in front of Elvis's rather modest mansion with a candle in my hand, along with my family and the thousands of other lunatics who had come to pay homage to the King. After three hours of worship, I was fantasizing about fried peanut-butter-and-banana sandwiches when my older sister, Nevia, snapped me out of my reverie. She asked me to take her picture with a suspiciously effeminate Elvis impersonator. Like a true king, he grabbed her by the waist and started serenading "Love Me Tender." Her squeals of delight caught the attention of my other two sisters, Yvette and Bianca, who ran up and joined in the fun. After the impromptu performance, they cheered and clapped loudly. "Elvis" bowed his head humbly and mumbled a "Thank you, thank you very much." As they huddled into a photogenic position, I realized this particular Elvis had breasts. Hmmmm. Either no one noticed or, more likely, no one cared. As I peered through the camera at the three girls and the lesbian Elvis, I saw the truth. No matter which road I travel, all paths lead me back to my crazy family.

We weren't always lesbian Elvis worshippers. The second of four daughters, I had a pretty typical Mexican-American childhood in San Antonio, Texas, replete with dance classes, annual road trips to California, and even a pet goat. I was always thought of as the good daughter. At parties my mom was fond of boasting to friends and relatives about my straight A's and other achievements, as Nevia dug through my mom's purse to steal the car keys.

Nevia is six years older than I am, so while I was playing with dolls, she was toying with boys. My little sister Yvette is three years younger, and Bianca, the baby, is seven years younger. I've always thought we were spaced perfectly. Close enough to play together, but not so close as to suffer the horror of actually attending school simultaneously. We got along as could be expected. After school Nevia smoked cigarettes and hung out with her friends. Without her as our babysitter, I improvised, emceeing our eighties version of *American Idol*. (Yvette and Bianca were particularly fond of belting out ballads from Whitney Houston and Lisa Lisa and Cult Jam.)

If I was feeling particularly evil, I would inflict tickle torture on them, or give them nightmares by telling stories of La Llorona, a woman who drowned her kids, or La Chusa, a crazy devil bird that ate children. When I felt especially sisterly, we would scrounge the house for change and run to the corner store for dill pickles and chamoy.

Those carefree afternoons ended when I was thirteen. My dad was diagnosed with pancreatic cancer. I knew him as a hardworking man who barbecued every Sunday and took us to the park on his motorcycle. He had two degrees, in political science and biology, and in his day he was into "Brown Power" and the Chicano movement. My good grades put me in his good graces, and he enrolled us both in an evening computer course. Every Tuesday after work he would come home and change, and we would take off in his van to the local high school. We always stopped for a snack before, usually donuts and coffee (Coke for me), then attended the class, where I was the only kid. Having to always fight for attention with my three sisters, I truly treasured this time spent alone, this special attention he paid to me. I relished my role as a good girl.

At the end of my eighth-grade year, my father complained of stomach pains and was initially misdiagnosed with gallstones. When they operated to remove them, they discovered it was in fact a malignant pancreatic tumor. They informed him and my mom, who eventually told Nevia; they felt that, at nineteen, she was old enough to understand. Nothing was ever explained to me and my little sisters, but intuitively we knew. I would round the corner in my house to find my sister and dad embracing. On the way to school, my mom would cry in the car. My dad's religiously fanatic sisters would come over with a bizarre entourage, forming a prayer circle around his bed. We began to live in hospitals. Once, I was ordered to keep him company and, as I sat by his bed, we watched TV in silence. Bored and uncomfortable, I excused myself and climbed onto the roof from a waiting area window, where I read for the rest of the afternoon. When I came back my cousin was with him, so I went home. He told my mom not to bring me back. I was a worthless sitter. He died on Valentine's Day, ten months after being diagnosed. He was forty-seven.

It was a violent and unexpected departure in the framework of our family, and our lives would forever be characterized in terms of before and after. Before our father's death, we seemed to be a relatively normal family. After his death, we five girls (Mom included) were left alone, and we developed a serious dependence on each other that formed the basis of our relationship. To this day, I have spoken with either my mom or one of my sisters (or all of the above) every day of my life.

After the death, we moved, and I was transferred to a predominantly white school that seemed like 90210 to me. They had school-sponsored ski trips, huge pep rallies, and kids named Sunny and Tyler who drove BMWs. It was a huge change from the all-Mexican high school I just left.

I went from being vice-president of my old school's freshman class to eating lunch by myself. Eventually, I created a role for myself as a smart, well-mannered girl and eventually fit in by joining the debate club and dating a Jewish boy named Mitch. I wasn't the only one having a hard time adjusting. Since my father's death, Nevia had basically locked herself in her room with a stocked mini-refrigerator and a duffel bag full of drug paraphernalia. When she did crawl out of her cave, she or one of her druggy cohorts would inevitably embarrass me in front of my new friends.

My little sister Yvette, who was only about eleven or twelve, fell in with a bad crowd and ran away from home. She was not just a run-to-the-grocery-store-and-then-call-your-mom-to-come-get-you runaway, she was actually gone for two weeks. Of course I was concerned, but I was also super-embarrassed by the flyers that were posted everywhere. Her picture was even on the news. Classmates would ask, "Is that your sister posted at 7-Eleven?" To which I would reply with a sympathetic "No, but I hope they find that poor girl." During all this time my mom was occupied with a relationship she dove blindly into months after she lost her husband of twenty years.

Her rebound relationship lasted longer than we all thought it would, and Mac eventually became our stepdad. In my mother's disoriented emotional state, my baby sister Bianca was virtually ignored. At age seven she would make her own dinner, consisting of Top Ramen or the Domino's Pizza she had ordered with my mother's stolen and forged checks. Very little was ever mentioned of my dad. By the time I was nineteen, we had firmly chosen alcohol over therapy. When we got sad, we would drink tequila and listen to my dad's favorite songs. Things got pretty messy and resulted in a lot of fighting and sobbing. In a shining moment of our family history, we were actually the catalyst for an airline law to be instituted, which prohibits inebriated passengers from boarding planes. It all stemmed from a particularly rowdy night during a Christmas spent in Las Vegas. My mother had followed Mac there, who was pursuing his dream of becoming a Dean Martin impersonator. Yvette and Bianca lived with them, while Nevia and I stayed in Texas. Nevia booked a redeye return flight for herself, probably because it was cheaper, and we had the brilliant idea of partying until she boarded, so she could immediately pass out on the plane and sleep through the entire flight. We ended up drunk enough, all right, drinking "Blue Nile" cocktails in the lounge at the Luxor Hotel. By the time we took Nevia to the airport, we were so drunk we burst into the airport like a maniacal circus. We were smoking, laughing, and being all-around obnoxious. Yvette and I found a discarded wheelchair and she jumped in as I pushed her, running full speed down the corridor. We crashed into my mom as she was examining the monitor, trying to find Nevia's gate, and she started cursing at us while hitting Yvette with her purse. Shocked bystanders gasped at the crazy woman beating a disabled girl.

We carried our show to the gate, bumping into people and bullying our way to the front of the line, where passengers were already boarding. When it was Nevia's turn, the airline refused to allow her to board. The Indian in our blood and the tequila in our veins possessed us. Yvette threatened to kick the airline stewardess's ass, while I donned some fake glasses and pulled out a pen and paper demanding names. "I'm a lawyer!" I slurred, "I'm gonna own this airline!" I furiously jotted names, sneering, "James Smith, I hope you enjoy your last day at work! Well, Betsey with an *e* Roberts, good luck finding a new job!" (The next day I found the crumpled paper with incoherent scribble and quickly threw it away.) My mother tried to control us, but our lunacy was contagious, and she called the threatened stewardess an "old bitch." Dignity lost, my poor mom deserted us, and the police were called to escort us out. Nevia, who at this time was crying hysterically, told the airline officials she had no idea who we were and could she please board because she had to get home to her poor husband who was waiting for her, so they could spend their first Christmas together. She was eventually allowed on, and we cheered as we were led away, but our victory was short-lived, as a minute later Nevia made her way back from the plane, sobbing and humiliated. She had been voted off, *Survivor*-style, by her fellow passengers. Rejected and dejected, she returned the next morning, without us, and boarded meek as a mouse. After that debacle, we continued to have tequila-induced outbursts, but like aging rock stars, we began to outgrow our own ridiculous antics.

At age twenty-seven, Nevia had married a respectable, hardworking, and infinitely patient husband. They bought a beautiful house, a shih tzu, and a Lexus. It was like Joan Jett moving to the suburbs. She still has a penchant for bad eighties rock (like .38 Special and Krokus), fake nails, Regis and Kelly, and singing big-mouthed basses. I, after a little longer than the customary four years, finished college. I am still thought of as the smart one, although I am also regarded as airheaded, selfish, somewhat delusional, financially irresponsible, and codependent. I know this is what they think of me because we once played a game called "Five Things I Like About You," which quickly turned into "Five Things I Hate About You." I must admit they're probably onto something. Yvette got "knocked up" at sixteen, and I now have a ten-year-old nephew, Zachery. Sweet but odd, he's Mac's karaoke protégé, and often wears one glove, sunglasses, and Mardi Gras beads. (When asked about this ensemble, he'll coolly tell you this is what he's about right now.) My youngest sister, Bianca, got the hell out of San Antonio as fast as she could and moved to New York City. Tired of slacking in Austin, I quickly followed.

We immediately fell in love with New York and all its possibilities. We turned into full-fledged *Sex and the City* wannabes. She enrolled at the Fashion Institute of Technology, and I soon became employed at a popular fashion magazine. I felt I had hit the big time. I embraced the cool New York world of fashion shows, wine tastings, and super-cool boîtes with doormen and lists. We sampled the sample sales, and my sister became a British designer's apprentice. She started to hang with a too-cool Brit crowd and even affected a Madge accent. I, in turn, became a Francophile and fell in love with a handsome Frenchman with dimples. Never mind he was from Brittany, not Paris, and my wine knowledge exceeded his. My new role was New York "it" girl.

The farther away I got from my family and the less I saw of them, the more insane they seemed to me when we reunited. To my sister and me, from our cosmopolitan pedestals, they appeared brash and gauche. Our trips back home became increasingly strained. Our usual forms of amusement and bonding, like getting soused and singing karaoke, ceased to work. We weren't connecting anymore. I thought I was worldlier than ever and had outgrown them. For over a year, every time the family got together, a hysterical drama would unfold. I yelled at my sisters about their shitty lives. I chastised my mom for smoking or eating greasy tacos for breakfast. I criticized Nevia's dated wardrobe and hairstyle. I accused Yvette of being a bad mother. I felt like a defector.

Things came to a head on New Year's of 2002. My entire family came to visit from Texas, and I demanded that David, my boyfriend, hang out with us the whole night instead of attending the fete he really wanted to go to. We celebrated at my cousin's downtown restaurant, and things went smoothly until around two in the morning, when David got tired of clapping as my nephew Zach karaoked "New York, New York" for the fifteenth time, and my sisters kept insisting on yet another New Year's tequila toast. I lied and told him I didn't mind if he left us to go to his friend's party. I stayed to watch the Moreno New Year's Extravaganza and downed my own bottle of champagne.

The next morning we all went for brunch. Hungover and pissed, I tried to eat my omelette as Mac smoked, and my mom announced she wanted to visit the World Trade Center site again so she could buy some more morbid souvenirs. I sat there seething at my caricature of a family and my selfish boyfriend, whom I vengefully locked out and punched upon his late arrival. Nevia finally set me off when she asked, "What time did David come home last night?" Whether she had asked innocently or provokingly, it didn't matter. I had had it. "He wouldn't have wanted to leave if you guys were normal!" I screamed loud enough for tables to turn around. Their faces registered shock and hurt and something I mistook as remorse. In retrospect I now realize it was pity. They saw the real me that morning, without drinks and cleverness, hungover and tired. Not clothed in my usual role of "fun girl" or the more recent "pretentious bitch," I was left with my sadness.

I could not see that it was really me that was the caricature. I continued to pine for a distinguished family with a father who was a powerful lawyer and a mom who dressed impeccably as she gardened. I wanted a family I could bring a boy home to, with a nice house and a big dining room table, where after a four-course epicurean dinner, we would sip our port wine and talk politics or art. Instead, I went back to a house with every room painted a different color of the rainbow because "Oprah said color's in," and Mac keeping me up all night while he karaoked until the wee hours of the morning. (For Christmas one year he gave me a tape of him singing his favorite songs. He dedicated it "To Robyn with love.")

My superior attitude was soon dealt a tremendous blow when I was laid off from my power editor job and plunged into a late-twenties crisis. This was a tough time for all of us. Yvette became separated from a husband she never lived with because he was sent to Kuwait and then Iraq. Nevia was facing baby pressure, and even little Bianca lost her big job. I had always considered myself lucky, special even. The kind of person that makes things happen, that great things happen to. Losing my dream job left me unhinged.

This perceived failure opened the door for future failures. I began to listen to the voices of doubt that I had always confidently pushed aside. That year I bounced from freelance job to freelance job. Set loose from my role as a successful cosmopolitan chick, I was left directionless and scared.

My grandfather became very sick in May of that year and my mom thought it wise for Bianca and me to come home. I landed in San Antonio's very little international airport, and for the first time in a long time I was glad to be home. My aunts and cousins had flown in, too, and at my grandparents' house we talked and laughed, and I indulged in all the rich and comforting Mexican foods I had discarded. My grandfather, more than anything else, looked just plain exhausted. One afternoon, as he sat peacefully watching a boxing match, I was seized by the feeling that I wanted to know him. I sat next to him and began to bombard him with questions: "Grandpoo, when were your parents born?"; "When you met Grandmoo was it love at first sight?"; "Were you scared during the War?"; "Are you sad you never had a son?" He answered some questions disinterestedly, and the rest not at all. I sat there frustrated and desperate to learn something, to understand. A pet commercial came on, and quickly I said, "Grandpoo, what do you like better, cats or dogs?" He finally looked me straight in the eye, and said nothing. Embarrassed, I apologized for bugging him and asked if he wanted something to drink. Then I kissed him on the head, and as I went to get his water I realized that in my life many things would be left unsaid, and the rest I'd have to figure out on my own.

Eight months later, David and I broke up. He was "confused and needed space." Two months after that, I lost my job again. One snowy morning afterward, I sat in my apartment alone drinking coffee, feeling lonelier than I ever had in my life. I got up to refill my cup and paused at my fridge to look at a family picture we all had taken at Graceland. We looked really funny, wearing oversized matching Elvis sunglasses. And happy. I took a deep breath and exhaled. I was going to be okay.

My entire familia came to visit for my thirtieth birthday in June. We took over my cousin's restaurant (the same one from the New Year's hell the year before), and while I had a day of beauty, my sisters and mom decorated the place. When I walked in they had erected a tent (like a wedding nightmare, rain was forecast) and decked out the patio with banners, balloons, and even a piñata. I joked it was my double quinceañera. That night I had the best party of my life, and when I looked around I almost didn't recognize my sisters: Nevia, the loudmouth, sat very regally, charming all my friends; Yvette, the "problem child," was standing with her new serious beau, coolly surveying the scene. "When did she get her shit together?" I thought. Then there was Bianca, whose sarcasm and mean temperament made her the tyrant of the family, lovingly bringing me my cake. Has she always been this gentle? And my mom, after a lifetime of struggle, looked content and dignified. A respected matriarch? What happened to the girls I knew? And what about me? After seventeen successive years of boyfriends, I was alone . . . and kinda happy. Had we finally broken free from our life-long roles or had we been changing all along, and I was too busy or stubborn to notice? Maybe we just grew up.

The truth is that even now we're still adjusting, but that night I had a glimpse of our best selves. And so I hang that picture with the rest. While we may not always agree or live up to each other's expectations, the only constant is us, for better or worse.

This year for Christmas, instead of celebrating in San Antonio or New York, we've rented a condo in Taos, New Mexico. Never mind there'll be twelve in a house for eight. We're on our way. David's back in the picture, and he's coming, too. The Moreno show in New Mexico? I'm keeping my fingers crossed. But I know it's going to be fun.

JUST US GIRLS

BY MICHELLE
HERRERA MULLIGAN

I t happened on a routine visit back from New York. Things
had been strangely peaceful all week. My mother had re-
frained from the usual comments about my weight, hairstyle, and shoddy "libertina lifestyle." I even started to feel
at ease as my brothers and I settled in for a night of junk television. But then she came out of her bedroom carrying a black
off-the-shoulder sweater and shifted her eyes nervously as she
suggested we go to the mall for a little "Christmas shopping."

She asked me to try the sweater on. A surprise attack. I
turned to meet my brother's eye but he just looked away. I was
on my own this time.

"Why do you want me to wear this?"

"Just be quiet and put it on, I don't want to hear any of your
mouth."

"Mom."

"You'regoingtowearitbecausewe'retakingglamourshotsjust
usgirlstogetherandIneveraskyouforanythingandyoucando
thisonethingforme."

"No . . . but Mom . . . *Glamour Shots* . . . ," I said weakly,
slowly backing away. My brothers laughed in the background.
It seemed too absurd to be true. But it was settled.

The reality of where we were going didn't set in until we arrived and approached the "studio"—complete with the famous before and after shots—denim, teased-up hair, fake pearls, and all.

It was as if my mother wanted one last chance to immortalize my youth and vitality before obesity and ambivalence captured me for good. When we got to the mall, I felt confused, angry that she took me there, yet weirdly proud that she thought I looked good enough to be photographed.

I wasn't giving in so easily. I took one look at our "photographer's" feathered mullet and acid-wash jeans and exploded. After a brief yet heated argument, I set the terms:

No denim, no chiffon, no teased hair.

The photo guy flipped back his frosted hair and encouraged me to find my "inner hottie." I ignored him and turned away in disgust at first. I simply accepted my punishment with the little dignity I could muster given the "exotic locales" being arranged behind me. The regrettable outcome of this ordeal involves my mother and me in cheesy vaudeville "Judy and Liza" shots, and portraits of my mother in green chiffon and me in black lace. My brother says my piercing stare in the "intimate" portrait haunts him to this day.

Despite my loathing for physical exertion and women's fashion, my mother maintained an unfailing optimism that someday I would be the fit and attractive girly-girl she always longed to be. As a kid, I spent gymnastics class hiding with a book in the corner, with one arm lazily bent over my extended leg to simulate "stretching." My mother ignored this little hitch and enrolled me in every fitness/activities class she dreamed of attending as a child: tap dancing, aerobics, you name it. I even had a disconcerting stint as a Girl Scout in training. I was dismissed after the first day for refusing to make crafts the boys could use on an upcoming camping trip.

As a baby, I practiced my future calling as a wanton woman. I enjoyed traipsing through the house in plastic heels and diapers, and nothing more. While she pictured me pirouetting across imagined stages at four years old, I fantasized about drinking martinis during sloppy nights in bohemian neighborhoods. My mother had my ears pierced when I was six months old, had dresses made for me by the time I was two, and bought me every doll I desired by the time I was old enough to attend elementary school. By the time I turned five, she stuffed my legs into itchy pantyhose and sprayed my hair stiffer than a Jersey City hooker's for special occasions. I resented this, using every opportunity possible to turn her efforts on their head.

One day, when I was about nine years old, she brought a "surprise" home from the Mexican store. It was hanging, covered in plastic, on the back of her bedroom door. I surveyed it curiously, determined it had nothing to do with me. I then returned to my strict afternoon program regimen (*Diff'rent Strokes, The Facts of Life, Family Ties*). "Look what Mami brought for you from the store," she called out excitedly. I dragged myself up and sauntered into the room. She had pulled off the plastic to reveal a stiff, multilayered Pepto-Bismol-pink dress. I crinkled my nose and muttered, "What's *that* for?" My mother's face fell for a split second, then hardened into a familiar resolve. "This is the dress you're going to wear to the birthday party this Saturday, *y no empieces.*" After whining for a minute, I sulked back to the TV set. It was just beginning.

When Saturday came, I put on my favorite T-shirt and a pair of overalls, hoping that my mother would forget our conversation as she often did. She didn't. "Ponga ese vestido y no me digas nada!" She yelled. "I don't have time for your big mouth." After shedding tears of anger, I forced the scratchy, uncomfortable "Mexican torture dress" over my unwilling head, then wiggled into an equally distressing pair of white tights and Mary Janes. Now thoroughly miserable, I presented myself to my mother. Her eyes shone and she gave me what would become a rare compliment. "Mira que bonita es mi hijita." I paid her back by lifting my skirt every time the relatives pointed their ubiquitous cameras at me. But my attitude didn't matter. In her mind, my image was pretty and carefree, everything she wasn't at my age.

My mother was born in the late forties in a crime-ridden border town. My grandmother left her in charge of her five brothers and her sister at the age of twelve. She always dreamed of starring on television as a great singer and dancer, but instead of taking lessons after school, she spent her afternoons mopping up classrooms to support her siblings' education. She pictured being called up to an amphitheater stage, handpicked from the crowd to accompany pop star José José ("Esta noche una niña muy especial cantará con nosotros . . ."). Instead, she was the stuttering vagrant that everyone ridiculed in class and the role model her siblings looked up to. She spent her evenings making dolls out of the garbage that accumulated outside of concrete, makeshift homes. She begged for dimes on the bridge to make ends meet, yet she always dreamed of finding something beautiful. It seemed the more her grandmother, an intermittent adult presence, beat her with a hairbrush for vanity, the more she resolved to defy everyone's expectations. Each amateur beauty or talent competition was a step toward stardom. When she was old enough to find a job, she bought wigs from dime stores and practiced the latest dance moves with her brother or by herself, always glancing back as she turned before broken mirrors.

Then she had me. Her only daughter. (She assures me that, conceived in a time of marital stability, I was the only planned one.) I was born with a markedly pointed head, short, bony legs, and brown, wrinkled skin. (My father even threw out the newborn's Polaroid.) My idea of an afternoon's fun was playing quietly by myself, plotting against the kids down the street. I grew up to be a finicky, accident-prone girl, and I avoided both food and exercise. My family affectionately dubbed me "la flaca." "Don'play too rough with la flaca," my mother would cry. "She's deli-cat, se va a romper la pierna!" She seemed determined to protect me in the way her parents never did. At school I cowered from the girls that mocked me, and the boys that threw volleyballs at my head, but at home I was an aspiring bully who would silently scheme to crush all that opposed me, even if at times that would include her.

When it came to my "beauty," tensions seemed to approach a standoff between us after my parents' divorce. My father had custody for the first couple of years, and mornings were marked by awkwardness. On Sundays, she came over to help dress my brothers and me for church. Sometimes she would arrive late, in time to face clothes strewn over unmade beds, our aimless wandering, and a growing silence between her and my father. My father tied his tie and addressed her with friendly ambivalence. She responded with a painted-on smile, and my brothers and I would take turns distracting her, arguing and tormenting each other, if just to give her something to do. When they finally submitted themselves for inspection in crisp shirts and dress pants, I quietly hung back until the last minute, and hoped the image of people glaring as we shuffled into the back pews at Santa Monica Catholic Church would win the war for her attention over my faded blouse and slacks. One benefit of our custody arrangement, I believed, was my ability to choose my own clothes. But she was just saving me for last. While combing my little brother's hair, without glancing up, she stated her regulations in a clear, firm voice. "Take off those ugly things y ponte el vestido bonito que te compré. Do you wan' everyone to think yoor poor! And put on cream or something en la cara. You look like a cad-ah-ver." She'd dismiss my brothers and switch her attention to me, disappointed at my ineptitude. Then she would start pulling my hair into bobby pins, spreading bright pink blush on my cheeks until I felt as limp and clownish as a rag doll.

A year or so later, she won custody and moved back in with us. After her return, she seemed to slip away somehow, as if her physical presence allowed her some room to drift. When I wasn't ditching classes, helping to take care of my little brother, and generally flunking junior high, I devoted my energy to reeling her back in. I didn't balk when she suggested a layered perm, even when it involved a late-eighties, Debbie-Gibson-inspired bang cut. On the first day of the eighth grade, I wore a hot pink shirt and rose-printed jeans, parading around the house and asking my older brother if I "passed" the unspoken junior high inspection standards (to which he muttered, "You look fine," with a pronounced eye roll). My eighth-grade class seemed to disagree, and the year went as miserably as the previous one had. Most classes left me doodling in margins, staring blankly in response to my teacher's snide remarks. (Are you with us? Blank. Maybe you'd be more comfortable in hair-dressing class, with the rest of the "chicas" from your neighbor-hood. Blank). My mother was with a boyfriend I hated, she dressed seductively on weekends, and made out with him in cars. Conversations with her now ended bitterly: "You don't care about my life!" I would scream. "You don't care about mine," she would say. I started to drift, too.

The one good thing seemed to be my new job as a busgirl at a Mexican restaurant, where I worked with my mother. Deter-mined to make my mark in high school the next year, I decided my newfound wealth merited an opportunity to create my own sense of style. After a summer of racking up twenties, I went shopping and found the perfect skirt hanging on the wall of a trendy, independent shop at the local mall. It was multimedia, part white denim, with black and white ruffles on the bottom, cutting-edge, I thought, Cyndi Lauper–like. The perfect thing to assert stylish independence. The price tag read $60, an unheard-of extravagance at the time, but I had the money and I went for it. On the first day of school I proudly sashayed the halls of my new high school, taking the looks that followed me as compliments. Things seemed to go well until lunch rolled around; I'd registered too late and got stuck in with fourth pe-riod, the dreaded first shift destined for losers that eat between 11:00 AM and 12:00 PM, where none of my few friends would be caught dead.

My plan was to get my lunch to go and eat on the back stairs, exuding a solitary fabulousness. I got in a short line, and two pockmarked, gangly boys quickly slid behind me. They glanced at me sideways, then laughed and pushed at each other. I didn't look back at them. Instead, I nervously picked through the potato chips and stared at the specials of the day; I suddenly wished one of my friends were there to talk to. As if magically, one of the boys appeared just behind me; I could feel his breath in my ear. He reached his hand under my skirt and underwear and squeezed, whispering, "Nice skirt." Then he and his friend burst out laughing, and I walked out of the line and forgot about my lunch, holding back tears. When I arrived home that night, I stood in front of the full-length mirror to reevaluate my outfit. My image seemed mocking. I was a lurid, overstuffed doll, wearing a tight black T-shirt over garish ruffles, another version of the Pepto-pink dress. I did wear the skirt again once or twice, but the free feeling it gave me was gone.

Later that year, I began to embrace what Mother perceived were "puras locuras." I announced that I was trading in the few skirts and dresses I owned at the thrift store for a used pair of combat boots. And much to my mother's horror, it wasn't just a phase. Freed from the constraints of her marriage to my father and her relationship with her ex-boyfriend, she loved her new sense of freedom and femininity and couldn't understand why I concealed mine. She would spend hours preparing her makeup and outfits to go out salsa dancing on a Friday night. My brothers and I rated her clothing and assured her that her slinky off-the-shoulder tops and tight black skirts looked great, as a pounding merengue throbbed from our tiny stereo and she forced our unwilling bodies to dance with hers.

I, on the other hand, wore looser- and looser-fitting T-shirts in the hopes of hiding my recently acquired breasts. My new punk identity did wonders for me, freeing me to wear black, ditch gym class, and turn my back on my increasingly confused mother.

When I wasn't writing for the school newspaper, working as a hostess at the restaurant, or organizing several student activist groups, I'd plop on my friends' floors and pig out on junk food, with absolutely no thought of calories. During frequent arguments with her, she called me gitana, libertina, and jeuvona, hoping to shock me out of my rebellion. She modeled her sexy outfits and taunted me by saying she was the hot one, while I looked like an old lady in my lace-up Docs. But we both knew these conversations were in vain. No one called me la flaca anymore.

I got older, went away to school, and it began to appear that we couldn't be more different from each other. The more I learned about "the patriarchy and Latin America," the more I wrote off her superficial evaluations of my character. To my surprise, she cleverly found an advantage when I went abroad to study in Mexico for one year. She sensed my fear of the nose-in-the-air fresas (spoiled rich girls) that seemed to rule the roost on Spanish telenovelas. On one last-minute trip to the mall before I left, she detected my nervousness and pounced. "The geerls in Mexico aren't like they are here," she warned. "They expect you to be nice and arreglada, and you," she said, pausing to look me up and down for effect, "you might have troubles there." I pictured a clan of laughing blonde vixens mocking me in Spanish (Mira la pocha fea!), and soon I was buying enough sweater sets and preppy shirts to give Eddie Bauer an orgasm. (Of course, she took advantage of this time to "accidentally" donate all my old clothes to the Salvation Army, a tragedy I discovered when I returned the next summer.)

When I settled in Mexico, I found that Guadalajara had a lot of steep hills and unpredictable public transportation, so I found myself walking more than I had in my life. I lost about fifteen pounds and looked girlier and thinner than I ever had.

(By the way, I discovered that there were college kids with green hair there, too. Many of them became my friends.) One day, I was walking down the street in one of my seemingly endless supply of plaid skirts and long button-down vests with books in hand when I saw myself in a bank window. I looked just like the rich little fresa girls that I was afraid of. And it occurred to me that I resembled the girl my mother wanted to be. (In fact, she often refers nostalgically to that time whenever I'm particularly overweight or unfashionable: "Well, nothing's like the time when you lived in Mexico . . .")

When I came back to the United States, I promptly gained the weight back and reengaged my frumpy, alternative lifestyle. I moved to New York to work in magazines, where my hatred for all things related to fashion and fitness seemed to deepen ironically. The more the froufrou girls around seemed to obsess about their appearances, the more they resembled the fresas I'd left behind so many years ago. I resolved to resent them and live my fashion-minimal lifestyle as a form of protest. My weight started hitting unpredictable peaks and valleys; I seemed to yo-yo the same twenty pounds, hinging on my alternating spurts of alcohol abuse and gym obsessions. (Hey, you can't live in the fashion capital of the world and not let it affect you a little.) I felt reduced to an adolescent when I would see my mother during those times. She would purse her lips and look me up and down, sneaking in suggestions on how to improve my diet, listening from her bedroom to hear the refrigerator door open. We were cooking dinner together once when she suddenly filled with rage. "You're too young to look like this," she said, slamming her rag on the counter, as if it were something she had pent up inside.

One day, nursing a hangover on my bathroom floor, I was surprised by a sudden thought. I was at the top of what had become a thirty-pound peak, and I realized I was sick of feeling nauseous and bulging out of my clothes. Inexplicably, I decided to take up salsa dancing. At first, I was nervous and awkward during the classes, cursing the lack of rhythm my birthright should have guaranteed. But I began slowly to lose weight, gain agility, and feel more comfortable on the dance floor. On a really good night, I'd forget myself in the music, picturing a long skirt whipping around me, everyone watching as I twirled in perfect rhythm.

One night I caught my reflection in the mirror and suddenly understood my mother's hidden desire. In my lightness and forgetting, I was freeing myself of the preconceived image I had in my mind. Looking back in the mirror I looked beautiful and young, and no one could touch me. In that moment, I realized that ultimately, she only wanted this freedom for me, too. Since then I've ditched the salsa class, continued my yo-yo diet, and still think I'm allergic to my treadmill. Yet, somehow, though we never speak of it, when I'm feeling insecure, I simply picture my mother, full of pride, dancing by herself in an empty house.

After the Glamour Shots, it was as if she and I had reached an unspoken understanding. I finally fulfilled her fantasy (my image looms in every room of her small house). She points them out all the time. She particularly enjoys the shots we took together, all plunging necklines and mesh. When I look at them now, they mostly make me laugh. At times they make me angry, especially when I think of my mother's conversion to evangelical Christianity, and how this still doesn't stop her from mentally assessing my pant size every time we meet. I work at major fashion and beauty magazines now, and I still struggle with my own definition of beauty. Sometimes I grab all the cosmetics I can find on the giveaway counter, sometimes I want to throw them all away. I don't like taking photos that much, it never seems like me when I see them later. My mother, however, seems calmer about my appearance, she has the Glamour Shots to appease her. As for me, I imagine someday I'll see a glimmer of our real selves in the photos, posing in our most flattering light.

ESOS NO SIRVEN

BY DAISY HERNÁNDEZ

My mother and tías warned me about dating Colombian men: "Esos no sirven." They would say the same thing about the 1970s television in our kitchen. "That TV no sirve para nada. It doesn't work."

As a child, I thought that being married to a Colombian man would be like fighting with that old television. It didn't get all the channels, but we made it work because it was the only one we had. We switched among the three channels it did get by turning the knob with a wrench. We spun the antennas in circles, and when one pointed at the sink and the other out the window—past the clothesline with my aunt's three-dollar pants—we found that it did work and we had the telenovela *Simplemente Maria*.

My mother and aunties taught me that it was easier to believe the worst about the people you knew best. Although their six brothers stayed in Colombia, phone calls between New Jersey and Bogotá brought stories of my charming, whiskey-drinking philandering uncles, and all the evidence for why Colombian men "no sirven." From the kitchen, my mother and aunties dictated Spanish warnings like dark nursery rhymes: Colombian men get drunk, beat their women, cheat on their wives, and never earn enough money. They keep mistresses, have bastard children, and never come home on time. They steal, lie, sneak around, and come home to die, cradled in the arms of bitter wives.

So by sixteen, I knew better than to give my phone number to Manolo César Rodríguez. He was Colombiano, twenty-one years old, and had been in the States for a few years. He cooked hamburgers at the McDonald's where I had my first after-school job. He smiled at me, and while I knew about Colombian men, I had been reading Harlequin romance novels since fifth grade. I had been waiting for a man to smile at me. Men looked at beautiful women, and beautiful women were always happy. They did not work at fast-food places. They spoke English perfectly and French as well.

Manolo spoke to me in Spanish. Querida, mi amor, mi biscochito. In Spanish, there were many words for loving a woman. When things were slow in the kitchen, he stood behind me at the register and helped me with the orders. He said Spanish words with carelessness and precision. "Ya mi amor, I got that for you. Get the next order."

I gave him my phone number and waited for him to call.

My Colombian mother and aunties may have raised me with tragic notions about our men, but they also schooled me as the American child of immigrants. I believed anything could work in America, even Colombian men.

The women in my family did not marry their own kind. My mother chose my Cuban father, Tía Blanca went with a Puerto Rican, and Tía Carmen with a Peruvian. And my tía Elena never bothered with any man, since God was the only hombre that really worked. Except for her, they all married citizens, men with papeles.

Having grown up with little money and six brothers in a country famous for cocaine and civil war, my mother and tías were determined to lead easier lives. They taught me a complicated pattern of what works with men. My father's alcoholism was better than womanizing, beatings, or, worse, a man who could not hold down a job. My Peruvian uncle was machista but he owned a Chevrolet and drove us to Great Adventure, Action Park, and Niagara Falls. My Puerto Rican uncle had kids with other women but he read tarot cards and cooked a good arroz con pollo for Thanksgiving. Finally, God did nothing to stop the war in Colombia, but he was reason enough for my tía Elena to awaken early every morning and have something to think about other than the violencia over there and the unemployment over here.

My mother and aunties advised me against dating any Latin American, even the kind they married. They constructed a careful list of what worked: A Latino with a college degree works best, but choose white over black, since no one sees the diploma on the street, in churches, or at the supermercados. Ask to meet his relatives. Forget Caribbean men. They want sex all the time, speak Spanish with missing syllables, and if they are not black, their grandmothers might be. Forget Central Americans. They want sex all the time, do not grow any taller, and if they are not indios, their grandmothers might be. Consider Argentines. They want sex all the time but most are white, have law degrees, and if they are not Italian, their grandmothers might be. Remember to ask if he grew up in the capitál or some no-name campo. It is the difference between marrying Hialeah or Palm Springs.

In church, we learned that marriage is a holy sacrament. At home, marriage was not so much a union of blessed souls as it was a decree of what kind of street you would end up living on. A good man, one that worked and held a savings account, was a semi-sure sign that you would live in an aluminum-sided two-family house on a tree-lined street next door to Korean, Brazilian, and Italian families. My mother and tías had worked as teachers, seamstresses, house cleaners, and home attendants, and they wanted me to have an easier life. They dreamed of the suburbs.

At sixteen, however, I definitely did not want to marry any hombre to live in the suburbs, sacred land of stiff lawns, my Catholic high school, and girls with new Nissans. Even then I sensed it would not be a fulfillment of my mother's dream but a betrayal of what I knew to be home. The distance between school and our house, her hopes and my hesitations, was long and unexplained, and it often made me anxious. But the year that I turned sixteen, I had something else to think about—riding in Manolo's fixed-up Camaro, kissing for hours, and loving like in the novels and telenovelas.

When Manolo began calling, I was thrilled and got under the bedcovers with the telephone receiver for privacy. My mother and aunties smiled, so sure that it was just a passing interest. They were certain that I would marry American. Anything made in America worked. The cars, the washing machines, the lightbulbs, and even the men.

Of course, they heard the same accusation, Esos no sirven, hurled at American men. They even knew a woman who left her Nicaraguan husband and children for an Americano. Months later, the gringo dumped her.

"No better than a Colombian," declared Tía Carmen. "He wanted her for you know what y nada más."

But it was the Colombian men that my mother and aunts knew best. So in our kitchen they were the guiltiest.

Manolo was initially a paradox for the family. He had hazel eyes and white skin and looked more Americano than the Italians who owned my mother's factory. He called my mother Doña and returned from fishing trips with trout for my father. My mother was suspicious. My father was delighted to get free seafood.

Six months later, my tías and mother didn't know what to say. The last time a woman in our family dated a Colombian, it was decades earlier in a country where that was the only choice. My mother gave me an accusatory look that called to mind the writings of Achy Obejas: "We came all the way from Colombia so you could date this guy?" It was one thing if the Coast Guard could not keep Colombian men from crossing the border in 1991; it was another thing for her American daughter to open the front door.

I continued dating Manolo because I knew it would cause no more consequences than several rounds of acerbic reactions. Despite my mother and aunties' insistence on good men, our primary ties were to each other as mujeres. Our working-class lives and cultura meant that we relied on each other for the cleaning, the shopping, and the respite of a good chisme. Familia was not a cliché but something I smelled when the house was crowded with aunties wearing Ben-Gay for their dolores.

Even as they scolded me for dating a Colombiano without a college education, the tías demanded to know the detalles of his single mom, who kept a string of love affairs, and his dear old abuelita, who was, of course, una pobrecita and an angel.

As the relationship evolved, I continued holding high court at home. The three aunties had no children of their own, and as my mother's firstborn, I was treasured and criticized. I lacked the polite manners of good Colombian girls, according to my tías, and was a complete American brat, una pretensiosa. But hey, I was their American brat. Accordingly, I could get away with anything—or at least with not saying "muchas gracias, señora." That get-out-of-jail card extended to dating a Colombian man. Everyone—my mother, my tías, and I—we all just blamed it on my American side.

My own concerns had to do with another border. I was a virgin and Manolo had said he would wait until I was ready. I expected to be ready soon.

The women in my family did not talk to me about sex, and women's magazines did not mention poverty or ethnicity. My mother and tías told me that men either worked for you or they did not. Romance happened between seven and nine in the evening on Spanish soap operas. Sex happened later.

But at the supermarket, I read the truth about multiple orgasms in *Cosmo*. My friends and I relied on Judy Blume's book *Forever* to tell us we could have sex with the boy and not marry him. Something could happen between a broken hymen and baby showers. College and a career, of course. But mostly it would be a lot of sex. My best friend and I spent the better part of the summer before high school reading Judith Krantz novels and watching the porn videos from her father's secret hiding place. We saw that women could have sex in outdoor swimming pools, in hotels with different men, and with each other. Fresh out of eighth grade, we watched, analyzed, and came to our final conclusion: sex was good.

By the time I watched women have sex with each other on my friend's nineteen-inch TV, I had already heard about mujeres like them.

I was ten years old and sitting at the kitchen table when a friend of my mother's came to tell her and the tías the latest chisme: the woman they all knew on Walker Street had left her husband and children to be with another mujer. Gasps made their way around the kitchen table where café con leche was being served.

"Can you believe it?"

"She's that way?"

"I never would have thought it!"

Everyone was shocked, not sure what to do with the information that a woman had been so moved by love that she moved toward another woman. It felt terribly romantic to me: the notion that love could move you beyond what everyone else said.

I was also not exactly sure why the women in my family were so startled about a woman going with another mujer. Besides discussing how Colombians didn't work, all we ever did at home was talk about women.

There were two types of women. The telenovela woman was a fair-skin lovely who worked as a maid, suffered public humiliations, and married her man in the last episode. Then there is Iris Chacón. Think J.Lo but bigger.

On Saturdays, my family gathered to watch a variety show

on Spanish-language television, where Iris Chacón was all se-
quin panty thong and big brown ass, and salsa was just a side
note. She was a curve of glitter on the screen, an exaggeration
(turned into art) of all that was mujer, and we were all very
much in love with her. Or at least my father and I were. Like a
good Latina family, we did everything together, even watch
women with big butts and tetas at eight o'clock on Saturday
nights.

My mother and tías talked endlessly about Iris Chacón.

"Look at her tetas!"

"Qué grandes, no?"

"Look at her backside!"

"Cómo lo mueve!"

They discussed other dancers and actresses, debating who
had silicone implants and fake behinds. I stared at the screen,
trying to figure out how real Iris Chacón was. The fact that
she was on television, a fiction available to us any Saturday
evening, only made her seem more real and made me feel that
I was in control of my desires, that I could choose who I would
love and who I would marry.

"She might as well wear nothing!" my mother declared
about Iris as if to chastise us for watching.

My father and I nodded but kept our eyes on the screen,
grateful that for once the reception was good on this old TV
and that Iris Chacón looked so very real.

After a year of dating, I was very much in love with Manolo, his
Camaro, and the tender way that he kissed me. He took me to
the beach at night when it was flooded with stars and crashing
waves, and the world felt so much bigger than what I had ever
imagined. I was seventeen and in love.

I was also lonely at school. Often the only Latina among my peers, and the only working-class one at that, I was an outsider. Manolo, all open-hearted and romantic, was a perfect antidote. He reminded me of family. His Spanish tilted like my mother's, and being with him I felt at home, closer to the parts of me that were invisible at school.

So I was angry with my mother and tías for finding any fault in a man who took me to the movies, the mall, and upscale versions of McDonald's like Houlihan's. The more they raised their dark eyebrows and asked if Manolo ever planned to attend college and amount to anything more than a job at McDonald's, the more I called him and told him I would love him forever.

Sex was a different matter.

Growing up in a small town where love easily meant nine months of gordura and no high school graduation, I was determined to not become a teenage mamita, despite how good sex looked on TV. I told Manolo that it would happen after my high school graduation, when I was on my way to college with a four-year scholarship.

It did, and I discovered that sex with a man was exactly like it was in a Harlequin romance novel. There was suspense and blinding lust, need, aching and throbbing. There was also a beginning, a middle, and an end, and when it was over, it was over.

By the time I started wearing a faux-gold chain that said "Manolo [heart] Daisy 2-14-91," my mother and the aunts refused to speak to him. It only made me want him more. I went to college, and for another two years I loved him against all odds, or at least against my mother's wishes.

When we broke up, Manolo said that my mother was right. He had feared what she desired: that I would leave him for the guy with more money and a better car. Guilt-ridden, I told him that the other guy just understood me better. He was also in college, studying D. H. Lawrence and training as a journalist.

But Manolo was right. The other guy had a better car, did not immigrate from Colombia, and had the money to attend college. He was not Italian but his grandmother was.

Those questions began nagging me: How did I end up heeding my mother's warnings? Were the romance novels wrong?

To the degree that I was disturbed, my mother and tías were delighted. Finally, I was listening to them. I was commuting to college, living at home, working part-time with gringos at an office, and dating an American. Unfortunately for them, college did not just introduce me to American boys.

The sign in the student center was straightforward: Workshop for Women on Sexuality at 2:30 PM. Hosted by the college's feminist collective.

I would like to say now that the moment that changed my life was charming or at least cinematic. But it comes down to this: one night, I was going down on my new boyfriend, and the next afternoon, I was sitting in a carpeted room with white girls, giggling, fully clothed, and drawing portraits of our vulvas.

The facilitator, a woman from Planned Parenthood, was eerily cheerful and unfazed by our work. "That's it, everyone! You're doing great!" she said. "Mary, that's just beautiful! I love the colors. Cheryl, keep going! We've got crayons for everyone!"

It was all I could do to not blurt out "Lady, we're drawing pictures of our pussies, not a schoolhouse!"

The many shapes and colors of the vulvas, I have to say, not to mention the sizes and detail work of the clits some women drew, demanded my full attention. So much so, in fact, that I almost snapped at the other Latina in the room who started talking to me. She was the president of the collective, wanted to know everything about me, and insisted I come to the group's weekly lunch meetings. I smiled absentmindedly, keeping my eyes on her magenta-colored rendering of her pussy. I figured she could see mine, I could see hers. Hers looked like strawberries, sliced ones at that.

Then she introduced me to the white woman sitting next to her, saying, "Oh, and this is my girlfriend."

Maybe it was the rich colors of her vulva or just something about the way she said the word "girlfriend," but I understood her immediately. And as I shook Girlfriend's hand, I snuck a glance at her drawing. Her pussy looked like a swirling river of siennas and periwinkle.

The idea of two women together was not a novelty. I had watched enough porn to know it was possible, but as I smiled at them, I just thought, "I have never met one." Lesbians were something that happened on TV like Iris Chacón and telenovelas. It was not real. The idea of actually kissing a girl had never occurred to me. And as the two women pecked each other ever so lightly on the lips, I felt so embarrassed and enthralled that I frantically looked around for a place to put my eyes. Finding nothing, I just stared down at their vulvas.

I began to wonder what was wrong with me. Qué me pasaba? Why had it never occurred to me? A girl. I could kiss a girl. On cue, the facilitator passed by, murmuring, "Daisy, honey, why don't we add some colors, open it up."

My eyes widened. How did she know? I looked down and it was all there for the world to see: my vulva. I had drawn a small brown mound, speckled with black curls. No fruit or rivers here.

I attended feminist meetings the way I had once gone to church with my mother. I dressed in what I thought were my best plaid skirts and I didn't miss a session. We talked about sexual abuse, organized our school's Take Back the Night, and analyzed the significance of lube. The women's studies professor gave us impromptu talks about the fluidity of gender identity and desire, and it was all I could do to sit still next to the girl that looked like a boy.

It was the mid-nineties and multicultural everything was in. So, I had the books, the teachers, and the new friends to teach me that my sexuality was about as normal as me being a Latina at a predominantly white college. Sure, we were outnumbered, but now the laws were on our side and we had a visible though small community. The more I listened to the feminist collective's president talk about her lesbian life, the more comfortable I also felt. The woman knew about Audre Lorde, arroz con frijoles, and threw in a Spanish word into the conversation every now and then. She invited me to parties at the apartment she shared with Girlfriend, and although all we had in common was sexuality and ethnicity, it was more than enough. She was close enough to be home for me—the equivalent of my mother and aunties in one woman, with the lesbian and overtly feminist parts added.

The more I thought about being with women, the more I

recognized its perks. It meant doubling my wardrobe and having whatever size penis I could afford at Toys in Babeland. It also meant spending entire weekends at a time processing our feelings, having a lover socialized to take care of my needs, and talking about what names we would give our cat if we had one together.

While I didn't know if I wanted to spend my life with a woman (let alone have a cat with her), I was sure that I needed to try it. Luckily, my mother and tías spoke Spanish and I kept my diary in English.

The worst part about trying to date women was that I didn't have my mother's warnings. There was nothing to rebel against. No indicator if I was doing it right or wrong.

True to lesbian social codes, I graduated from college, joined a group of women writers, and ended up in bed with a friend. I couldn't tell what was more exciting: her naked large breasts against my own A cup–sized ones or the inversion of gender roles. I was now the one buying dinner, picking up the flowers, driving us upstate. My days were spent figuring out how to please her and it was intoxicating to feel so subservient. She was, of course, the kind of woman that you'd fall into. We'd talk endlessly about politics, writing, our childhoods, and every time she spoke Spanish and English in the same sentence, I felt a part of myself fall in love.

Within months, however, the relationship soured. I was ready for more experiences and we were better suited as friends. But still unsure about what to do, I tried dating another friend. She e-mailed me that she wasn't interested.

I then dated a Puerto Rican butch who drank about as many

Coronas as my father. My mother and aunties would have been horrified. I was, after two months.

Going out with a Dominican femme was not any better. She drove an SUV, had her hair straightened once a week, and kept another lover in the Bronx. After three times in bed, I got tired of always being on top.

After dating a transgender Jewish boy, I got tired of always being on the bottom.

I went back to what I knew and tried dating a Colombian woman who lived in New York City. But I lived in New Jersey and she didn't want to invest in long distance. I decided it was too much work.

I persevered, though—answering personal ads and drinking flat Diet Coke at lesbian bars—because I had read the romance novels, seen the movies, and believed the songs. Love was supposed to overcome everything, even the taboo of lesbians and bad Colombian men. It was supposed to work out no matter what job you had, what nationality you were, or which street you wanted to live on. It was supposed to work even if you kissed a woman.

And it did work for a few months. I fell in love with a dark-haired woman who had a way of tilting her bony hip that gave her ownership of the room. Men would hit on her and she would coolly reply, "I don't think my girlfriend would appreciate that." She was the most feminine woman I had dated (hours were spent daily concocting outfits) but also the most masculine. She carried my bags, bought me overpriced jeans, and would lean in to kiss me. I found in her a kindred spirit, a woman who had an ambitious career streak that matched my own. We plotted the films she would one day make and the books I would write.

She was equally self-assured about her sensuality and un-apologetic of needing me, at times following me into the dress-ing room at the store to whisper that I looked so beautiful, that she wanted to go down on me right there. Any of my attempts at being coy fell apart when she'd beg, "Please, I like it when you scream. I need you to do it like this morning. Scratch my back when I'm fucking you. Please." I had heard the same line before but it was different this time. Something inside me moved, fell into place.

When she dumped me, I didn't know if I was crying over her or my family. I had been so moved by this woman and had not been able to share it with my mother or tías, the first women I had loved. Instead I told them that it was the rigors of graduate school that now made me sob hysterically while watching *Sábado Gigante*.

I had cried about other women, and maybe all of it was adding up. This time I had to tell.

My mother made it easy to come out. She lived by the marian-ismo social codes of Colombia, circa 1955: Speak when you're asked. Smile politely. Raise eyebrows when you disapprove. Even with your own daughter. And, of course, be a good mother by adoring your children even if they date Colombian men or demand the time to do impractical things like write poems. So as much as I searched for love with both men and women, I was always sure of my mother's love—and that while she might faint, she would certainly not scream or kick me out of her house when I delivered the news.

It also only worked to my advantage that at the time of my coming out, I myself was following Colombian social codes, circa 1955. I was twenty-five, living at home, getting a graduate degree, being una niña buena, leading a life any mother could discuss with her sisters and neighbors.

After another night of crying about lost love, I called my mother into my bedroom. Unsure of where to begin, I chose the logical. "Mami, you know it's been a long time since I've had a boyfriend."

She nodded and gave me a small smile. No boyfriend meant no possibility of sex.

"It's been years now since I dated Manolo and those boys after him weren't very interesting."

She nodded again.

I looked at the pink wall of my bedroom, the writing awards, the Ani DiFranco CDs, and then I just said it. "Well, Mami, the thing is I've been dating women."

Her mouth opened but no sound came out, and I was sure that God had punished me by giving my mother a minor heart attack. But no, that wasn't it. She was clutching at her heart, all right, but it was to strike a pose similar to the one of the Virgin Mary that hung over the bed she shared with my father.

"Mami, are you okay?"

"Sí, sí, ay, dios mío, dios mío."

The silence that ensued was worse than her plea to God. So I filled the space between us with a concise history of the lesbian, feminist, and civil rights movements that all combined had opened the door to higher education, better laws, and supportive communities of otherwise marginalized people. "So, you see, Mami, it's all because of how hard you worked to put me through school that I am fortunate enough to be so happy and make such good decisions for myself."

By this time, she was trying to catch her breath and fanning her face with her other hand. She then spoke the only words she would come to say to me about the subject: "Ay, dios mío. I've never heard of this. This doesn't happen in Colombia. In Colombia, I never saw anything like this."

"Mami, you haven't been in Colombia in twenty-seven years."

"But we never saw anything like this."

It is not too much of an overstatement to say that my coming out ignited about the same familial outrage as a bombing in the middle of Bogotá.

In the days that followed, my tía Elena accused me of trying to kill my mother, quickly adding with grim self-satisfaction, "I watched a pornographic movie and I know what you do now."

I tried to protest, but all I could think of saying was, "No, really, I haven't dated anyone with breasts that big."

But before I could speak, she declared, "It's not going to work, you know? You need a man for the equipment."

For this I was ready. My consumerist upwardly mobile inner American brat replied, "Tía, por favor, you can buy that!"

She broke out into a Hail Mary.

My mother meanwhile developed a minor depression, anxiety, and a vague, persistent headache. She was not well, the tías snapped at me.

"Don't say anything to upset her!" barked Tía Carmen. "The way this woman has suffered, I will never know."

But she did know.

Tía Carmen threw away a birthday gift from me because she could see that the present—a book on indigenous religions in Mexico—was my way of trying to convert her to lesbianism. Tía Elena began walking into the other room when I would arrive home. The third auntie, the oldest of them and now well

into her late sixties, simply began alluding to the vicious ru-
mors the other two aunties had started about me.

That my romantic choices could upset my mother and tías
was a given since high school. A lot could be said about a
woman who married the wrong man. But that had an explanation: not listening to your mother and tías. Dating the same sex
was different. There was no explanation.

My mother now wants one, though, because she is hurt.
More than anything now, she hurts. I keep thinking that if only
I can tell her how it works with women, she would understand.
The problem is I do not know. Why, for example, can I still feel
attracted to men but prefer the way a woman squeezes my
hand? Why is it that a woman can do everything a man does
and it is always so much better, so much sweeter?

The closest I get to finding an explanation for what it feels
like to love a woman is a Frida Kahlo painting, the one where
her insides are exposed, and she is sitting next to her twin, who
holds her heart, an artery, and the scissors. That is how I think
about loving women, like she can dig into you and hold the insides of you, all bloodied and smelly, in her hands. She knows
you that intimately. But it is nothing I can say to my mother,
who already thinks Frida is beautiful but odd.

Instead, I show her pictures of old lovers, hoping that the
faces of the women I have loved will explain everything. But
she stares at them blankly and gets a headache. My photo
album is not the life she wanted for me. In some ways, it is better. With a college degree in English, I do not need a man or
woman that works. But la seguridad, the fewer worries she and
the aunties had hoped I would have is hard to imagine now
that I am sharing lipstick with my new girlfriend and getting
harrassed on the subways by men.

What hurts most is knowing she would adore my new lover, who, it turns out, is a cross between Telenovela Maria and Iris Chacón. Kristina is a good woman like the telenovela star (a social worker by profession) with a Chacón bottom and thongs to match. She paints corazones for me, calls me mamita, and encourages me to buy the red dog collar with the spikes. She loves museums, has a college degree, and can talk extensively about Mexican murals. She is not Italian but her great-grandmother is.

When my mother visits my apartment these days, I catch her looking at Kristina's framed picture. In that moment, everything is in my mother's face: the years she worked with her hands, the houses she bought with my father, the money spent on schooling me, la esperanza de algo mejor, her desire that I have a good life. It all feels ruined by that one picture.

And I want to tell Mami that it is not like that. Everything she did is not lost; it just turned out differently.

YOUR NAME IS
SANDOVAL

BY LYNDA SANDOVAL

I grew up the youngest in a family of three girls. My eldest sister, Elena, got perfect grades, kept her room spotless and organized, hung up her clothes promptly, and spoke politely to everyone. Loretta, the middle child, flew under the radar most of the time, but was also my dad's hunting and fishing pal, the son he never had. I will admit I was envious that Elena was a source of pride and Loretta the chosen buddy. I love my sisters, though, and never resented them for the roles they played in the family. I saved up all my enmity for Dad, and my role was being the unrelenting thorn in Father's side.

By preschool, I knew two things with absolute certainty: my father was an alcoholic, a "bad word" that I only understood to mean he drank cheap jug wine with my uncles until I was embarrassed by his slurred speech, and his "disease" was something I would never be able to admit to my friends without dying of shame. I realized he'd never be the dear ol' dad of greeting card and sitcom lore, and I felt cheated out of the kind of daddy I believed every little girl deserves.

My first memorable disappointment came when I was a three-year-old student at Sunny Corners nursery school. One day, a fellow student, Norman, yanked my long hair back and planted a big wet kiss on my lips. I did what any self-respecting young girl would do after such an unwelcome assault: I cold-cocked him. The school administration frowned on this use of violence and punished me by scheduling, of all things, a *marriage* ceremony for me and Norman the Victimizer the following day. I was horrified, but I had faith my parents would put the kibosh on the wedding when they picked me up. As a teacher himself, surely my father would disagree with Sunny Corners' ludicrous marital punishment idea. This was before the days of time-outs, but couldn't they just spank me?

That afternoon my teacher told my parents the whole ugly tale and the planned punishment. Now, my dad was an odd mix of liberal Renaissance man educator and stereotypical Latino male. Literally from our diaper days, he raised us to become educated, self-sufficient, independent, critically thinking, Democratic-voting women . . . as long as we followed his rules to the letter. Still, I truly expected him to stand up for me and balk at the notion of marrying off his toddler daughter to a socially inept, sexual-deviant-in-training. To my horror, he didn't. On the contrary, during the drive home, I got a lecture about being "ladylike."

"I don't want to hear about you punching other children," Dad chastised from the driver's seat. "It's not how a girl should act. You should be ashamed of yourself."

"He pulled my hair and kissed me!"

"That's no excuse. And you'll have no television tonight."

Defeated, I went the route of passive protest for the heinous wedding ceremony. I wore an orange yarn wig and a death scowl for the duration, and refused to say "I do" or hold Norman's slimy, groping hand. I have one snapshot of the fiasco as proof, and I look grim. The experience was abysmal, except for the cake and Kool-Aid reception, of course.

This was the first in a long line of valuable lessons about what to expect in the way of paternal support, and it left me bitter. I chose to act out that residual resentment through a string of planned and spontaneous rebellious acts. I let out my first rebel yell at the age of six. My sister Loretta was seven and much more obedient. She was, however, open to going along with my evil plots, and I could be damned persuasive. One evening, my mother went to a bridal shower, leaving us in the care of my dad. Instead of Chinese checkers or story time, Dad chose to nurture glass after glass of red wine. My oldest sister, Elena, was the "grown-up" at age nine, but she was sucked in by some old movie on television and left Loretta and me to our own devices.

I remember glancing up at my dad sitting on the couch, listening to old Motown music and sucking back hooch while Loretta and I played alone on the floor. His feet, still ensconced in the black dress socks he wore during his sober workdays, rested on the edge of the coffee table. Maybe he just didn't know what might be fun to do, I thought.

"Want to play Candy Land, Daddy?"

"Play with your sister."

"We can play Chutes and Ladders, then."

No answer from Dad.

"Or checkers."

Nothing.

"Can we get a dog?"

"No. Just play with your sister!"

Eventually, his glass went from full to empty, his attention from barely there to nonexistent, and position from upright to slouched. Not long after, he'd propped one of his sock-clad feet on the back of the couch, and his snores carried through the house. When I was sure he was "asleep"—read: passed out—I eyed that omnipresent jug of Gallo wine and turned to my sister with a Grinch-smile on my face and a subversive idea in my mind.

"Let's drink some of Daddy's wine."

Her big brown eyes went round. "We shouldn't. We're not allowed."

Like I cared about *that*. I glanced at him snoring open-mouthed on the couch, completely unaware of our needs, and the anger building inside me. "Who cares? If he can drink it, we can drink it."

It turned out to be a good-enough argument for a seven-year-old. We proceeded to get shitfaced on cheap burgundy drunk from tiny paper Dixie cups while my father slept. I don't remember how much we drank, only that I was flat on my back on the living room floor and couldn't lift my head when my mother returned from her event.

"Goddamnit!" she said, as she shook my father semiawake. "Look at these girls! Can't I leave them with you for one evening?" My mother never used profanity; this was huge.

Nonplussed, my father looked around. "Where's Elena? She should've been watching them."

"They're *your* daughters, too!" my mom yelled.

"I didn't give them permission to drink," snapped Dad, flashing an accusatory glance at me. Not at us, though Loretta was as wrecked as I was, but only at me. I'd been the instigator; everyone knew that. Loretta would never have suggested such bad behavior. "Talk to your daughters about the drinking, not me."

Mom shoved aspirin down our throats and literally dragged us up to bed. The next morning, nursing a bitch of a hangover, hunched over a bowl of Captain Crunch, I just wanted to forget the whole night.

"What the hell were you thinking, drinking my wine?" my dad growled at me over his newspaper.

Fury licked up inside me. "You drink all the time. Why shouldn't we?" I growled back, letting the disgust and disappointment show in my eyes. The conversation ended there, but from that day on, I felt a low-grade level of distrust emanating from my father. In his mind, I was edgy, rebellious, and disobedient, and I decided to play the role to the hilt.

In addition to all the regular adolescent stuff like swearing, talking back, and skipping classes, I went the extra mile to annoy him. At age thirteen, during a sleepover, a friend and I lit up a joint we'd copped from a local burnout and blew smoke out my bedroom window. My parents didn't say anything, but shortly thereafter, my dad brought home cigarettes, cigars, and some marijuana and said my sisters and I could try all of it as long as we did it at home. I guess he was trying to be an enlightened, open-minded parent. The same thing happened after my friends and I began standing outside local convenience stores and asking adult men to buy us beer. Dad said we could drink at home if we wanted to, but none of us did. Where was the fun in that?

Where drugs and alcohol failed, I turned to the one thing I knew would get him: my sloppiness. My room was such a pit that I once actually lost a fast-food taco once, only to find it moldy several weeks later. Try as he might, my father wasn't able to discipline me into being as neat as Elena. But then again, no one, save Martha Stewart, is as neat as Elena.

One evening the issue came to a head. I was visiting a friend when the call came from my mother: "You'd better come home. Dad has had it with your messy room." Her words were cryptic, as always, in her desire to avoid rocking the boat further. Was I grounded? Did I have to clean it right then? Was he going to whup my ass?

I wish. My dad had flat-out snapped. Fueled by the copious amounts of Gallo cream sherry flowing through his veins, he had thrown all my belongings out onto the front lawn. *All of them.* Like I was being evicted before I even paid rent. He even broke my beloved Polaroid camera during this frenzy, a camera I'd saved months to purchase. I remember feeling cold and shaky with unexpressed fury, but what could I do?

I was probably fourteen at the time. I wanted to run away. I wanted to kill him. I wanted to set the cops on him when he drove drunk. I wanted to be an orphan. I felt helpless and trapped and mired in deep-seated loathing for my father. But I did nothing. I shut my mouth and took it.

My mom and I reassembled everything, but that's no surprise; she always made up for what I deemed "deficiencies" in my father's parenting. My camera was permanently fucked, which I never really forgave him for. The room got cleaned and life went on.

I got used to his alcohol-induced episodes, but one aspect of my father's personality confused me. With us, he seemed distant and unaffectionate; he got a pained look on his face when we tried to kiss him good night, and he held out his arm for us to kiss the back of his hand instead. Yet with friends and strangers, he could be amazingly giving. Once, as the director of the local Head Start program, he visited a family so poor, they were forced to eat boiled weeds they'd pulled from a field.

He returned home visibly distraught. "I can't simply stand by and watch that. We have more than enough. They have nothing." He proceeded to empty our pantry and refrigerator and delivered the food to them. Another day, a vagrant, wearing only jeans and holey Chuck Taylors, came to our door soliciting for God knows what. The man admitted he didn't have any other clothing, and I watched in amazement as my father removed the shirt he was wearing and handed it over.

I admit feeling proud of him at those moments, but his selflessness didn't generally extend to his own family, which frustrated me. With us, he was stern and punitive, rarely giving us the benefit of the doubt. Every now and then he'd brag about me to others or tell me I'd done a good job at something, but the praise felt hollow. "You did a good job on that report for school," he'd say, calling me over to sit on the arm of his chair. "Thanks," I'd say, reluctantly crossing over and taking a seat where he'd indicated. He'd pat me on the back, the equivalent of a big friggin' bear hug from other dads. But I always knew what was coming next. "You know why you got an A?" he'd ask, chest puffed out and his goddamned omnipresent jelly jar of Gallo cream sherry resting on his rounded belly. "Because your name is *Sandoval*." "No, it isn't," I'd fire back, unable to appreciate the praise. "It's because my name is *Lynda*." Things would generally escalate into bickering from there. He'd be a jerk, I'd be an ungrateful brat, blah blah blah.

I can look back now and understand that he was trying to instill familial and cultural pride into me, but it felt like he took credit for everything positive or chalked it up to the fact that I was Hispanic—a Sandoval—completely discounting the "me" factor in my accomplishments. I hated that. It forced me to deny my Scottish/Irish/Swedish mom's genetic contribution to the person I was, and it removed my hard work from the equation completely. He could be infuriatingly ethnocentric this way, which caused me to rebel against my own culture.

For the longest time, I thought the whole Hispanic thing was a pain in my ass. I wanted to be (1) a platinum-blonde WASP with mile-long legs, or (2) black. Oh, sure, my cousins and I sang "Feliz Navidad" for the grown-ups at Christmas to earn brownie points (and money), and we scarfed biscochitos with abandon. We intermixed Spanish words with our English, without even really knowing we were doing it. I learned to make tortillas from my grandma after my poor mother's attempts resulted in batches of tasteless, partially burnt crackers shaped like the state of Florida. Still, my dad was into the "Chicano power" movement at the University of Northern Colorado in the early 1970s, and I wanted nothing to do with any of it because of him. I used to tell people I was Italian, ignoring their strange glances.

My dad had enough cultural pride for all of us, I thought. He actually went so far as to joke that Mom was "Hispanic by injection," a concept with an exponential ick factor. Why did she need to be Hispanicized anyway? She not only converted from Baptist to Catholic to marry my father, but from Colgate to Crest, which I'd always felt was the bigger sacrifice. She'd compromised so much for her marriage, I thought—why her heritage as well? I was as proud of her culture as I was of my Hispanic roots. Though he did revere her, from my child's perspective Dad seemed to devalue anything but Brown Power. This soon became another quality on a long list of things I disliked about him.

One of the things that topped that list were inconsistencies and broken promises. He'd promise a day at the zoo, then renege at the last minute. He'd promise to quit drinking, raise our hopes, then enter a treatment program and sober up only to go back to drinking six months later. Sobriety in my father was never the epiphany I'd hoped it would be anyway. He didn't turn into Super Dad, but rather into a dry alcoholic who desperately yearned for a drink; I could feel it, and it hurt. We always tried to pull him into the family during his nondrinking days, but it didn't work.

During one stint of sobriety, we all went walking through the woods to a small lake near our house. It could've been the perfect outing, but Dad was distracted, stern. He didn't want to chat, couldn't give a shit what this plant or that tree was. It didn't take a genius to know he didn't want to be there, or anywhere, without the ubiquitous jelly jar of sherry to take the edge off.

"What's wrong?" I asked him. He and I always walked faster than the rest of the family, so we were several yards ahead.

"Nothing," he growled. "Just enjoy the goddamn walk."

In the dappled sunlight, beneath the canopy of trees, I saw the truth. Dad was going to drink again. My stomach sank, but I walked along in silence, I wanted to avoid the torturous anticipation before he'd actually start. *Just get it over with*, I thought.

Two days later, my mom, sisters, and I returned home from shopping to the familiar image of my father, glassy-eyed and unfocused, the bottled love of his life on the table next to his chair. I looked at him with defiant anger, but part of me felt relief. At least I didn't have to wonder when it would happen. I'm sure I made a caustic remark, but I don't remember it.

I do remember my dad looking at me with a dictatorial gleam in his eyes. "Take off my shoes," he said gruffly.

The last chance I gave my dad was on my twenty-first birthday.

"Pick any restaurant you want," he said. "This is your twenty-first. It's a big deal."

"Really?" Should I allow myself to hope like this? "Will you promise not to drink?"

"Of course. It's your birthday. Whatever you want."

I'm embarrassed to admit my gullibility, but I actually held out a flicker of hope that he meant it.

I chose a Moroccan restaurant with belly dancers and waiters who set teacups on the soles of their lifted feet, pouring tea over their shoulders and never spilling a drop. Despite his earlier enthusiasm, he was distracted and less than interested the entire time. Halfway through the meal, he escaped to the car and drank sherry he'd smuggled along.

It was that night—ironically, on the birthday I supposedly became an adult—that I realized he would never be the father I wanted. He was, however, the only father I had, and somehow that knowledge released me. I can't even explain it, but I suddenly knew that he wouldn't make an effort to repair the tattered fabric of our relationship. If I wanted any kind of contact with my father for the rest of my life, it was up to me to ply the needle.

I took a break from him for months, doing things like attending Al-Anon meetings and working out to bolster my self-image. I joined a church, made some new friends, and started to think of myself in my terms and not his. I wasn't stupid. I wasn't a slacker. I wasn't a slut. I wasn't a "good-for-nothing who would amount to jack shit."

Only when I started to truly believe this did I begin to take adult control of our relationship like I hadn't been able to when I was a child. If I was at his house and he started in on me verbally, I left. I surrounded myself with the people who had actually brought me up. I began taking back my dignity.

I had no choice about living with an alcoholic as a child, but I did have choices now. I started to understand that my father didn't really believe his own harsh accusations; he was just as reactionary as I could be. We were like gasoline and flame. I struck out at him verbally about his drinking and disappointed him with my behavior, so he struck back with hurtful words meant to knock me back in my place. I still don't know which came first, but it became a vicious circle he and I chased each other around for years. Coming to terms with this was a big lightbulb moment in my head.

As a teenager, the thing I had hated most of all was being compared to him, especially considering I felt there was no basis for it. As an adult, however, I'm starting to make some connections that make me feel differently.

My dad used alcohol to avoid deep, interpersonal relationships; he put people second in importance to drinking. He made promises and grand plans, only to break them in favor of drinking. I used my computer to avoid relationships, neglecting people to concentrate on my writing. I promise phone calls that I never make and schedule lunches and get-togethers with friends and family, only to cancel them in order to stay home, glued to the keyboard. When I'm immersed in a book or on deadline, I put writing before family, friends, social contact, grooming, eating, taking care of my health—everything, regardless of the disappointment this causes for others. Our addictions actually aren't so different.

At age twenty-three, I dropped out of college, sold off my meager belongings, and bought a one-way, standby airline ticket to Germany. Although I wanted to go live in Europe for the experience, I admit I also felt satisfaction knowing that dropping out of college would probably piss off my dad once again. As an educator, he was all about education.

The day I told my parents, I hitched my chin defiantly. "I'm moving to Germany." I was certain Dad would flip out, so I'd steeled myself against the litany of reasons why a young woman like myself shouldn't run off to a foreign country alone. It never happened.

Mom sucked a quick breath. "Oh, honey. Really? That's so far away. And what about college?"

"Nonsense," Dad told her. "Living on her own in a foreign country will teach her more than a year or two in any college ever could."

"Really?" I didn't want to believe this career educator actually supported me dropping out of college, but it turned out to be true. He started buying me German language and travel books and doling out salient details about the country in which I would live, and I realized my dad and I shared another trait—wanderlust. He embraced new cultures, and so did I. I had, amazingly, done something of which I was sure my father wouldn't approve, and I'd been dead wrong.

Living on separate continents did wonders for our relationship. I grew up, by necessity. I didn't have anyone there to pay my way or get me out of jams, and I had to obtain residency and work permits, housing, a job—you name it—all on my own. My newfound maturity, and the confidence that came with it, eventually afforded me a clear, objective perspective on the most tumultuous relationship of my life.

My dad was as much of a rebel as I'd always been. Had we switched places, I knew he would've reacted the same way I had to his parenting—testing limits, questioning authority, striking out on his own path. I theorized that my father was extra hard on me because he recognized our similarities and was scared shitless by the addictive personality we both shared, terrified that his own weaknesses would manifest in my life. I believe he saw in me all the opportunities he'd once had, and he so desperately didn't want me to squander them by losing focus, starting to drink, living life in his image.

Did he ever tell me any of this directly? Nope. Not even indirectly. But he had raised all of us to be critically thinking women, and I could finally see past my own anger, past his penchant for alcohol, to what I now believe is the core truth of our relationship: we were more alike than different, and that scared us both.

Alcoholism killed my father while I lived in Germany, just a month after I'd turned twenty-four. We had talked—really talked to each other like two adults, for the first time ever, before it happened. He called me—a first—and I could tell he was plowed already in the middle of the day. Strangely, I didn't immediately snap into my familiar anger reaction, I just wanted to understand him better. For whatever reason, I empathized with him like I hadn't ever done before. He was in the midst of a rambling story about his middle school students and the current semester when I interrupted him.

I sank into a chair by the phone and closed my eyes. "Dad," I asked softly, "why don't you just stop drinking?"

He sighed, and his answer held no anger either. "Because I can't. If I could change my life, I would. Believe me."

I did believe him. For the first time, I didn't think he chose drinking over my siblings or me. I didn't superimpose his alcoholism over the map of my life. I saw it as his blight instead. I suddenly saw my father as a separate person with his own imperfect life, not simply as a player in mine.

The rest of our conversation involved language studies, German culture, the weirdness of middle school kids, and other various topics of interest. My dad was a brilliant conversationalist, a well-read and interesting man. I just hadn't been able to see around our contentiousness to the truth of that.

A huge bouquet of flowers arrived at my door not too long after that phone conversation and with them a card. I've since lost the note, but I'll never forget the words:

> I know I wasn't always the father you wanted, but you were always the daughter I wanted, even when it didn't seem like it. You go after life and take risks to get what you want, and I'm proud of you. Keep learning German, and maybe someday Spanish. Write books. I'll always love you and be proud that you were my daughter. Love, Dad.

Less than a week later, he was dead at the age of fifty-one.

It could've been a case of too little, too late. One candid phone call and words scrawled on a single card. But it wasn't too little, and it's never too late. Maybe it's easier to forgive people who've died, or maybe I'd felt his love and respect in some deeper place all along. All I know for sure is, distance and time had caused a shift in our relationship and opened my eyes.

My stubborn, bossy, persuasive, charming dreamer of a father had somehow managed to raise me, kicking and screaming, in his image. I couldn't be angry about being compared to him any longer, because I was finally happy in my own skin, proud to be the woman I was. He set limits, which I always tested, laid ground rules I always questioned. He kept me on a tight leash because he wanted me to be the best person I could be.

Believe me, I don't think broken promises and cameras, broken hearts and spirits add up to great parenting, but I don't judge his methods any longer. He was what he was and did the best he could at the time.

Almost two decades after my father's death, I've made peace with his life. Whenever I accomplish anything, I tell my mom, "Dad would be busting with pride," and I mean it. I wish he were here to celebrate my successes, because I finally understand him and his contributions to my development as a person.

If he were here, he'd surely sit back and say, "Do you know why you turned out okay? Because your name is Sandoval."

I might allow myself a quick eye roll, but I'd be able to answer him honestly and with pride. "You're right, Dad. Because my name is Sandoval. *Lynda* . . . Sandoval."

BALANCING ACT

BY LAURA TRUJILLO

Henry and I are dashing to his preschool classroom: he's asking me about whether SpongeBob, SquarePants—if he lived with us—would have to live in a fishbowl, or could he sleep in his room? I'm guessing he would have to live in the fishbowl, I tell him: my reason, of course, is that SpongeBob needs water. Henry is five and he always needs to know why.

But really, I'm thinking about my work meeting, the one I'm almost late for, the one that, if I hit all the lights on the way in and maybe speed a little and then land that dream spot near the bottom of the parking garage, I'll actually walk into on time.

Henry rushes into class with a see-you-later-Mom, and I throw his lunch box into the bin, hang his Scooby backpack on the hook, and sign my name on the drop-off sheet. "Those are nice shoes, if you have to work," says a voice behind me. "Hmmm," I say, turning around, half thankful that someone noticed that I was dressed up, half confused as to which one of the eight moms standing behind me said it. "Thanks," I say, "I guess."

Another woman dressed in a tiny white tennis skirt and

tank top smiles, a nodding poor-her smile. Another mom in her knock-off Juicy sweatsuit and flip-flops with a baby—one of those adorable babies that looks like he should be in a Gap ad—gives me a look that I immediately interpret as "you're-a-bad-mother."

I dash back to my car, engine still running. I wonder why three generations of women before me haven't figured how to work *and* be mothers. It feels cliché that even at the new millennium, this discussion still exists. Women have juggled it and cried about it for decades. Sacajawea carried her baby on her back while leading Lewis and Clark. Two centuries later *thirtysomething* tackled it with the usual angst. *Cosmo* told us we could have it all and still have the energy for sex before collapsing to sleep.

Each generation likes to believe that our moms had it easier. And telling ourselves that story allows us to live the lives we do. My friend Kelly dashes out of work, late again, to pick up her daughter at preschool (add $5 per minute), exasperatedly saying "It never was this bad for my mom." Sure, in our mothers' generations, we wouldn't have had the choices we do now, but that's just the point. At least they didn't have to choose. It's easier for me to believe that my mom had no choice, that she graduated from radiology school after Catholic high school, fell in love, got married and pregnant, and then had to stay home.

My dad was from a traditional family, a third-generation American from Mexico, after all. That's what you did—stayed home and raised the babies.

That was then. My dad worked hard, never forcing his life on his daughters. He wanted us to have a choice. Still I can't seem to make it.

My friends say the same thing about their moms, with pity, of course. We like to think they had no choice and that we're the ones who have to make the tough decisions. We think they must have resented us a bit and hated their lives. The way my mom's revolved around shuttling me and my sister to softball practice and Blue Bird meetings, making sure clean and ironed shirts hung in my dad's closet and that dinner was on the table at six every night, with all the food groups represented.

That's why I was so surprised when my mother informed me that I was wrong. She recently told me that even though it meant that she wouldn't graduate from college until she was fifty-eight, after she raised two daughters and had to go to night school, she knows now that she wouldn't have changed her decision, even if she wasn't happy all the time. "No one ever is," she says. But it doesn't mean she wasn't happy, too. My mom and many others had the choice and were strong enough to make it.

So why do I have to juggle so much to be happy?

I check my voice mail while waiting to turn left. What did that woman mean, anyway, by "have to work"? Do I have to work? Yes and no, I think. Yes, maybe to buy these shoes— nothing special, just some strappy ankle-strap shoes, the shoes of the season, and the brown buttery leather skirt I splurged on from Banana Republic. So sure, I laugh to myself, I have to work to buy these.

But that's not what she meant. No, I guess, I don't really *need* to work.

After all, we could live on my husband's newspaper editor's salary. We could downsize; I imagine us living in one of those cute little bungalows, small enough that I can actually keep clean, the kids sharing a room decorated with the hand-sewn duvets with airplanes and helicopters that Martha had taught us how to make (no matter that I haven't sewn since junior high). I could make my own organic applesauce, do laundry before we run out of socks and I'm forced to dig through the dirty clothes hamper before school starts. I wouldn't be late all the time. I would never have to tell my toddler that I didn't have time to read a book before I rushed to work. I wouldn't have to call him in the afternoon because I missed hearing the way he says "frusterated."

I could actually attend those PTA meetings at the elementary school, the ones so smugly scheduled at 9:30 AM on Tuesdays, virtually assuring that none of the working moms will be there. When I volunteered at preschool, I wouldn't offer to clean the class water bottles in the kitchen so I could secretly make phone calls for work. I wouldn't feel schizophrenic all the time. I could join those eight moms at the preschool with their slightly superior attitudes. We could go to Starbucks together after the playgroup.

And then for a moment, I wonder if maybe what we should have done was waited to have kids. Not forever, left to be one of those women hoping her eggs are still good. But just a few years. After all, the maternity clothes are so much better now. Where was Liz Lange when I was wearing all those leggings and tunics?

John and I got married when I was twenty-five. I'd graduated from college, had a great career, and we'd dated for two years. When I talk to some of my friends from school—Regina, the oncologist who waited until she was thirty to marry, medical school after her master's degree—I'm almost embarrassed.

Because to many, it sounds crazy. I got married at twenty-five, and by thirty-three, here I am with three kids.

As much as I thought I'd be different from my family (I'd be the one coming home only for tamales at Christmas), I began to realize that maybe I'm more like them than I thought. And so we gave up our great jobs in Portland, Oregon, and moved to my hometown. We bought a house ten minutes away from all of my relatives—to see my nana, dad, mom, sister, cousins, and aunts. My husband teases me. Is this a Latino thing or a family thing? I mean, doesn't everyone's aunt live next door to their dad?

But if we waited, we'd be one of those cosmopolitan couples with money to buy cheap short-notice tickets for vacation in Paris, living in a downtown loft with metal open stairs (stairs that a toddler could never race up without injuries), and able to go to dinner without finding a babysitter. On Sundays, we could read the whole *New York Times* and maybe even finally refinish the old mission desk we bought. Maybe I'd be the one with the Nieman fellowship studying at Harvard this year. (Okay, maybe not, but I need some excuse.) I could bounce from job to job, moving to New York or Boston, not caring which school district we lived in. We would have the nanny's salary, the preschool tuition to buy the Ralph Lauren leather sofa, the Marc Jacobs bag, the DKNY suit before it goes on sale and all the size sixes are gone.

But if I'd waited, would I have *these* three beautiful, healthy children? And would my nana and family be alive to enjoy them as long?

No, apparently I really am glad we didn't wait after all. So if I don't have to work because we need the money, then it must be that I choose to work—that I want to be more than just a wife and mother. And maybe that's not something I want to know about myself. That I have to work to be who I am. That I pay someone else to help me raise my children. That my son called our nanny Mom for a year. That maybe I'm not good enough to stay home. That maybe I am good enough, but it's simply not what I want.

I turn and immediately get stuck in traffic. Fiddlesticks, I say, seriously, because I made the mistake of saying something much worse around my toddler, and you know the rest. I'm going to be late.

I was never one to want to be a mom. Not someone who coveted baby dolls. I rarely babysat, preferring to mow lawns. I always figured I'd have a great job as a reporter and someday would have a family, I just never really thought about the practical part—you have to have a baby first.

But a year or so into marriage, John and I decided we were ready for a baby. Nine months later, there was Henry. And then, just like all those books said, I turned to mush. Suddenly, here was this little person who grabbed my pinky and smiled—smiled!—and that was enough. He even seemed content when I read my favorite book, Joan Didion's *Slouching Toward Bethlehem*, out loud to him, instead of nursery rhymes. He changed my life, and if I'm lucky, I'm helping change his, or making his just as good as he made mine.

And so I decided to work and stay home. To work part-time. To manage both lives, because I couldn't leave either one behind.

And so it turns out that this tomboy, this girl who never dreamed of dressing up a baby in all those little ruffly clothes, now has a row of three car seats in the back of a Volvo station wagon. We never discussed how many kids we wanted to have. But once Henry got to be about two and even more fun, we decided we *needed* another baby, not because we wanted another baby, but because we wanted another kid. It's that feeling of realizing that your children are the most amazing people you'll meet. When Henry was three, we had Theo, the most adorable curly-haired baby. Henry said he'd rather have a skateboard.

We thought we couldn't be busier and wondered why we felt stressed or pressed for time with one kid, let alone two. And when Theo was just a baby, I decided I wanted one more. And we figured it would be good to have the kids close together. They could stay home together and grow up together. Our friends told us we were crazy and asked if we were simply "trying for a girl."

And I never could fully explain why we wanted a third child. I joked that three was the new two, that all the moms were doing it. But the truth is, I love being a mom. I love my husband even more when I see what a wonderful, caring, and fun father he is. I wanted Theo to be as good a big brother as Henry was to him. I wanted Henry to have another brother, not just now for the T-ball and soccer games, but for when he's thirty or when he's fifty, and John and I are crazy, so he'll have someone to call and laugh with.

I wanted another kid who would be a part of me, so much so that we gave each of them my last name, Trujillo, as a middle name. Maybe it was my way of passing my culture to them, even if it seems like just a gesture. I wanted them to feel like Trujillos, too. So I'm trying to teach them Spanish, with the help of Sandra Cisneros's books.

When I'm not making sure my kids are clean, healthy, and bicultural, I edit a fashion magazine at my newspaper. It's a full-time job that somehow I've persuaded my bosses into letting me do part-time, working from home half the week. My husband often leaves for work early, rushing off so he can come home early and I can stay through copy-editing and page proofs. The mornings are a blur, me trying to blow-dry my hair while reading Madonna's newest morality tale to my toddler and dodging the Cheerios the baby is throwing at us from his high chair.

Henry, the five-year-old, has just opened the debate on whether Tony Hawk or Bucky Lasek is going to do a 980 at the upcoming X Games when Gaby, my saint of a nanny, arrives, saving me from the life I created. Or maybe what she does is allow me to have this joyful mess.

I rush into the meeting, late, where editors already are discussing what should go on page one. Nixed is a story about unsafe playgrounds, the one story I might read tomorrow. And with snot on the bottom of my skirt, the snot I saw before I rushed out the door pretending not to notice, I take notes and wonder if I can finish editing photos to get to Henry's class play on time. Laura the editor and Laura the mom sit in the meeting together, planning the day, but some days it feels like neither Laura can get things right.

Recently I had a very busy day at work. My son had soccer practice that night. If I left on time to pick him up and my other boys from home to dart to practice, I'd never finish editing the magazine. It needed to get done. And when my nanny called to tell me that Henry ate his dinner early, put on his shin guards and cleats, and was ready, she put him on the phone to ask about practice. I told him practice was canceled. I'd be home later. I lied to my son to finish a project. Then I cried all the way home.

Another day, I was rushing to get dressed when Theo, my cherub of a two-year-old, tugged at my leg, saying, "Read to me, read this." In a minute, I told him.

Just read this, he said, placing the *I Stink* garbage truck at my feet. I grabbed my clothes. Maybe Gaby can read it to you, I said. When she gets here.

"I like Gaby better than you," he said, smiling.

I stopped, suddenly finding the time to pick up his book.

"You mean she's nice to you, just like Mommy?" I said hopefully. "Yes, Gaby's nice to me and takes care of me and you're nice to me and take care of me," he said.

"So you really mean, you like Gaby the same, the same as Mommy, right," I say, knowing if I were in a courtroom I'd be accused of leading the witness.

"Yes, I like you both," he said, laughing.

His baby brother toddled by and Theo darted off with him, leaving me in a worry. I relay the conversation to moms at work, looking for the obvious—yes, he really meant he likes both of you. I felt slightly better. Besides, many of them work full-time, I must be okay.

One month, the mothers' lounge at work was nearly full as we all sat in a room and pumped breast milk. We edited stories and proofread spreadsheets and felt like a dairy. I wondered why we pushed ourselves so hard.

I guess for me it's because much of who I am and how I value myself is in my work. There's no paycheck for raising your kids, there's no quarterly review or annual raise to tell you you're doing a good job. The kids will say thank you for reading the eleventh book on crocodiles or for making them dinosaur-shaped chicken nuggets, but not for trying to make them thoughtful, sensitive, loving, and hopefully bilingual.

The worth comes in quiet moments every day, like when I'm washing the dishes and hear the boys playing in the family room—happily. I can hear Henry reading a book to Theo about a boy on his bike. Then he stops and I hear him describing to Theo how he's going to teach him to ride a bike. "But not till you're four," he says. "Or you'll get hurt." Despite these moments, I want more. I want to make decisions at the newspaper, edit stories and work with young reporters, even enjoy lunch now and then with my friends at work, and have a life outside of home. My job allows me to cope. And it makes me a better mom. Working full-time away from home three days a week makes me love the four days a week I'm home with my kids.

So right now, this is how it is. You don't do things perfectly. The day goes on, with or without my self-examination. Questions are answered. Phone calls are returned. I finish editing the week's issue and rush to get out the door with my husband on time for the class play. I call the preschool director from my cell phone and ask if she can hold the play for five minutes because I'm late, and she does. All the moms are there, cameras in hand. Not just their video cameras but the digital ones, too, the ones that likely will be turned into scrapbooks with stickers, thoughtful notes, and acid-free paper. And I realize I'm the only one without a camera.

But then I tell myself it's okay, that I'd rather remember the good and the bad, the messy and all, because that's life, right? And Henry says his line, with only a little prompting from his teacher.

No, I don't really belong in either world. But I float in and out of both, seamlessly at times and with much more angst at others. I do really want to figure it all out, this netherworld I live in. But just not today. Today I've got to figure out if SpongeBob SquarePants is going to eat the crabby patties in the fishbowl or not.

II

"And After We Kissed . . ."

ON THE VERGE

BY ANGIE CRUZ

The day of the 2003 blackout, I went to meet my friend at a quiet café on Greenwich Avenue, and as soon as we sat down, the lights went out. We went to another café across the street, to find that the entire avenue was without electricity.

"Oh, it feels like DR," I said to my friend, and thought back to a conversation with a young man in the Dominican Republic, who asked me, "Is it true that the lights never go out in New York?"

"Never," I said, not bothering to mention that the lights did go out three years ago in Washington Heights. It happened during a heat wave. We all imagined that Con Ed chose the Heights over a neighborhood like power-hungry Forty-second Street because the Dominican community, for the most part, always talked about returning home to the island. And when don't the lights go out in DR? It happens so often, it's part of the lifestyle. When the lights go out, we take a break, sit outside, and delay our plans. We use up all the ice in the fridge, and those who can afford it eat the meat in the freezer and feast with whoever is around. But downtown New York City without power? How could Con Ed be so cruel? It could only be temporary. Or so we thought.

We decided to get something to drink and head to the park until the electricity came back on. There, we spent two hours in the sun talking about traveling to another country, and maybe living somewhere else, where people worked to live and didn't live to work. Where people greeted each other on the street and weren't afraid to look in each other's eyes. A country with an antiwar government, where the disparity of the wealth wasn't so extreme? Did such a place even exist?

"So why don't you move, then?" she asked.

"I don't know if I'm brave enough," I said, surprised at my answer.

My parents came to the United States with a few dollars in their pockets. They didn't have a network or speak the language. They moved here in search of a "better" life. Was it okay for me to transplant myself to another country? Or was a choice like that screaming traitor to the familia's overall plans? Wasn't it my duty, as the daughter of immigrant parents, to strive to live the American Dream in all its splendor by getting married, finding a job with benefits, and earning enough money to help my mother in her old age?

At thirty-one, I was not married. I was a writer, so the hope of making enough money to take care of myself let alone my mother seemed dismal. And benefits? My biggest benefit as a writer (if I had a writing gig to begin with) was that I could move anywhere I wanted to as long as I could plug in my laptop. So why did the idea of moving to another city seem so radical? I had lived in Washington Heights for most of my life, and I always told myself that it was because the rents were cheaper. But deep down inside I was afraid of leaving and abandoning my community, which was tied to how I identified myself. More so, I was afraid that if I left no one would notice I was gone.

As a child I had always assumed that when I left the hood, it would be on a horse and carriage with the sign JUST MARRIED attached. In my early twenties I moved out of my mother's apartment and assumed that once I found a partner (we didn't exactly have to get married), we would go on adventures together around the world. I also assumed that Washington Heights, with so much of my family living on one block, would always be there for me to return to. Now in my thirties, I was thinking of good friends that would make great co-parents and I accepted that maybe the man that I fell in love with might not necessarily be the man I would have a family with. And that maybe I would have to take my adventures in life alone. I also knew that the community I called home was changing, immigrants being pushed out by university students and yuppified New Yorkers. If I left for too long I might return to the Heights and not recognize the place. Just the thought made my heart beat faster.

My friend and I parted ways with much on our minds. She headed toward the train. I headed toward a bus. We didn't bother to check if there was electricity or not. I didn't notice that the stoplights weren't working. There were hardly any cars on the streets. Only when I saw the crowds waiting for buses did I think that something was wrong. I asked a woman at the bus stop if she knew what was happening.

"The entire East Coast is blacked out. You have to get home any way you can, before nightfall," she said. I recognized the fear in the woman's face as she struggled with her cell phone and attempted to hitch a ride uptown. Her face screamed terrorism. The crowds on the streets reminded me of 9/11. I saw the panic in people's eyes.

My first thought was that I should've moved out of New York City when I still had a chance. I had planned on leaving New York after 9/11. But I didn't know where to go. I definitely didn't belong in the Dominican Republic, where my cousins called me alternative because I refused to blow out my hair. I felt like I was living neither here nor there. If I hadn't read Gloria Anzaldua's book *Borderlands*, I would have been wandering the earth in search of a land I could call mine. Thanks to her I could at least claim spiritual and emotional citizenship on the "borderland."

So on the night of the blackout, while most people looked very sure about where they were going, I felt I was at a crossroads. I was caught between calling my mother and calling my ex-boyfriend/lover/friend, who knew me better than anyone else at the time and who was my latest refuge. I stood on a barbwire balancing the two worlds that meant the most to me. I knew my mother was probably trying to reach me and that she was worried. The latter was up in the air. After dating him for a year and three months, I wasn't sure if he cared.

We had just broken up. Again. As if one could break emotional ties like one closes a bank account. Months before, when the United States went to war with Iraq and the city was on high alert, I asked him: "Sweetie, if something went down in New York, who would you choose to spend your last hours with? Your ex-wife and child . . . or me?

"That's not a fair question," he said. "I can't believe you would ask such a thing." The blackout came just a couple of months later. Okay, it wasn't as if we were on the *Titanic* or the city were on orange alert, but still, there I was, standing on

Twelfth Street and Seventh Avenue, feeling very vulnerable, five blocks away from my boyfriend's apartment. I could either find a way to get uptown to my mother or just walk over to his place and wait for him to get home. I panicked.

I jammed the circuits trying to reach my mother, who was on the other end of the island of Manhattan. I was wearing uncomfortable shoes and couldn't imagine walking 150 blocks. It was getting dark. I had my ex/etc.'s keys in my bag. We weren't really in a relationship anymore. We were trying to be friends. But there was no one that I wanted to be in the dark with more than him. I felt like a fool for feeling that way because I imagined him with his ex-wife and child. *His family.*

Mi familia was my mother. My mother, who didn't have a husband or partner that I knew of. At that moment I identified with her. What it must feel like for her to sit alone in the dark, possibly afraid that no one was coming home. Or maybe she wasn't afraid, maybe she was just wishing for some company to shorten the dark hours without television, radio, or lights. Maybe she was fine. Unlike me.

I didn't go uptown that day. I walked toward my ex/etc.'s apartment hoping that he wouldn't mind but knowing deep down inside of me that I didn't care if he minded. The day we broke up he didn't ask me for his apartment keys. I didn't ask for mine. We both decided that we were in two very different places, wanting very different things. He was an overworked film-industry guy who yearned to spend more time alone, and I, after writing in isolation for eight to ten hours a day, desperately sought a playmate, a partner, someone to go out with and experience the world.

"Even though I love you, I don't think I can do the relationship thing right now."

Those were his last words to me.

I thought about the fact that his father was staying with him. He was visiting from Mexico. What if his father found it inappropriate that I showed up unannounced? Was using his keys without his permission a line I shouldn't have crossed? I thought about what it meant to be a good Latina woman. Not someone that just showed up or stayed over in her ex-boyfriend's bed while the father was in the other room sleeping on the couch.

I looked over at the crowd waiting for the buses. The buses were full and not taking any more passengers. I looked toward the west side and saw the sun slowly come down. I envied the joyous-looking people, drinking it up at the bars. I saw all the people embracing, finally finding each other after their long treks home. Parents were carrying their children. Lovers were holding hands and putting their heads on each other's shoulders. Vendors were giving away ice cream. I was terrified of being alone. But worst of all, I was afraid that no one wanted to be with me.

I was mad at myself for having such feelings. I'd been on my own for twelve years. But what was wrong with accepting the need to want someone, to trust someone, and to have someone in my life that would help me do some of the lifting? Maybe some of the women in my family were able to live life without partners and still look sane while they were at it. But I was on the verge that night. After everything I'd lived through, was I going to see the end of the world alone and without someone to love me?

I continued to call him and couldn't get through, but I finally did get in touch with my mother.

"I'm staying downtown," I told her.

It was our code for "I'm staying with my ex/etc.," whom she still thought was my boyfriend, possibly my future husband. How could I explain my predicament to her—after being with a man a year and three months. My mother had warned me that a divorced man with a child would never be fully mine. At least not until he was ready to marry again.

"I'm glad you're safe, mi'jita," she said. And told me she had her feet in a vat of water after walking 120 blocks to get home from work.

I could have also taken that walk. But I didn't.

I made my way into his apartment and sat down to wait for him in the dark. There was no radio, no phone in his place. My cell phone was out of range. I didn't know if he would come home that night. I wondered if he stayed at work, or if he was over at his ex-wife's and chose to stay there with his son. I waited in the dark contemplating if that was what I wanted my life to be like. Not knowing if the man that I loved even wanted to be with me in an emergency situation. That if we were on a sinking ship, would he choose his ex-wife and son before me?

I had obviously watched too many movies. I decided that as soon as he showed up I would tell him that maybe with time we could be friends, but right now I needed a healthier relationship where I was certain the man I loved was coming home to me and I to him, especially if the world was coming to an end. I sat in his living room feeling like a trespasser, even when my photograph was still on his bulletin board and my toothbrush in the bathroom.

I thought about all the relationships that grew closer or fell apart after 9/11. Those are the moments when things become clear. Whom we love. Whom we care about. What we want.

And I knew then that I wanted to be with him. And in the midst of seeing people feel their way down the streets, holding candles and lighters to make their way up stairs, I thought how he hadn't even left a message on my cell showing that he was concerned.

At that moment I craved someone to take care of me. I started to fear not being able to have children if I waited too long. Even if it meant being in a dysfunctional family, I wanted one anyway. I romanticized my grandmother's relationship with my grandfather. They sacrificed to have a large family. I imagined her at home with all her children around her table, reminiscing about their lives in DR. I wished I had chosen to walk uptown in time before the sunset to be a part of that. Little did I know at the time that my grandmother was also sitting alone at home. And her relationship with my grandfather was far from romantic.

I laid down on my ex/etc.'s sofa. The sun was finally gone, and I heard laughter and lively conversation from the streets. Who were all those happy people laughing? I envied them. They sounded secure. Why shouldn't they be? The U.S. government was going into debt to secure everyone against terrorism. I wondered if President Bush might also be sitting in the dark in D.C., afraid of living in a world where no one loved him, of losing everything that made him feel secure. Maybe that was what made him declare war in such haste? Was it the fear of vulnerability, the fear of change that led us to war? Was it possible to secure a country from terrorism any more than it was to secure a person from feeling alone with a ritual like marriage? And was that why my ex/etc. and I had such a hard time committing to each other, because we knew that no one could make us feel less alone unless we felt secure within ourselves first?

Instead of trying to battle aloneness in a dark room all by myself, maybe I would be closer to achieving my desire, to share and receive love, by surrounding myself with people.

I grabbed a candle and some matches and decided to go meet the neighbors. They weren't my neighbors, but what the hell, I needed to find out what was going on. I tried to open the door. Somehow I had locked myself in. The door handle was loose and slipping off the socket. I looked around to feel the darkness creep around me. I banged on the door with the hope a neighbor would help me out. Not only was I alone, I was really trapped in the dark. My phone flashing NO SERVICE with a few minutes of battery life left. I was inside his apartment, among his things, without his permission.

After a few hours my ex-boyfriend/lover/friend walked in with his father to the apartment. He rushed to me and held me for what seemed like a long time.

"I'm so glad you came here," he said. "I left you messages. Didn't you get them?"

Only hours later did my phone beep to show that he did leave a message.

That night we lit candles and ate the ice cream in the fridge. His father read poetry to us. We talked about art and life and commented on how silly it was that in a city that was supposed to have so much wealth, there was so little time to sit and talk. Without the radio or television we were engrossed, content. I was present and wasn't thinking about the future. I was enjoying his father's words, my ex/etc., the beautiful lighting, and trying to stay cool in the heat. Isn't that what life should be about?

The next day, I crawled out of my ex/etc.'s apartment and we walked into a crowd of people, wandering aimlessly. I felt more at peace. Not because he didn't ask for the keys to his apartment back, but because the terror of ending up alone without anyone to love was tucked deep inside somewhere. It was a new day. I allowed the future to unfold instead of pushing for the script I had already written in my head.

After fourteen hours, no one seemed to know what was going on exactly, or when the electricity was coming back on. A part of me wished the lights wouldn't come back on. The city was free from traffic, the stores were cool because all the appliances were off, and strangers were striking up where-were-you-when-the-lights-went-out-stories. I rushed over to buy the *New York Times*. I got the last copy and a man offered to pay me five times the price. I was no fool. I kept the newspaper close to my heart and ran over to stand on one of the long lines to use the public pay phones to call my mother. I was relieved to hear her voice.

"We've had electricity for an hour," my mother said, shocked that the downtown folk were still in the dark.

Admittedly, I was also shocked. When did us uptown folk ever get the better deal? I read the *Times* and learned that investigators didn't think terrorism played a role in the blackout. Another article blamed New York's old transmission system.

"At least it's not terrorism," I overheard a lady saying on her cell phone.

"It definitely wasn't terrorism," a man said on the line to his friend.

I thought back to the last blackout uptown, and the late-night conversations on the front stoop with my neighbors and cousins. I missed them. I didn't know these people downtown. My family felt very far away in a city where the trains weren't running. I started to think about the conversation I had with my friend about leaving this country. It felt like ages ago when I was sitting in the park, when the lights first went out. I started to think about all the fears that had ripped through my heart and head in a fourteen-hour span and I laughed to myself. At least it wasn't terrorism. As if the terror we have in our hearts weren't enough.

I caught a bus heading uptown. I wanted to be around my family and walk into a home I knew I was always welcomed into. Neighbors greeted me on the street and I realized how I took my community for granted. I was so busy trying to make my ex/etc. mi familia, I had forgotten that I already had a family. I thought back to the conversation with my friend, about not being brave enough to leave the Heights and start over somewhere else. At the moment I wanted to be nowhere else. Nothing could be more romantic and satisfying than walking into the familiarity of my mother's kitchen, the noisy streets, into the cacophony of questions and wet kisses and embraces after a long trek home.

THE FIRST WIFE

BY SHIRLEY VELÁSQUEZ

They met on a balmy evening on an Upper West Side corner of Manhattan. She was on her way back to her hotel room, and he had just walked out of his mother's apartment. I'm unsure about the length of their conversation or the topics they covered, but I know it was her brown and thickly curled hair that caught my boyfriend's attention. M.'s eyes wandered in the springtime, but as summer approached, he was actively looking.

He came home late that evening, and I was standing over the stove, boiling water for lentils. "It smells great in here," he said, "thanks for making dinner." Maybe it was the way he said "great," or perhaps his overly friendly chatter, but I knew that he'd met someone.

"I want to meet her too," I said.

"Okay," he said. He didn't try to lie. He didn't tell me much about her, either. "But remember," he giggled, "you're the first wife." Then he kissed me on the cheek and headed back out of the kitchen.

"At least he knows I'm the only woman who'll tolerate this," I thought to myself. But then again, what if there were other women who were willing to accept M. and his harem?

And what if they received him without reproaches? I felt inadequate but I decided against revealing any vulnerability. The following day I found myself searching for poise. M. had invited her for dinner, and I needed to be bigger, wiser, and more beautiful than her.

Making believe I was thick-skinned was not new for me. It took only for me to tighten my cheek muscles and clamp my jaw to prevent me from betraying anger or fear. As early as nine years old I had practiced the skill of transforming liquid emotions into marble sculpture. Back in the mid-1980s, when Cabbage Patch dolls were the status symbol of third-graders, I pleaded with my mother to buy me the doll in exchange for better grades in school and more help with house chores. Not an even exchange, since my mother was a single parent at the time and rearing two children. The likelihood of getting the doll was rather small. But that Christmas season in 1985, I secretly rummaged through the shopping bags she had just brought home. And to my shock, I discovered "Michael" from the cabbage patch in Georgia, awaiting adoption.

"I knew it. I knew it. I knew it!" I uttered aloud. I would have preferred to adopt a girl but I was excited, and relieved, to be Michael's new momma. Then, before I could put the loot back into the shopping bag, Mother walked out of the kitchen and caught me with my Christmas gift in my arms. She came over, took the box and the rest of the shopping bags, and instructed me to get wrapping paper. "Why didn't she yell at me for seeing my gift," I wondered.

"Start wrapping the gifts," she said to me in Spanish, and then disappeared into the kitchen.

"This one too," I said, pointing to the doll.

"Yes, that's for Christina."

Christina was my best friend, and our mothers were also close friends. But Mother's intentions confused me. Why would she give Christina the one thing I wanted.

"Maybe she's tricking me," I thought. "Maybe she's punishing me for poking through the gifts."

I wanted to blow into the kitchen and tell her to stop teasing me. Why couldn't she be straight with me? She complained about being short on money consistently, but here she had just bought presents. So now, I also worried about my mother having enough to feed and clothe us. Since she took my complaints as personal attacks, I tried not to cry. Instead I wrapped the gifts and wrote out Christina's name on the Cabbage Patch box.

The first time I had noticed my boyfriend's lusty desires for other women was six months into our relationship. A pale blue envelope sat in his open schoolbag, and it caught my attention as I walked by. His name was delicately scripted on the front. I took the card out, and my finger rubbed off some of the card's red glitter. I remember only pieces of what I read:

"Dear M., We're lucky to have met each other . . . You are an amazing man . . . I'm excited to get to know you better. Love, C."

She had written her phone number down, right below her name, so I decided to call her.

"I'm M.'s girlfriend. Can I ask you a couple of questions?" My voice was sweet and pathetic, which is probably why she did not hang up on me. C., I found out, was an African-American psychology student in her late twenties.

"I met him in Central Park," she told me. "He was walking his dog."

"That's our dog," I said defensively, quickly getting to the point. "Did you guys have sex? Because from your letter it seems like something happened." I took a long puff from my cigarette before she finally responded.

"I think you need to talk to him. He never told me he had a girlfriend." She clearly wanted to get off the phone, but I managed to extract from her a final bit of juice—that on one of their dates they had kissed close to the mouth, but never directly on it. We hung up and I pounced into the living room, where he was sleeping, determined to find out every ounce of information on their little romance.

"Wake up!" I was crying. "I called C. and she told me everything that happened between you." I knew nothing, but I hoped some detail would help make sense of this nightmare.

"We only saw each other a few times, nothing happened."

"That's not what she said!" I yelled.

"Nothing happened. I drove her to school once and we hugged."

"How did you hug? Show me." He reenacted the moment for me and I played C.'s role.

"I don't believe you. What did you do with her? Do you want to be with her?"

"I don't know." His voice was quiet and exasperated.

He simply did not know what he wanted, that much was the truth. He went to bed again and I stayed up the entire night. Just because I had thwarted their liaison did not mean there were not more women to come between us.

M. and I met on a hot summer evening in 1996. I was twenty years old, a sophomore in college, and he was almost thirty-two. We were at the Theater of Dreams, on the Upper East Side, attending an interactive play in which audience members would explain inspirational dreams or recurring nightmares, then the performers would act out the scenes. He saw me as I walked in and sat down in front of him. I could feel his stare; I looked at him too. He was beautiful. Short brown hair and hazel eyes. At the end of the performance, he approached me.

"How did you like it?" he said. I was nervous and didn't know what to say except "It was fine."

He asked for my number and called a few nights later. We saw a lot of each other over the next month. While his mother was out of the country on sabbatical, M. had moved into her spacious Upper West Side apartment. He invited me often, and we made love more than we talked. He was a natural storyteller. I learned that his family had fled west through the forests of Eastern Europe during a pogrom at the turn of the twentieth century and settled on the Lower East Side of Manhattan.

His mother was a graduate school professor and had been a professional ballerina before joining academia. Where Mother's apartment smelled of carne asada, hers smelled like paper. The walls in her apartment were lined with books, some tattered and most with notes sticking out of them. Intrigued by this woman and her lifestyle, I began poking around her stuff.

Her belongings revealed specks of her interesting life, and without even knowing her, I became equally drawn to and intimidated by her. In her closet hung a red velvet turtleneck shirt and red velvet tight pants. Perhaps she had worn the outfit to one of her book parties, where another admiring author complimented her delicately stranded silver earrings.

In her living room hung paintings by a famous Mexican muralist, which the artist himself had dedicated to her. I had seen one of his paintings in MoMA. M. explained to me that his mother's relative had married the painter and that he and M.'s family had founded a taller in Mexico City. In his mother's bedroom was a photograph of her standing next to Diego Rivera in front of his studio. Here I was, an unknown, inconsequential, one of the hoi polloi from Queens in the museum-like home of prominent artists. What luck to have met a man like M., who had inherited what I had wanted so desperately: a mother who was also a trusted confidante, a legacy to share. In those succeeding moments I decided to keep M., to make him love me. He was my opportunity to get out of the oppressive atmosphere in my family's home. He would not have chosen me if he had known early on that my parents took on an extra job delivering the newspaper to pay for my high school tuition or that my father struggled to assemble coherent sentences in English.

When I finally met her, she was sitting in a café, wearing a necklace I had spotted in her jewelry box. She was a beautiful woman entering her sixties, and I absorbed her every facial and bodily movement. She enjoyed the gravitas of intellectual conversations, but I was too young and insecure to provide her with anything meaty. I was afraid of boring her with my stupidity, so I kept quiet, at least then I could feign mystery. She revealed little of herself that evening. It didn't matter. I was already obsessed with making her my own. She was precisely the mother I had fantasized about.

Only two months after we met, M. asked me to move in with him and I readily agreed. I was eager to create the bright, cultured home I had imagined. I would fill shelves with the books my parents should have had that would have taught me about Latin American art and maps of the ancient Incan empire. But M.'s infidelities quickly began to threaten my dream, and I became determined to stop his other women from robbing me of my home and the man who gave it to me.

It is possible to be addicted to a person, to a lover. And as with any addiction, the body twists itself in discomfort until it can indulge in the drug again. Comparing myself to other women appeased my addiction to him; my body would itch until I compared her defects to my assets and vice versa. She doesn't speak English well; she never read Pablo Neruda's memoir; she has big tits, but her ass is sagging. Whereas: I do M.'s laundry; I keep our apartment clean; not only did I read Neruda's memoir in Spanish, I also carried a Spanish-English dictionary in my bag to look up the words I didn't know. "So I'm better than her," I concluded. And soon after my mind had injected its assessment of the situation into my body, my fear was temporarily soothed. I had gotten my fix.

I had heard before that the first time a lover strays, it can pass for a mistake. But M. had not erred. And for the next few months, I pictured what the next woman would be like. In one fantasy, she was taller than me, had long golden hair, and a tight body. Maybe he would meet her at the organic supermarket in his mother's neighborhood as she picked up the last of her grocery bags from the cashier counter.

"Let me help you," he'd say. Then he'd walk her home, four or five blocks away. During the walk, she'd tell him that she lived with her parents and that she was a fine arts student. He'd compliment her on her smile, and she'd giggle softly. There would be nothing brusque or crude about her. Unlike my parents, hers would have never confided their financial struggles to her. Instead they'd discuss her ideas about a subject she wanted to paint or they'd share their comments and thoughts about a play they'd attended.

During one of our fights, probably about one of M.'s millions of flirtations, he looked at me and said, "How can you expect

me to be with only one person?" He said it with sincere conviction. His parents had taken lovers, after all. Was I the abnormal
one here? I suddenly realized then that in order to keep him, I'd
have to welcome those other women into our lives and eventually into our bed. I could not force him to choose me and only
me. He was not capable of it.

When he met U., I had already stopped nagging him about
the women he seduced. No more catching. When he met S., I
told him to see her as often as he wanted. He was a free human
being, after all. My love had stamina and my plan was to wait
until he realized what a good girl/woman I could be. And what
did I get out of it? Well, I eliminated M.'s need to lie. I felt a
surge in vitality because my man and I were living in reality.
All by myself, I'd found the intestinal power to keep M. I knew
how to please him. I was going to experience the other women,
firsthand, by seeing and touching them. I'd understand why M.
was attracted to them. Maybe I would emulate a gesticulation
or braid my long black hair like theirs. Perhaps if I incorporated
one of their oft-used words into my own sentences, he'd like
me better.

When I wasn't obsessing about M. and his women, I had
college to deal with. It was impossible to seek refuge in my
studies, though I wish I had been more selfish with my time,
worrying less about the outcome of our relationship. Just before
graduating university, I landed an assignment as a business reporter that took me to Hong Kong for an entire summer. We
spoke a few times, and led separate lives. For the first time in
my life, at the age of twenty-four, I had my own bedroom. The
first two weeks were difficult as I developed a routine that did
not include him.

Luckily, my work at the paper demanded enough of my concentration to keep my mind off what M. was doing without me to question him. I took the bus to remote areas, finding the right words and gestures to get me to an interview with local businessmen. I had friends and immersed myself in Chinese culture. Away from the chaos of living with M., I had a sense of myself.

Then I returned to New York. M. had been unsure if he wanted to continue living with me, and part of me dreaded facing him when I arrived. I came back with no job or place to stay; I refused to move back with my parents. The strength I developed in Hong Kong faded to increasing insecurity and anxiety. M. and I went on an intense summer's-end trip to Maine. Among honeymooners and jagged rocks, we resolved to make a fresh start. I moved back in, and soon enough, he slipped back into old habits.

I thought this over as I finished preparing dinner for M. and his new girl, D. She's a twenty-two-year-old architecture student from Brazil, and when the doorbell rings, I step into regal character. I open the door and in sotto voce welcome the slender trigueña. She walks in and bends toward M. to embrace him. "She's inside my home," I think to myself. "In the flesh," I say aloud, with a forced smile. We get to know each other. She's a warm woman with two dimples dotting each side of her big mouth. I don't sense that she's attracted to M., but as we eat dinner, I'm anxious. I realize that, among us, I've drunk most of the alcohol. We talk, I can't remember what about. Then we go into the bedroom and close the door behind us. I'm nervous and can't believe I'm about to see my boyfriend fuck another woman. M. is naturally charming and proposes to give us both massages. She plops into the middle of my bed, and I head into the bathroom to wash myself down there again—to make sure I don't stink. I look in the mirror. My face looks yellow and wide. My nose twists to the right and my left breast sags heavier than my right one. "I'm still here," I think to myself.

When I return she has already taken off her clothing and is wearing only pink gingham panties. Her breasts are full, luscious, and the nipples are brown and hard. I hesitate before taking off my kimono. "I think I'll keep it on for now," I tell myself. M. has already doused his hands in almond oil and begins to rub from her stomach to her breasts. He massages the entire breast. I want to touch her too, but I don't know how or when to do it. Then I want to hurt her. "What am I doing here," I ask myself. "They don't care if I'm here or not." I'm drunk and curl into the corner of the bed and pretend to fall asleep. I fantasize about being ten again: My mom picks me up from school and we make our way back home through quiet streets. The sounds of sex break my reverie and when I look behind me I locate the source of the sound—his hands rubbing the oil on her legs. I'm too nervous to participate. So I put my hand on his rear, squeeze it a little. I give the whole affair my blessing. Within moments I've descended into deep, dark sleep.

The following morning I was embarrassed at the stupidity of it all—having a horny boyfriend, touching his women, burying anxiety in pseudo-philosophical conversations. In fact, shame would become the common denominator of the "the morning after," and there were many mornings after.

Slowly, I began to find small escapes from my home life. I got a job as an editor at Ms. magazine, even sitting next to Gloria Steinem at meetings at times. I attended art history classes at the Metropolitan Museum of Art and took tango lessons, where I allowed flirtations to grow.

So when we attended my friend C.'s birthday party, I did not panic when M. struck up a conversation with A. She giggled a lot and leaned her body in, toward his seat. Instead, I continued my conversation, with whom and about what I cannot remember. All throughout the evening, as the flirting between them peaked and ebbed, a little voice echoed in my mind. "He won't leave you for her. She is fatter than you. She wouldn't do for him what you do." The playing continued between them, and I secretly hoped no one would notice.

Two weeks later, I saw my friend C. again for dinner and she struggled to tell me something. "I'm mad at M.," she finally said, "he was really inappropriate at my birthday dinner." It turned out people had noticed their banter that night and now C. was about to give me secondhand information about the nature of his relationship with A. My thoughts raced. Had they stolen a kiss that night while I was in the bathroom? Had they had a tryst or made love on my bed while I was at work?

"What happened?" I asked. She scratched her chin for a moment and said, "At one point in the evening, A. realized there was nothing casual in the way you spoke to M. So she pressed him for questions about your relationship."

I pressed him for questions about our relationship too. All the time. And we usually ended up screaming at each other. But apparently that night he talked gaily and only to her. C. continued, "When she asked M. if you were his girlfriend, he replied 'I guess you could say that for now.'"

C. stopped to give me a moment to digest what she was telling me. "And when she asked M. if you lived together, he said 'we have a living arrangement.'" C. proceeded to apologize for delivering disturbing news and said something about how I needed to leave M. In the echo of her voice, the decision stepped into my mind as an imperative. It was not a question, it felt surprisingly factual and unsentimental. The spectacular moment I had been waiting to arrive for years came unexpectedly while C. dipped her nacho chip into a bowl of guacamole.

Stories about the relationships we leave take on their own personality. Whenever I tell mine, it seems like a different story altogether, as if it belonged to someone else. Or as if I were a crew member watching the play from backstage. Sometimes I give a detailed account of the thirty days it took me to pack my clothing and some books. Though I did not know where to go or how to leave, I knew I had to move out and on. Other times, I focus my story on my friends' pep talks. "You need confidence, you need to feel sexy again," they'd say. One even suggested I find another lover. Un clavo con atro sequita. Eventually I did.

I went through another phase where I would tell my story a lot, to whomever would listen. Once, while at a Duane Reade, I confessed to the cashier that I missed M. and thought I would expire without him and his family. Another part I think about is how in the final days of our relationship M. sniffed my body, everywhere. He suspected that I was seeing another man, and the idea roused his jealousy.

"Where do you go when you don't come home? Who are you with?" he yelled.

"With friends," I responded without a trace of remorse.

"Which friends?"

"New ones."

"You need to leave this house. You can't stay here anymore."

With relief, I agreed. But the one thing I never said to him was "I'm hurting you, because you forgot me."

In the end I never asked why it was okay for him to cheat and not me, because I didn't want to admit that I had betrayed him and myself by sleeping with a random stranger. I didn't choose a clean break.

I'm still angry that M. lured me into a damaging lifestyle. But ultimately it had been my choice to follow him. Yet from the six years I spent in the couple, I marvel at my persistence. It's one of the qualities I like about myself, but I'm careful to not let my insistence color my judgment. I'm at ease knowing that if I want something, I will take the opportunities as they appear. That's how I got my Cabbage Patch doll in the end. For my tenth birthday a few of my friends gave me money and I bought the doll myself.

Even though for many years I could not extract myself from the fear of M. leaving me, I continued to develop as a woman. All along I had been defining the honest companion I still aspire to be. It occurred to me that our separation was not about one outgrowing the other, but about my ceasing to make us fit.

STRADDLING DESIRE

BY ADRIANA LÓPEZ

I inherited my grandmother's stallion strut: back straight and chin up, glide, glide. And at the age of eleven, I pranced around in a two-piece bathing suit with my shapely aunts at Jones Beach, even if I didn't have anything to strut. I was as carefree as any girl at the seashore, amid a carnival of oiled-up, unclad bodies parading around like Greek gods. Studying them, I dreamed about growing up into a va-va-voom woman like Rita Hayworth, who could just kick up a knee, shake her mane, shoot a sly, knowing smile, and melt all the boys with the power of her sex appeal.

But when I found myself becoming a woman, standing in front of that white-lacquer trim mirror that I so adored, I saw a gangly Olive Oyl with two sticks for legs, a concave chest, and an oversized head, marked by a shiny forehead as expansive as the Great Plains. My heart pined for a medieval cleavage, hips as wide as a galleon's mast, and thighs as strong as Wonder Woman's. I worked harder than the other girls in my grade to compensate for my lack of corporeal swellings. While the other girls found the boys in our class boring, stupid, or crude (or a combination of all three), I had no trouble engaging them in conversation, putting up with their inane prattle while my mind wandered elsewhere. At least I was close to them, I thought, those lean, hairless, inexperienced boy bodies. My only goal back then, other than juggling my social butterfly life (a frequent complaint for my mother to deal with in parent-teacher conferences) and finding time to do my homework, was figuring out how to pique the attention of the opposite sex.

I had my chance one Saturday afternoon when I was eleven years old. I went over to play at my next-door neighbor Karen's house. She and her male cousins were playing the "run around in a dark room and feel up whoever you can" game. After the groping had come to an end, and the lights were turned on, her wise guy cousin David publicly acknowledged what I had feared others would notice. He played the blind boy, slamming his palms up and down the flat white wall of the room, calling "Adriana, is that you???" A reenactment of feeling me up. While everyone laughed, I stood there, hiding under my heavy bangs, girlish in little Daisy Dukes and a flowered halter top. My cheeks burned, but I laughed along, only managing a bright "Shut up!" in response. I boiled inside. The joke played over and over in my head in the years that followed. I started using the skit at parties to poke fun at myself, before anyone else had the chance.

Mom would try to boost my ego by insisting that they were merely shallow boys who couldn't see the profundity in my "dark eyes that danced with the mystery and witchery of love," the definition of the name "Adriana" from the *Name Your Baby* book she had consulted. I knew someday, when I finally developed into Rita Hayworth, I'd make boys like him beg.

But I never developed into the woman I had anticipated. Everything that I still struggle with now began in my adolescence. Choices I face appear as polar opposites, and I constantly fight my desire between recklessness and restraint, the intellectual and the carnal. The more I fought my raging libido, the more it erupted haphazardly without warning, leaving me regretful for my behavior the night before. I have always been fighting an urge to behave like any man naturally has the right to without any fear of stigmatization. I constantly bite my tongue, stopping myself from sounding vulgar and voicing my sexual desires. I longed to remain the good girl in public while keeping a secret bad-girl life in private. When I was that raging hormonal teenage girl, I would have pounced on a free TV offer for an all-inclusive boob and butt job package to make me feel wanted, if only so that people would look at me and fantasize about what I really wanted to do.

When I was seven years old, I enjoyed flirting with men of all ages at my parents' parties in our new home in suburban Long Island. I would twirl in poofy party dresses and giggle when adult men tickled me, whipping back my long brown ponytail over and over again. The feeling they gave me intensified when my parents later divorced, and my mother suddenly became a dating single gal. I started studying her moves at eight years old, absorbing all I needed to know about attracting, teasing, and conquering a man. Mom was not an intellectual but she was cultured, well-spoken, and extremely attractive. She was small-busted like me, with a round behind and full thighs that drove men wild. She avoided wearing outfits that were too revealing and chose the bars she frequented and the words she used carefully. She was aware of how to put her numerous male suitors on the spot. It was the art of delivering the wise-ass comment with a benevolent smile, keeping them out on a ledge.

It was hard to criticize her. She woke up at seven every morning, always scrubbed and polished in her blazers and long skirts. When the sun went down, the outfits effortlessly transformed for happy hour. A sleeveless blouse under the blazer, extra eye shadow and lipstick in her purse, and open-toe sandals to replace the pumps. In my post-divorce mini-depression, I envied her happiness, yet felt acutely conscious of her in my friends' parents and teachers' conservative social circles. Back then I was still one of the few children of divorce in my class, and my elders laid on the sympathy. I milked it.

Before my mother remarried, I would regularly sleep at her rich divorcée girlfriend Marlo's house during school nights. Marlo lived in upscale Garden City, and I'd hang out with her spoiled, jaded kids when they snuck out at night. They taught me how to get in and out without getting caught. My mother slept elsewhere those nights as well. I never knew where she went, but the next morning she would pick me up, running late as usual, in her white, shiny Camaro. Her curly brown hair with henna streaks still air-drying in the wind and her eyes hidden behind her large round sunglasses, she would offer lethargic chitchat as we drove to school in the next town over. I slouched in her red leather bucket seats, envious of the attention she was giving some other man over me and annoyed at the interruption of my everyday school routine. She'd drive fast as if to escape the reality of her double life, which glared at us under the harsh morning light. As we flew through the perfectly manicured lawns of Long Island toward my quaint junior high school, we seemed to shed the naughtiness of the night before. She was never apologetic, and I held back tears as I rolled into school tardy, again. But once inside the abandoned hallways, I was fine. I had a nightlife that the other kids dreamed about.

Life with my mother and her clan of divorcées showed me a whole new board game of life: seduction. I'd listen to their conversations when they didn't know I was there, recording their laughter at their bleeding-heart boyfriends in the back of my mind. Mom would take me to all-night Colombian parties on the weekend, and they would gather in a circle, pulsating their gaits to the rhythms of the cumbia. They were beautiful and unafraid. I remember thinking of how they were seemingly unconscious of how they tortured the men around them, just as the boys at my school tortured me.

My mother was married and pregnant by age twenty, and she was determined to stop me from following in her path. She enrolled me in every after-school activity in the "keep your child distracted" manual: horseback riding (bad choice), tennis, track, gymnastics, dance classes, soccer, orchestra club (Warning: Pachelbel's Canon in D is extremely erotic)—but they didn't distract. The conquistador force inside me quietly grew.

When I was thirteen, I seduced the paperboy. After school I'd listen for the hum of Phil's ten-speed approaching. When I heard the Long Island *Newsday* hit the front porch, I'd swing open our front door in nothing but one of my mother's silky robes. I'd start up pop culture conversations about Depeche Mode, gossip about Keith Haring. He was a nerdy art geek with the pink streak in his frizzy hair, and my strategy was to slowly build his confidence and prove I wasn't out to hurt him like other bitchy kids in our class. He was afraid to touch me, so I made the first move by stroking the inside of his hairy and fleshy pale thigh. Just a few steps from the door, so he could still watch his bike with its metal basket overflowing with the dozens of newspapers still undelivered, we sat and explored one another on my mauve carpeted staircase. It was no work of sexual genius on his part or mine, but accidentally, I experienced my first orgasms from his clumsy-but-ambitious petting. It gave me that fifth-dimension feeling, time became a light wave rippling by in slow motion. Suddenly, it seemed like the sport I most wanted to practice. I was hooked.

I decided to seduce his older brother, Morris, who was already in high school and would never leak to his friends that he was messing with a junior high chick. And if Phil told anyone about us, nobody would have believed it, since everyone thought he was gay. Morris was also an effeminate art geek but slightly better-looking in his frumpy tallness. He was a big shot in the fashion design cliques and heavy into British glam rock. And just like little Phil, he was interested in dressing me up a la Madonna punk. We leafed through copies of W magazine together, traveled to Manhattan on the weekends to shop vintage downtown. They adored my obnoxiousness, my flat chest, flat ass, and no-hips body of a thirteen-year-old boy. Perhaps I was the girl they would have liked to have been if they were born girls themselves. I found neither of the brothers attractive but learned how to close my eyes and imagine Andy Gibb on top of me. By just using them, I was building up my confidence for future heartthrobs. Only my best friend, Deborah, who wrinkled her nose in grossed-out bemusement at the thought of us, knew about these somewhat embarrassing escapades with the Panelli brothers. It would have been torturous to explain to my cheerleader and student government friends my sexual slumming with zeros like the P brothers. These were the women who could set me up with football players or surfer gods. I didn't want them to think I would settle if nothing better stepped up to my plate.

I glided by the school routine, effortlessly maintaining above-average grades and a studious demeanor in class. But after school, I continued to devise complex strategies to compensate for my corporeal inadequacies and lack of studly suitors. I aimed for semi-geeky guys (a notch above the Panelli brothers) who thought I was a catch even though I didn't look like the pinups they locked themselves up with. As usual, I'd relax their nerves by befriending them first, laying down the groundwork of familiarity, and then later I'd quickly jump bases with them. Knowing that these Atari-loving dorks didn't know the first thing about coordinating fool-around sessions, becoming the master planner fueled me and gave me a sense of control over my sexuality. I'd meet Nick for feel-ups right after school at the public library, coordinate group make-out sessions at friends' basements to be with Billy, and sneak Tim into my house, past my nosy Italian neighbor, Louise, who ultimately ratted me out to my mother. I was shameless, but after my mother found out about my after-school entertaining, it was a living hell at home for several months. She threatened boarding school, a convent in Colombia without men in sight for miles (we weren't even practicing Catholics). She canceled our subscription to Newsday.

During those years I was glued to my bathroom's fortress of full-length mirrors under 500-watt fluorescent lighting, perfecting the come-hither stare I emulated from the fashion and porno magazines. I wasn't allowed to wear makeup aside from clear lip gloss, so behind my mother's back I sneaked on unflattering blue eyeliner, globs of black mascara, frosted pink lipstick, and peach blush on my olive skin, so I could make my devastatingly innocent moon-shaped good-girl face (which earned me the benevolent "cute" description rather than the more lustful "hot") into a weapon as deadly as that of any raven-haired bad girl from the soap operas. Because it was always the brunettes who were bad girls, right?

Dating was challenging—on the whole I wasn't curvy enough for Latin or black men, and I wasn't preppy or blonde enough for the overly white ones. Let's just say the boys in high school found my looks passable but weren't knocking down my doors. So I used what I had—my sense of humor, and a resourceful ingenuity—and continued to knock on theirs.

It didn't make things easier that one of my closest girlfriends, Tina, was the hottest girl in our high school. I thought that if I were seen with voluptuous girls that perhaps I too would be seen as voluptuous in a certain abstract light. Even our middle-aged teachers squirmed, blushed, and fought to not look down below her neck. Standing in their rounded shadows, I watched how men's eyes were magnetically locked onto her, and I felt powerless.

Tina taught me all my seductress skills. She was a beautifully odd-looking creature and the only other Latina in my class. Unlike me, she was actually born in South America and had a slight accent that made her shy about speaking up in public. Tina, née Maria Cristina, was my body's antithesis, and she worked hard at exploiting that because early on she knew she had to be famous. She was gossiped about because she had an overflowing neckline, a butt shaped like a heart, and a waist so thin you would have thought she was wearing a corset. She informed me early in our relationship that our respective countries rivaled each other in the Miss Universe competitions.

Colombia made it to the nail-biting finalist run plenty, but our beauty queen only took the crown once, when the already over-the-hill Luz Marina Zuluaga won way back in 1958. Between 1979 and 1986, Tina bragged, Venezuela was on a hot streak and grabbed that damn crown three times. She was competitive with me, the only other Latina in our crew, but I liked it because it meant that maybe I had that certain something even though I still resembled a lollipop. In her cat eyes, I had become a threat.

I hoped that Tina's Aphrodite genes and her way with men would rub off on me somehow. Behind closed doors when she didn't have her public persona on, she talked to me like I was her little sister (she was left back a grade because of the language). She gave me boy advice, stood up for me in the girls' bathroom one time when some metal girls didn't like the way we looked, and taught me how to roll my r's correctly in Spanish. Around Tina I began to feel the power of being dark, being Spanish, as we called it back then, different from the rest of the girls in school. When she yawned it was sexy, when she accidentally wrapped herself up within the long spiral phone cord, she was electric. Anything Tina put on was tantalizing; sweats and an oversized T-shirt looked like lingerie. She was everything on the exterior I felt was locked up inside of me. She wore her sexuality on her sleeve. Mine was suffocating in my brain. I was still too self-conscious of coming off as easy. I still liked imagining myself as hard to get.

In public she rarely liked to hang out like one of the girls, which I loved doing. She became removed, positioning herself a good distance away from me and the rest of our underdeveloped posse trying to get noticed by strangers. Her permed long-flowing black hair, light green eyes, and pushed-out pouted painted lips, open ever so slightly, attracted older, sometimes downright sleazy men who walked right up to her, possessed by the sex they imagined she'd give them. Though people may have found her to be a little slutty, she rarely went all the way. I, on the other hand, had become more sexually active, though no one would suspect it. Tina was into classic rock and metal, while I chose baggier, frillier clothing. And as smart as she was, she could appear cheap, making her extremely unpopular with the girls at school, and the men became never-ending sprinklers of lewd comments. She didn't know how to Jekyll-and-Hyde it like I did. Her parents didn't make her hide her sexuality and it went with her to class, to church, to the grocery store, to family gatherings. It was out there for everyone to see and to make a move on. Tina was *allowed* to get picked up for dates and go out alone. No one cared what time *she* came home or too much what the guy behind the wheel looked like. I, on the other hand, wasn't allowed to go on dates with anyone, not even a boyfriend, until my senior year of high school. Creeping in the door after a date, I prayed Mom would be asleep or out so I wouldn't have to receive a full inspection: a sniff of the hair and critical eye on the lips, trying to detect make-out swollenness. Mom was no idiot, she was at it herself. So I had to work quickly and surreptitiously at parties and sleep over friends' houses as much as possible to get any action during high school. Let's say I ruined plenty of great pants with grass stains, having no place to go.

When I got into the college of my choice, I bloomed with a new intellectual confidence. I blindly joined a sorority dominated by weight-conscious and neurotically funny white women. And at the height of the Kate Moss era, in North American, non-Latino circles, thinness, and not roundness, was a good thing. During my second semester as a fresh-meat freshman, I was dragged away from a keg at a mixer and delivered the news by two older and intimidating sorority sisters. "*Ay-dree-ana!*" they screeched. "We want *you* to represent *our* sorority for Greek Week as this year's Greek Goddess!" As the message slowly registered in my inebriated brain, it started to sound like my beauty queen dream come true, my official arrival as a sex symbol. Visions of a crown, sash, and red roses flashed in my head when I was interrupted with a nasally demanding "*Well??*"

"Yes, I gladly accept," I slurred back, always the mannered lady.

Once I sobered up in my dorm room, I learned that claiming my throne entailed choreographing a sexy number with a Mr. Greek God in a dance/strip contest for the entire Greek establishment. Though I had my momentary trepidations, it was a role I felt I needed to try on while it was still being offered to me. But without knowing it, I had been cast in the stereotypical role of the exotic Latina. No, stupid, not the maid. The hot-blooded sexpot I always wanted to be, the one who can naturally shake even a flat ass and be their Charo for the nineties.

The Greek God whom I'd been teamed up with turned out to be a beefy, light-skinned West Indian with dance-floor pelvic thrusts as deadly as a washing machine on final rinse. I was humbled. I met my fellow god a few nights before the big event to create a sketch and practice our bump-and-grind moves in that echo-filled and dimly lit corridor of the humanities building. He came prepared with a boom box filled with R & B and house cassettes, directing me like Bob Fosse: "Like this, baby, feel the music, that's right, loosen those knees and hips, give me some more pout." He demonstrated both the boy and girl role and I mimicked my part, loosening up, acting sexy, feeling confident.

You could scarcely call it a brainstorm, but we finally came up with an idea for the dance skit where he would wait, bare-chested and flailing in a cage, and I, the bespectacled temptress, would saunter onto the stage in a secretary outfit. Once I turned the lock and set the beast free on me, he would tear off my outfit to reveal nothing but a black bustier, miniskirt, and high heels. To best express our stifled lust onstage, we chose George Michael's emblematic "Freedom 90," with its subtle Latin beat and climactic buildup. On the night of the show, my sorority sisters did my makeup and poured me shot after shot of Jägermeister before I zigzagged to the auditorium. When showtime finally arrived I had sobered up. I stood cold and alone in my fishnets in the wings of the stage. My heart pounded in sync with the thundering bass beat of the ridiculous porno rodeo act before ours. Then my cue to strut— the sexy piano prelude from "Freedom 90" blared—and I took the stage, tiptoeing in my stilettos like a frozen ballerina with stage fright. Suddenly, under those bright lights, I knew that I didn't belong there in that outfit, alongside beef boy, amid all the testosterone wafting in the air. I felt the straight man playing the transvestite, doing a bad imitation of a sensual woman. Greek God sensed he was losing me and moved up and down my stiff body in double time while I attempted to shake my little booty back at him in front of an overwhelming crowd of chanting frat boys yelling "Take it off!" In the words of Sir George Michael, "When you shake your ass they notice fast."

I don't even remember what place we came in, but what I clearly remember was feeling cheap the next morning. My witchy dorm mates cracked jokes, bowing and kneeling, calling me Goddess. I was now a mini-celeb, recognized by those within the Greek circles on my quad, so walking anywhere or going down to the dining room disguised in a baseball cap and sweats for meals was excruciating. I was in my own jail cell of whispered catcalls. It was then that I started to realize that even though I wasn't born with curves, just being Latina or a woman of color with darkish looks in American society denoted a sensual mystique. I had never felt like the other, but all this had an uncomfortable resonance with my Latino Studies 101 class that semester, which dissected Rita Moreno's role in *West Side Story* as the sexually potent Latin spitfire.

The wrong kinds of men saw my pathetic dance, imagining me to be like some friendly babe in an exotic travel poster. The kind of man who wasn't into talking was walking right up to me now. But in the glaring light of day, the public recognition wasn't as sexy as it seemed. New to this role as sole sex object, I thought I could just step on the gas without caution like any man and enjoy the fast ride myself. But the hunt, the lay, and the insecurity in the aftermath of the act began to eat me up inside. At first, I didn't play the sexual game well enough with the older boys on campus who ate me up and spit me out. But soon enough I reinvented myself and grew from it. That sexually free girl with massive self-respect urged me to drive my steamroller over the opposite sex for a while. Cold and calculating, I'd seduce then sting, I was the one who was laughing in their faces, blowing them off, making them uncomfortable, commenting on *their* physique.

I soon dropped out of that mindless sorority and started hanging with a new crowd that gravitated to bars with grad students or people's homes, where you could hear yourself speak.

Being looked at again straight in the eyes and having literary debates was a whole new turn on.

The one-night empty fling became boring, and I craved monogamy, striking up a relationship with a tall hurly-burly poli-sci major named John with a penchant for skydiving and scotch. He stalked me on campus for months and I became impressed by his determination. Confused by my feelings of repulsion and kinky attraction for this overconfident psycho, I finally invited him into my dorm room. The sex was addictive, I stopped seeing other men, and we became inseparable. But by my junior year I began to tire of him appearing at every place I went and craved new adventures. He'd constantly be popping up at every girls' night out when he wasn't supposed to and force his friendship onto every single acquaintance of mine. I applied for a semester in Spain, a trip he was fully against, which made me more determined to go. Once in Madrid it was heaven; I was speaking Spanish full-time and feeling a whole new kind of linguistic sexy, and I completely forgot about having a boyfriend once an older law student at the university named Miguel began to ask around about me. In his red jeans and button-down oxford there was nothing J. Crew gringo about him. Yes, John had forced me to look him in the eye and promise that I wouldn't be with anyone else, but this was too tempting. I was unfaithful and guiltless, until John surprised me by showing up in Spain (I had asked him *not* to come). He waited with his luggage, all spread out on the steps of the school's locked entrance. As the sun rose, I came home, stepping over him. I consoled him as much as I could, but what could I say? I had broken my promise. We decided to call it quits after a miserable tour through old and rustic southern

Spain. The more John cried, the more detached I grew from him. He'd try making me jealous but it didn't work; I felt restless again.

I graduated college with honors, and a lot more escapades followed in my postcollege life in Manhattan and my travels abroad. I heard a rumor after graduation that Tina had been secretly videotaped having sex with some sleazeball and that the tape was circulating around her college's campus. The rumor must have been true, since soon after, she dropped out of school and moved to California to pursue her Hollywood dream. I've seen her in some small parts in B movies looking as gorgeous as ever, wearing bustiers and bathing suits. No speaking roles yet.

I lost myself in New York's nightlife, escaping my mother and the reality of full-time employment. But eventually, the thrill of the booze, drugs, music, and men dissipated, and I wanted to become serious. I still needed to decide what I was going to do with my writing and find the time alone to sit down and do it. Around that time, my mom underwent a second divorce and was grieving again but ready to take on the single life. She never settled, reinventing herself with each lover, convinced there was that perfect companion out there waiting for her. The men just came and went. Now both single, we lived together for some time in her two-bedroom apartment in Manhattan (she divorced well), until again we became too much for each other. I desperately missed school and wanted to start feeding my mind again rather than my body. So I dove into my writing and editing career and said good-bye to the gypsy life, committing to an older brilliant man who provided me with shelter, with whom I could journey and learn things about the world. I chose to keep that bad-girl side of me secret from him. I loved him so much, I wanted to occult my wild side. That was a mistake.

I concentrated on my career and forgot about the thrills of flirting. It was like a low-grade coma, suppressing all that sexual energy into discipline. I fell in love with my newfound order, the quietness of the writing life with a steady, attentive partner who also read and wrote.

We lived, breathed, and argued for eight years about the world of Latino letters, arts, and politics. He was the first partner with whom I practiced my Spanish, the first Latino boyfriend I had had, and that was new music to my notion of romantic love. My mom, terrified that I had impetuously moved in with this leftist poet, older man, once told a friend that she feared he and I were planning to breed little Che Guevaras and Frida Kahlos.

We holed ourselves up in his tiny and cluttered studio apartment, watching foreign films, making our own avantgarde films, listening to jazz. These nights blurred right into hundreds of long afternoons of reading and writing and tender lovemaking. He even liked to cook for me. This was a plus, since my specialty back then was fried eggs and toast. I immersed myself in him and stopped seeing my friends as much as I used to. Back then it seemed as if all my girlfriends lived these chaotic twenty-something lives and were involved in courtships filled with needless torture in comparison to our heady and cool commitment.

I was just beginning my life as a writer and he was already an established writer. There were endless invitations and free passes to concerts, plays, art openings, international conferences, movie screenings, and so on. Our free entertainment kept us busy and thankfully gave us a social life outside of our nest.

There was no competition between us and our work. He would give me gentle critiques on my fiction writing that were hard to take seriously because I knew he didn't want to bruise my ego. But he let me have it when it came to the ethics and art of good journalism. Toward the end of our relationship, I was giving him my opinions about his work. During those years, I can say that I enjoyed not being available to the opposite sex. I imagined a sign that hung around my low-cut neckline that read "taken" or "off-limits." *You can talk to me, but you can't have me.* It was another sort of game I enjoyed in my head with men I found attractive. Like an athlete, I thought this composure helped the intensity of my writing and editing life. Though we chose not to get married for the sake of rebelling against the in-stitution of marriage, we lived an old-fashioned, straight kind of love. Despite all my fierce feminist beliefs, for a time I was happy being "kept" by a loving man who allowed me the free-dom to do as I wanted. That is, except be with other men.

Throughout this time my friends reminded me about my past promiscuity, incredulous at how I became so settled. And deep down I also questioned my behavior, fearing it was too premature to have found love so soon without having explored more men. But I held on, challenging my nonmonogamous self, trying to make it work, loving and honoring him all the more, despite having eyes for others. Though I never flirted openly or ostentatiously, I always subconsciously imagined my-self like a lone baseball player, standing on the mound, putting it all out there, without anyone bold enough to come to bat. I existed like this for years. Waiting. Until the last years when I started putting it out there more and more. I began to unravel.

Conversation had always gotten me into trouble, and soon I uncontrollably found myself engaging men I found attractive in sexually charged verbal debates and discussions. It would just come out of nowhere, and immediately afterward, I'd run home to him. Then I'd want to party more and find that momentary thrill again. Sometimes they'd find me by calling and I'd just chicken out. I never allowed it to happen, but I realized it could. That's when I needed to face myself, my fantasies, and the relationship I was in.

After eight years, I felt the cold metal bars of the cage pressing onto my flesh.

At thirty, in my New York office job in the world of books, I felt safe. But after a long, stressful, repressed week at the office, the weekend came along and those quiet, home-cooked meals I used to love having him cook for me now seemed dull. So one night he suggested going out for a meal in town to break the monotony. I was getting dressed, putting in my dangling gypsy earrings I got in Spain, painting my lips into mauve perfection, looking at my thin but still sexy body in my black form-fitted dress, moving my hips to the Mary Jane Girls, and wishing I were getting ready to go somewhere else, alone, and search for an unknown someone else. While he was in the next room contentedly awaiting my final preparations, I saw the scene all in my head. I'd be at a party dancing with my gorgeous girlfriends, the stranger would approach me, engage me in tense conversation about some foreign literature. We'd dance a little, I'd tell him I was in a serious relationship, and he'd say so am I. Not to worry. He'd then convince me to go outside, and then I'd take over. We'd find an alleyway, a brownstone's lower entrance. We'd please each other terribly, and then I would walk away, never allowing him to know me.

I felt myself drifting back to my teenage urges, longing to seduce again. So the year I turned thirty, I said good-bye to a perfectly good man and ran toward the unknown, looking for the love of strangers. I now come home to a place of my own, write when I feel like it, and balance the good-girl, bad-girl irony like good theater. No mother to look me over, no boyfriend to ask me where I've been. It's a whole new mental space where I face my rampant adolescent desires in all the nakedness of broad daylight and strut.

AIN'T DISHIN'

BY MARIA HINOJOSA

Mujeres—let me be straight up. I ain't gonna dish about sex. You won't be hearing any fabuloso secretos de mi vida sexual because one thing I don't dish about is sex and I never will. (Okay, I have learned in all of these long years of my life to never say never. I have found myself saying and doing things I never thought I would—including in my sex life—and now I never know what I might end up doing.) The point is that there has never been a tradition of sexual dishing among the people closest to me . . . no dishing del sexo entre mis primas, mi hermana, mias tías, mi mamá—and forget about mi abuela.

Now, I have never looked up the term "dishing" in the dictionary, but the way I explained it to my Dominican hermanas, dishing is a form of gossip—with details. I said that dishing was like passing platos de comida in between girlfriends, it requires that level of intimacy.

Como niña, I didn't grow up hearing my mom and her family or her friends talking about love, much less sex. When we were together, there was an abundance of abrazos and kisses and apretones, and the first boy I ever kissed on the lips *ever* was my cousin—the cute moreno with jet-black hair and high cheekbones and a smile to die for. On the days when the entire family would get together for one of those interminable comidas del Domingo (which I looked forward to intensely), there were hours and hours of sex jokes that I was never old enough to hear until I had given birth to my own son. I have memories of those faraway pauses of silence in that corner where all the adults were—sitting with vasos de tequila at the ready—all hunched over, listening quietly to mi tio revving into the joke, and then a huge explosive bout of carcajadas and hooting and yes, real live hollering—and people saying me voy a morir de la risa! I am going to die from laughter! And I remember those as the first times I ever saw tears in my father's eyes.

In the Mexico de mis recuerdos de juventud, there were double entendre sexual stories scattered throughout my childhood—the double entendre precisely to mask anything too overtly sexual—and I didn't realize what they were even about until I was in my late twenties. The childhood sexual secreto story I like the best is the one about another equally cute primo who got his sixteen-year-old novia pregnant. I was only six at the time, so the only thing that bothered me about the wedding was that it was happening at all—thus ruining any chance I might have had to marry this particular cousin. I was convinced being in love with members of one's own family was totally normal, though I never heard any of my girlfriends talking about their cousins like potential mates. Getting back to my primo and his pregnant teenage soon-to-be wife: Her name was Laura, and after that shotgun wedding I used to hear my mom and tías talking about equally quick weddings by saying que la pareja se a-laur-eó—that the couple pulled a "Laura," I guess would be the closest translation. With my good but not perfect command of Spanish, I had somehow grown up thinking that *alaurear* was a real verb.

And no, I never had "the conversation" with my mother. She tried one time when I was seven and a half, but she only got as far as something about eggs in a woman's body and then my father called her: "Vieja! Donde guardaste mi corbata azul?" El caso es que, my mom, as was typical for her, dropped everything and went to atender a mi papa, y ya! The famosa conversación was forever interrupted.

No, I learned about intercourse by reading a little pamphlet that mysteriously appeared in my house. I had become interested in the subject because of my next-door neighbor. She was a mature eight-year-old, naturally precocious with long red curls and green eyes. She had a Polish mother and father who didn't appear attractive to me—her father's polio had left him with a pronounced limp and a deformed foot—yet they had a silent sexual energy that I think even I picked up on. My girlfriend was the first one to say "fuck" to me and then explain what it was, and I was so disgusted by even the thought of it— Mom and Dad doing that????—that when the pamphlet *Explaining Life to a Child* appeared, I instantly knew I needed something to be explained to me and took it with me to the bathroom.

I looked up the word "intercourse" in the index, re-reading it about three hundred times just to make sure. I used to go open the book in the middle of the day and then slip it back in the drawer in the foyer, making sure *no one* saw me. I never talked about this with *anyone* . . . no way. This was my secret pena—to know that people did something so weird, and yes, disgusting.

For me, the unspoken rule I picked up somehow—maybe it was my primas' ultra-chaste Catholicism—was that this silence about sex made it something shameful. I never heard these words—sex equals shame—come out of anyone's mouth. And yet, this is how I understood and interpreted the pena—the silent shame of desire, the silent shame of wanting something only because your body is telling you to, and feeling already at a young age conflicted.

After the sexual-literary-experience-with-a-pamphlet-as-a-teacher, sex came back into the picture when I got into fourth grade. I think some of my girlfriends were encountering the same silence in their homes—all of us immigrant kids—but one friend had a hippie brother who had long black hair, rode a motorcycle, and had once run away from home. This brother had brought some X-rated comics home after his runaway days and there it was—that whole disgusting thing lifted right from the pages of *Explaining Life to a Child* and brought to life in comic-book reality: women's breasts perked up and titillated and bulges in men's pants and then strange positions between naked cartoon characters, where you didn't see much but two bodies stuck together with Elmer's glue.

Inspired by all these images, my fourth-grade friend, who was a good little artist, created a group called the Bunny Rabbits (so seventies-*Playboy*-kitsch!), and we used to gather every week at a different girlfriend's house and go, literally, under the beds—all four of us: one Japanese-American, one African-American, one Canadian-American, and me—and we would draw pictures of boys with things sticking out of them like in the comics, and girls with teeny waists and huge tetas. (I have no ability to draw, so mine were the little stick-figure ones.)

My parents, the most tolerant in the world, will learn about this when they read it here, just like the rest of you. Because these things weren't talked about. No se hablaban. No dishin'.

That silence had its precio. I felt weird when a six-year-old friend of mine used to say "my pussy leaks" to me every time we went to the bathroom. I hated that word "pussy" but never told anyone about it. And I didn't have a name for "it" either in English or in Spanish.

There were other things that happened with this same girl-friend. Granted, her mom and dad, both psychiatrists, were going through a nasty public divorce—it came out on the local news that the two married shrinks were each going to a shrink themselves—so she ended up being cared for by her older teen sister.

Anyway, her downstairs neighbor used to do weird things con su parte. She came to school one day and told me he would rub himself against the hallway wall and then his cosa would look like a frozen hotdog and then something white would get all over his hands. I had no idea what she was talking about, but it sounded so gross.

I know now this boy was bad news, but my pena and silence about sex kept me from ever telling my mother about this.

There was this powerfully persistent pena about my body, too. Though I can't tell you one thing that my mother ever said that would have given me this message, I never really loved my body until I was quite old.

Everyone in my high school had these long, sleek bodies or the jockettes had those fabulous leg muscles and biceps, but I was the chaparra with the short legs and round bum. And I was, in my mind, the most flat-chested of everyone. As many times as friends said "let's go skinny-dipping," I never did. I felt too uncomfortable about showing my body in public in front of a mixed group.

There was a part of me that wished I could have feigned sensuality, but I just couldn't. It wasn't the fact that I had a round trasero. One girl was an immigrant from Iran and she had one like mine—bigger—but she owned her coy Arabian sensuality and exuded it. It's the exuding part that has been difficult for me.

There was also pena—which is a softer, "lite" version of shame, in my definition—about anyone's, but specifically my parents', nudity. I was mortified, marcada de por vida, after I walked into my mom and dad's bedroom on an early Sunday morning without knocking; nothing was going on but I did see my father's casually draped leg over my mom's body, which was covered under the sheets. I didn't see any action whatsoever, but the grito my father let out, me dejo traumatizada! I've always knocked on any closed door since then, and even when I get an answer, I still open the door slowly, giving people a chance to extricate themselves from an embarrassing position.

The consequences of this silent pena in high school were more difficult and left longer-lasting waves of misunderstandings about sex that have come up during different moments of my life. There were big and little things that happened, which in hindsight are so telling. One of my first boyfriends (I had just graduated from eighth grade, he had just finished sophomore year) was the brilliant son of German-born parents. I felt small compared to him, not in stature but because at sixteen this young man already openly called himself an intellectual. The first day he came over to my house I said, in all of my fourteen-year-old innocence: "Come to my room because I want to show you my beaver. I sleep with it every night." (I had proudly sewed a little beaver stuffed animal that I slept with under my arm—sin falla.)

Of course he started laughing uncontrollably and his friend

started to turn red, and I figured out that I had said something horribly wrong but didn't know what. And then finally he whispered what beaver means to a sixteen-year-old boy.

Me queria morir de la pena. I knew I was a prude through and through. I blamed it on the silence. But there was one boy who challenged my pena.

He was essentially the school slut. He liked all the girls. The pretty ones, the not-so-pretty ones, the tall ones, and then me, the short one. With him, it was all about mutual exploration. But I knew he was not a boy I was going to love and I knew he was not the kind of boy who I wanted loving me. So the physical part suited me just fine minus the gushiness.

He was the first boy who allowed me to see that you could get and enjoy the physical stuff without feeling que te tenías que casar con él. For weeks we would have a standing encuentro after my theater practice, up at his house when no one was home. I remember leaving his house red-faced and sweating from going to base this and that and then coming down the elevator of his building (he would never come downstairs with me), opening the door to the frigid Chicago winter air, and feeling like the cold had managed to wipe out the young orgasmic feelings I was having for the first time. It was just as well that those feelings got knocked out of me by the cold because it numbed me a bit more from the shame I felt as soon as I walked into our apartment and my mom would say, "Hola m'ija! Qué bueno que ya llegaste. Ya vamos a cenar . . ." And then she would kiss my cheek in the same place where just minutes ago a boy's lips had been.

But I didn't talk about these sexual stirrings or my mutual discovery sessions with the boy with anybody. Not my sister or my mom. Not with my oh-so-liberated teen girlfriends. I was so out of style with this guilt, even back then!

But then one afternoon this boy did something we knew was wrong, but you know, well, it just happened, and I guess I really did want to have something to "show" for all of those afternoons up at his place—because frankly, every girl would have given anything to be up at *his* place. He may have been the school slut, but the boy was fine and everyone knew it. So yes, one afternoon, he gave me a hickey. I tried the turtleneck-and-scarves thing and it worked, but then one Saturday I was getting out of the shower and who popped in to pick up the dirty clothes but my mom; she saw it and all hell broke loose.

The pena found a voice when my mom used that forbidden "p" word. She told me she wasn't going to tell my father because, poor thing, he would think his daughter was a puta. Nothing worse could have been said. The afternoon encounters were over. I was on my own to navigate teen sexuality and now I had some real emotional baggage. From silence to puta in a matter of minutes.

To survive, I chose silence.

But there was dishing all around me (never in Mexico with my primas), always with my Americana girlfriends, who ranged from Japanese-American to Jewish and everything in between. Instead of divulging my adolescent freakeo con el sexo, I listened to their stories about masturbation and the pubescent sex-capades of my amigas. I was intrigued but I always got pena ajena—I felt ashamed for my girlfriends who were sharing such intimacies with me. I would turn red for them.

To be honest, I was up for listening to any well-told cuento, and some of the stories were like telenovelas, but I never did ask for any detalles. I didn't feel I had any right to ask about any of this—especially because of my lack of experience.

But I would listen as one girlfriend told me about losing her virginity and another told of losing it—to my brother. I was not talking about that to anyone. Yuck!

These days, though, it seems with all of this mega-dishing about sex and people's sex lives on TV, on the radio (La Mega te lo toca todo!), and in the movies, that all of this overt sex talk is like some grand competition, and I just don't see my vida sexual as part of an international scoreboard.

As an older mujer, I decided not to dish less because of pena and more because of a certain kind of self-respect that grew in me as I got into my thirties—way too late if you ask me.

And it was just around that time I met a man for whom silence and chosen words—su dieta escojida de palabras y con quien las comparte—taught me all kinds of lessons. With Gérman, we rarely spoke of past loves—I mean, really hardly ever. I could not tell you any details about any of his novias because I don't know them. And he knows none of mine.

I fell in love with Gérman because he was able to keep his past privado. Yes, he was virile and sensual, but the fact that he was a private man who didn't dish and who didn't bring other women's karma into the bed with me made me feel that I could love and trust him. And ultimately marry him.

What primarily binds us together are love, mutual respect, and profound and honest mutual admiration. So while Gérman came from a very different geographic place and one that breeds a certain sensuality, he was able to manage the sexual configurations of a Latina-Mexicana-Chicago-raised-middle-class-former-Católica-intellectual-feminista-who-was-more-often-in-her-head-than-in-her-body type of woman, which I was.

It wasn't easy for me, though. It took me years to not feel radically threatened by the gorgeous, full-of-life, and often very sensual women in his country. These women had it going on. They were all part of the artists' and nature lovers' circle of Gérman's bohemian friends. His friends would often go skinny-dipping, but nothing ever happened. There were very special friendships down there. I felt so threatend by these stories and the women that my husband had to put up with bouts of childish nagging I'm-not-as-pretty-as-they-are-so-why-did-you-choose-me rants.

The long and short of it? My husband has the patience of a cow. (Don't get upset. I asked him to choose the animal for this metaphor.) Together we navigated the passion and lust of first love to the forced romanticism of a honeymoon in a tense and crime-ridden Rio de Janeiro. We have made it through the sex-as-habit period and crossed into the most passionate lovemaking in the world for me—trying to make a baby and procreate our animal species. My husband has been there when I have words and when the familiarity of silence beckons and is more appealing than a verbal analysis. He has shared my bed during the months of postpartum awkwardness and is at my side now, more than ever, as I try to become the most honest self I have ever been in my life.

And he has never stopped loving me. Or desiring me. He has let me be (though he has prodded me forward when I really needed it), and perhaps the sexiest thing about my husband is just that. He has the patience to see a woman come into her own. Without ever losing the ganas to be the lover that she needs at any particular time in her life.

And to do it in silence, si así lo mandan los Santos.

In the end, I realized that this silence was precious to me.

As a woman. Not as a teenybopper, not as a self-esteem-challenged Barnard college student, not as a let-me-be-in-a-codependent-relationship Latina in her early twenties . . . but as a woman, a mother, and a wife.

The boundaries that my own mother has silently laid out for me—were coming home now through my husband, who believes that one's essence as a human being has everything to do with how much you respect and love yourself. And, looking back now, the prudish penoso silence de mi casa had less to do with my parents' Catholicism and more to do with cierto respecto a sí mismo—a well-endowed sense of self-respect. That was just how it was expressed at the time . . . through silence.

Our parents had no idea how to talk to us about these things. And this whole tema just wasn't part of their equation growing up in Mexico. They, of course, could have no idea how much it would be for my generation. Unfortunately, I could have really used more family educational sex dishing and less silence and double entendres. Pero lo que pasó, ya pasó.

But these days, if there is anyone I do talk a lot about sex with, it's my daughter and my son.

I don't have much of an idea if what I am doing is what the experts recommend (and honestly, what mother has the time to read the three hundred expert books on raising your kids), but it feels right to me. I got a book called *It's So Amazing* and we read it together as a bedtime book. I took deep breaths and read with pause and tranquility the passages that once freaked me out as a seven-year-old. The whole process is just not so mysterious to them because we talk about it.

And I decided to initiate the mother-kid sexual conversaciones because sex is everywhere in their small world—starting with the magazine store ten steps from their school. One day, I ended up doing precisely one of those things I thought I would *never* do. I asked the owner to take the magazine cover, the one with the spread wide-open legs at eye level for a five-year-old, out of his display window.

I made the decision that I had to be the one talking to mis hijos about sex, otherwise they would learn absolutely everything about la vida sexual from TV—and that's just from watching the commercials. When I get together with younger women, let's say in their twenties, their wide-open vocabulary about their sex lives and trysts makes me laugh and still gives me pena ajena. But I enjoy it as a study of modern society and feminism at the turn of the millennium.

Even so, I think women talking about sex like this makes me feel they do it as a way of getting props—status. I don't know who they want to get props from except from other women who are looking for props too. Some of these sistahs talk about "multiples" the way I talked about going to second base. They boast about how their rabbit is never too far from their reach. One told me her friend was addicted to the rabbit. Another actually said, "Why stop with the rabbit. Hay un zoológico entero allí afuera!" (There is a whole zoo of vibra-tors!)

I love modern young women's street-girl frankness about sex, but I'm not convinced it means they are any more free and equal or any less traumatizada about sex than I was. Now these women are always on the prowl for the most amazing multiple orgasm ever . . . they can always keep trying to get higher. Pero y pa' qué?? So they dish about it the next day? And compete against their girlfriends?

The boundaries of silence my parents created for me are still here, even though my kids, my husband, and I talk about any-

thing and answer any question. But there is a borderline of si-
lencio that we each carry—a boundary that gives each of us a
sense of personal and private intimacy with ourselves and only
ourselves.

   Am I good listener? Absolutely. And between those of us
who dish and those of us who don't there should be no void.
Know that us quiet ones listen and learn and grow through you.
And know that we, at least, won't be repeating your stories to
anyone you never intended hear them.

STUMBLING
TOWARD ECSTASY

BY LETISHA MARRERO

Sensuality is a secret power in my body.
Someday it will show, healthy
and ample. Wait a while.

— ANAÏS NIN

I often wonder what my family thinks of me and my so-called love life. In my household, we lovingly, ignorantly embrace the Clintonesque military standard when it comes to personal issues: don't ask, don't tell.

As the elder of two girls—the unmarried one, to boot—I'm sure my father would like to cling to the hope that his no. 1 daughter is a thirty-four-year-old virgin. As for my mother, she could be wringing her hands over the remote possibility that her firstborn is going to hell in the form of a raging lesbian (not that I haven't dabbled . . . well, that's a different story for a different time).

In my twenty-plus of potential dating years, I am yet to have what would be considered the traditional class-ring-swapping, bringing-home-to-Mom-type boyfriend. The truth is, I'm more swashbuckling sex kitten than debutante. But I've kept all my sexual frankness and freakishness on the down low—until now.

Somewhere along the way, I dropped the requisite guilt that usually accompanies the pleasures of the flesh. But don't get it twisted: this is not exactly a lamenting confessional, since I'm not exactly Catholic. (A curiosity in and of itself: finding a Latina who isn't Catholic is as rare as Jennifer Lopez sustaining a meaningful relationship.) Oddly enough, though, I somehow relate to J.Lo's woes. Something fundamental about the nebulous man-woman paradigm has skipped past me, like forgetting to add baking soda to cake batter.

The end result is nothing but a flat, unappetizing Frisbee. Throughout our girlish youth, we're brainwashed to believe in that fabled moment when boy meets girl—that electricity-shooting-through-the-fingertips, walking-into-the-sunset type rapture that's supposed to transpire between the virile man and virginal woman who suddenly find themselves gaga in love with each other. That's soap-opera love—a concept with which I have limited experience: but hey, I'm not complaining. I have had my share of drunken monkey fun (emphasis on drunken). I've had so much that it prompted my best friend in college to quip, "You don't have relationships, you have adventures."

"There but for the grace of God go I"

No, I haven't found Jesus; that was the rest of the Marrero clan. Ironically, however, I've been digging into the crates of all the secular booty-shaking music I missed when I was trapped in the bizarre world of a Californian evangelical leper colony. Recently, a friend of mine turned me on to a 1979 hit by Machine with the same quixotic title. And in listening to the song's lyrics, I had this scary epiphany: Oh . . . my . . . God . . . my life is a disco song.

> "Carlos and Carmen Vidal just had a child / A lovely girl with
> a crooked smile / Now they gotta split 'cause the Bronx ain't
> fit / For a kid to grow up in"

See, in the spirit of assimilation, my wholesome, well-meaning Puerto Rican parents transplanted their wholesome, well-meaning Puerto Rican asses from the dirty South Bronx to the homogenized West Coast to start their wholesome, well-meaning family. They Anglified their babies' names and didn't teach their two girls a lick of Spanish, so as not to lend even the slightest accent to their daughters' would-be perfect English. The exception was the remedial dinner-table question-and-response session:

"M'ija, quieres aguacate?"

"Sí, papi, quiero aguacate."

And ta-da! A wedge of avocado would magically slide onto my plate.

Of course, this limited, produce-focused vocabulary (manzana, naranja, garbanzo) inevitably drove a wedge between us two, like, total California girls and Josefina, our paternal grandmother who lived with us for intermittent periods throughout my youth. Abuela's refusal to learn English challenged my parents' goal of complete American immersion. Sadly, I only learned to speak halfway-decent Spanish years after she passed away. So I never really got to know her, ergo my history. True to family form, everyone acted so surreptitiously about the past—on both sides of my family. The only grandparent I would ever know was a big fat enigma to me, literally: close to three hundred pounds, waving her flabby butterfly arms in praise of her God, wiping the perpetual sweat from her hairline. She seemed to me a miserable and irascible woman—she had her endearing moments, but for the most part, she represented my worst fears, which only caused me to resent her further. Because I resembled her slightly, I worried that I'd wind up like her—overbearing, oversensitive, overweight—waddling along, living vicariously through her children's success.

Little did I know that buried deep inside her, behind the dark mahogany eyes that I so clearly inherited from her, lay an insurgent wanton nymph whose own libidinous fire had been stamped out by the harsh struggle to make a better life for her children. Had I known I wasn't the only rebel in my bloodline, I might've found a simpática soul I could later relate to. Instead, the schisms between me and the rest of my family grew more and more profound.

> "And year after year, the kid has to hear / The do's the don'ts and the dears"

All my life I've felt beyond my years, as well as left of center. But there were so many rules, and so few explanations, as I questioned authority and the way of the world. I was left stuttering through life with a prepubescent perspective so retarded I should've had my own sexually handicapped parking space. Here's how things went down, and subsequently downhill, for me: One afternoon, my father summoned me downstairs to his home office, where he sat at his drafting table. Thinking I was surely in trouble for some random impish act, I stared down at my feet and nervously traced the patterns in the marigold linoleum. Daddy's Coke-bottle horn-rimmed eyes tried equally to avoid mine, as he awkwardly posed his question:

"So, uhhh, Tishie . . . what's your, umm, view on, ummmm, premarital sex?"

Obviously, Mommy had put him up to this. To this day, Pops can launch full-on dissertations on algebra and algorithms, and on world politics he could pontificate and postulate all damn day. But intimate and personal conversations leave him grasping at straws. Daddy's a sturdy, compactly built man with enormous calves and Paul Bunyan hands after years of manual labor, so even his attempts at a tender human touch back then seemed gruff and gawky around the edges.

"Ummmm . . . no sex till I'm married, Papá . . . ?" I said with all the earnest conviction of a ten-year-old virgin. Despite what I recited by evangelical rote, there was a hint of inflection at the end of my sentence. But Daddy didn't seem to notice.

"Good," he beamed, as if I just answered correctly in the fifth-grade spelling bee. Since he seemed all too relieved to return to his grid paper, I just scampered back upstairs, scratching my head in befuddlement.

Round two of Birds vs. Bees was yet another calamity: a few months later I found myself face-to-face with my mother in the family room, horrified because I had bloodied my tan polyester bell-bottom slacks. Sheepishly, I untied the sweater that was wrapped around my waist (thank goodness for those die-hard preppy days) and unveiled the brownish stain that occupied my crotch line. I was in tears, certain I was dying from some dreadful disease, smote by God for being such a cantankerous child. But rather than comforting me, Mama clapped her hands together, then hugged me: "Congratulations! You're a woman now!"

And thus concluded my two-part sex education class at home. The rest was up to the California public school system and my lonesome self. Ninth-grade health class was no help. It consisted of a scant academic study of *Gray's Anatomy* and pathetically out-of-date slide shows that left us all snickering. This pretty much left me on my own to figure things out.

My father was an engineer who sailed overseas on naval aircraft carriers for weeks, sometimes months at a time. He held this mystical place in my heart—part Superman, part Santa bearing exotic Oriental gifts. But his absences left an irreparable hole, because there was no solid male figure to consult during my crucial formative years. Mommy seemed more intent on keeping a compulsively clean household— occupying her time with laundry and ironing duties (which she continues to do every day of my natural-born life) like she was on some crazy self-imposed deadline. So really, it was just my younger sister and me. I couldn't exactly interrupt our doll sessions to spawn a healthy debate on Ken's genitalia, or lack thereof. Nor could I confess to sis that I used to lock myself in the bathroom and play Aqua Porno Barbie for some cheap adolescent shits and giggles. After all, I was the older one; I had a certain reputation to uphold of being the seminal source of information regarding the universe. (What can I say? The pobrecita looked up to me.)

"Let's find a place, they say, somewhere far away / With no blacks, no Jews and no gays"

Raised to be color-blind to the point of naïveté, I didn't even realize that I was of different genetic composition than my fair-skinned classmates. In my household, Isla Verde was a geographic location, not a cultural haven. And Abuela didn't have enough sovereignty in the family to demand any different way of child rearing. I have just one island memory from my only visit to Puerto Rico. I was three. I tried opening my eyes underwater while swimming in the aquamarine blue vastness of the Caribbean, feeling the salt water stinging my eyes. I sputtered to the surface—and reality—shocked that I wasn't a mini-mermaid who could parlay with the fishes. But I can't totally blame my parents for their reasoning: with so many stigmas attached to their race in the fifties and sixties, being Puerto Rican was a source of racial shame, not national pride. Watching *West Side Story* together on TV was as close to a family history lesson as we'd get. So rather than being encouraged to hold my head high because my aesthetic makeup is a striking mixture of placid Taino Indians, swaggering Spanish conquistadors, and robust African slaves, I simply believed I possessed an unfortunate fusion of character and facial flaws.

I was una gordita, a point that was driven home to me everywhere I turned, even in my own home. My parents were overjoyed when I tested as mentally gifted and talented (MGT) at age five: documented evidence that their daughter would achieve all kinds of greatness. But along that proud parental path, Mami and Papi forgot to remind their lil' prodigy that she might actually grow up to be a pretty woman. Instead, that was designated as my sister's domain. She got modeling classes (natural beauty); I got tennis lessons (get that fat ass in shape). I was driven to Weight Watchers meetings and force-fed rice cakes and cabbage soup before they became de rigueur for dieters. My parents' subtle prodding was cemented by Abuela's in-your-face accusations of "Why you so fat and your sister so skeeenny?" as a deterrent to browsing the kitchen cupboard. So my brilliant yet warped mind came to the conclusion that I was god-awful ugly.

Try as I mightily did to mitigate my defects—I pursed my lips, I fastened a clothespin on my nose for hours on end, I permed the curl out of my hair in hopes of feathering it—any attempt to beautify and anglify myself to Wonder Woman status was utterly futile. My nalgas would never squeeze into a pair of Dittos or Jordaches, so my social status as I knew it was mud. I wasn't taught how to work my feminine mojo, because honestly, I didn't think I had any. The only roundabout advice to attract the opposite sex was to perk up my surly personality. Hey, maybe develop a sense of humor! People will like you if you're funny! Occasionally, I'd get half-ass compliments from Abuela like, "Tienes las manos de tu padre." Grrrrrrreat. So I have my father's big ol' man hands. Gracias, Granny!

Unbeknownst to either me or Abuela, along with los ojos, I had apparently inherited her nubile, rebellious attitude. Legend has it that at the age of fifteen, she made the cardinal—and carnal—mistake of falling in love and running away with a black man. Oh, and did I forget to mention that Abuelita was in the convent at the time? Es la pura verdad. To risk eternal damnation over momentary bliss; that was the question. What's a lovesick nun-in-training supposed to do when her burning loins rub up against her burgeoning faith? Let's just say the dish ran away with the cuchara.

Excommunicated from the Catholic Church, Josefina only enjoyed four short years of connubial bliss with her beloved Ezekiel before he died of pneumonia. Somewhere thereafter, Josefina was clearly gettin' her freak on at other points in her young life. But, of course, no one talks about el escándalo behind my papi's two half-sisters: one bastard child and another from Grandma's second marriage to a naval officer who was just a few years older than my dad. But somewhere along the line, my grandma also found religion once more, this time as a staunch born-again Protestant—as if God had some kind of used-religion trade-in policy. And that's the abuela locked into my memory.

"And when she's ten years old she digs that rock 'n' roll /
But Poppy bans it from home"

Even though my parents first met in church as teenagers, they, too, enjoyed a somewhat secular period before becoming "born-agains." It was my unfortunate timing (or maybe theirs) to become a teenager when God became no. 1 in the house again. Suddenly, my dad, who used to eagerly down the beers I poured for him, became a teetotaler; and his fabulous record collection collected more and more dust. Only Johnny Mathis Christmas albums and new purchases from Amy Grant and Chris Christian were saved. As my breasts blossomed in double time (no training bras for me!), so did my taste for Donna Summer and Prince.

But alas, modern radio was deemed "devil's music." My family and I were ensconced in the evangelical influence of the church at least three days a week. I confess that the desperately lonely, longing-to-fit-in part of me bought into the religious clique and the social structure it provided. I was accepted, almost popular—something intangible in my mundane school life. So despite being a gullible pawn at first, I basked in their award system for memorizing chapters of the Bible. But another part of me, perhaps a voice from my nether regions, asked, "Is there more to life than this?" I was dissatisfied by the tendency to sweep the topic of sex under the virginal rug during sermons. Be like Mary. Save it for marriage, because the Bible says so. End of story. "Gloria a Dios," Abuela would echo loudly. Every once in a great while, I'd catch a glimpse of Abuela's once-youthful vivacity behind those weathered eyes—she had a robust, almost luscious laugh—but I rarely got to relish those lighthearted moments. I will never know what really happened to transform Josefina into an overweight, embittered old woman, who, by all previous accounts, used to be a free-spirited hottie. I kept hoping for her to look into my eyes with a glint of the same innate, libidinous fire lying dormant in our bellies.

It's only recently, as I've searched for a firmer sense of my Latina identity, that I've been able to wistfully pine over the kind of fantasy relationship that the firstborn nieta should have with her abuela—the fantasy where Abuelita would impart to me the culinary secrets behind making her arroz con gandules (hers featured little Vienna sausages) or her "swinging steak" (her chubby-cheeky phrase for oxtail soup) while I sat at the kitchen counter sipping a hot cocoa. As the steam rose from the pot to her face, I would notice her sly grin as a delicious memory would creep across her mind. "What is it, Abuelita?" I'd inquire.

With the distinct aroma of sofrito filling the air, she'd lower the flames on the stove to let the rice simmer and the soup stew waddle over to her well-worn recliner, and call me over to land on her ample lap, where she'd cradle me in those amorphous arms of hers. I'd put my head on her shoulder and she'd pull out the stack of weathered love letters she'd always kept near her heart, tucked inside the pocket of her housedress, tied together with a faded silk ribbon. After she'd repeat the last words uttered from her beloved Ezekiel to me, we'd share a sigh at the starry-eyed sentiments expressed in ink on worn parchment.

With rapt attention, I'd absorb, like a rice grain does water, Abuela's romantic regaling of the unbridled rapture with the grandfather I never knew—the dark-skinned, ebony-eyed mysterious man with the biblical name who caused her to lose her ever-loving mind and to betray her faith, her family, her morals, and all good reason to follow her palpitating heart.

Instead, this stringent vieja conspired with her daughter-in-law to sew me the most conservative buttoned-up wardrobe and brush my ponytails into such tight submission that even the baby hairs on the back of my neck would cry for freedom. Neither woman explained to me that there was a game to be played between the sexes. When my grandma went back to PR for a spell, we got an unexpected exchange student: my teenage aunt, one of the hush-hush latent by-products of Abuela's wayward wanderlust. Yvonne was only nine years older than I was, so I was psyched at the reprieve, hopeful that I was getting a shrinky-dink big sister to show me the ways of young womanhood. However, lil' Titi was too busy being resentful of the world for getting kicked off a tropical island, *Survivor* Puerto Rico–style. Yvonne wanted nothing to do with us, let alone be a role model to me. So instead of blooming into a sophisticated, worldly young woman, I pined like a spore on the underbelly of a fern leaf, waiting for the wind to blow some lovin' my way. Puberty by osmosis, I guess.

"Baby, she turns out to be a natural freak / Popping pills and smoking weed"

Maybe if sex had been revealed more openly in my household, I wouldn't have been so damn confused about what to do with all my embryonic emotions and advanced equipment. In the ensuing years, perhaps feeling burned by my aunt's antics, my mom remained tight-lipped about anything of the physical or sexual realm. Boys and subsequent crushes were never a topic of breakfast banter. I was never given any reasons as to why I was forbidden to use tampons—not even in an emergency beach trip situation—or why I couldn't wear black clothes or makeup, or why I got this crazy tingling feeling and moist undies when I read *Forever*, by Judy Blume ("What? This ain't no *Superfudge!*")

Left to my own curious devices, I thought I'd give masturbating a try . . .

By age fifteen, I'd mastered the art of phone sex, more than a decade before Monica Lewinsky put it in the national lexicon. I would mostly be the mute muse, listening intently to the dirty conversation prompted by a wrong number that carried a random male voice, just answering "Yeah" when cued if I would like to suck his cock. One afternoon, my mom actually walked in on me diddling away in my room. Horrified by the sight, she yanked the hand out of my crotch with one hand, the phone out the wall with the other, and screeched a slew of nonsensical phrases at me. My father was summoned to punish me. But I was entering uncharted territory in more ways than one. Just how does a parent discipline for something like that? Well, the obvious was eliminating my phone privileges. Then I was dragged to church that night to pray for my sins, and then to a child psychologist the following week to get to the root of my inexplicable turpitude. Of course, neither pastor nor paid professional was successful in exorcising the incubus that had spawned my "evil behavior." To this day, rather than opening up a mature womanly heart-to-heart about that episode, Mami refers to that act as "hurting myself." Ooooookay. (If she only knew how often I "hurt myself" these days. With new and improved accessories! Batteries not included.)

What no one would ever understand was that for the first time, I felt empowered: I could morph into anyone I wanted to be on the phone (this before the Internet came and changed the whole game of aliases and alternate personas). I could mask my ugliness and naïveté with the huskiness of my mature, surprisingly sexy voice, which could fool any horny man. However, what I failed to comprehend was that I, too, could be fooled. And so I became obsessed with a faceless Canadian named John who happened to be incarcerated in a Florida jail cell. With his frustrated rock-star, bad-ass attitude, he smooth-talked me into taking his collect calls, talking to me in ways I'd never imagined before. I racked up thousands of dollars in phone bills, enthralled at his most banal fantasies. Suddenly, I decided that in order to become a sophisticated, desirable vixen, my virginity had to go. I just needed to find a candidate.

None of my pimply jockstrap-wearing classmates could appreciate my non-cheerleader figure, but grown men were willing to take me for a ride. Of course, by their very cradle-robbing nature, these were usually unsavory types; I chalked it up to my emerging maturity. I was working at a local pizza joint when I met Tammy, twenty-two-years-old and one of the bosses. She was white trash personified in a beat-up Monte Carlo station wagon. But to me, she was everything I wanted to be: thin, bleach-blonde and confident, crass and comical, a Bud-drinking party girl who had men lapping at those perfect knees. For some reason, she was happy to show me the ropes of irresponsible young adulthood. The night I decided to lose my virginity, one of Tammy's many male suitors came by the restaurant with a friend named Dave. There was nothing memorable about him. In fact, all I remember is that he was a blond dude with a peach-fuzzy mustache.

After locking up the restaurant, Tammy poured quarters in the jukebox while I poured pitchers of beer, and the four of us started smoking and drinking. At some point, someone suggested the party go mobile. Driving two separate cars, I rode with Dave, because without any previous discussion, we'd made a pact the minute I slammed the door to his truck that we were doin' it. Before we even made it inside his apartment, he had his dick out. I acted nonchalant, like I'd seen nothing but dicks all my life. So, with a what-the-hell shrug, I mounted him in the front cab. I just wanted it over and done with. Dave was too dumb or too drunk to notice my inexperience, and it was painless. We even had a second round once we made it inside the apartment. I sneaked back into my house early before the sun rose, which was nearly impossible with Mama Eagle Ears. But I knew I could lie my way out of it. "Tammy's crappy car broke down." Whew. More important, as I climbed into my bed, I wondered what kind of spiritual retribution or reward was awaiting my sinner's soul after I'd done the dirty deed. Twice, even. Does that doubly condemn me? Hmmmm . . . The next morning, I felt no fireworks. And yet, I wasn't burned by fire and brimstone either. What's the big fucking deal?

I'd equate my sexperience to losing an earring: when you discover it missing, you temporarily mourn/curse the loss, and there's a smidgen of hope that you'll find its mate underneath a couch cushion or something. Each time you open your jewelry box you're reminded of that loss. After a while, you say "fuck it," chuck it in the trash, rendering one perfectly good earring meaningless. Meanwhile, you discover another pair to call your own, and before long, you've forgotten all about the original pair that you once held sacred. And then you think to yourself, Why the hell was I making such a fuss over such an insignificant accessory in the first place?

Actually, I've always been a fetishist. Earrings, purses, and—my Achilles' heel—shoes. During my new wave phase, as long as the shoe was cute, I didn't care what size it was. I was willing to suffer for fashion. I remember a pair of army-green ankle boots I had to have, but the only size left was a size eight. I didn't care: I shoved my size-nine feet in 'em. I didn't care if my toes were crossed. Just like my gluttony for the ultimate accessories (every fat girl's fashion crutch), I chose men, indiscriminately, despite the ill fit and discomfort. Each time a man slipped his dick in, I kept hoping to find Cinderella's slipper. No such luck. After I'd racked up a handful of dicks attached to assholes by age seventeen, I found myself going semi-steady with a twenty-six-year-old crank-abusing, suicidal construction worker who lived in his parents' backyard in a trailer (his name was Duke—no joke!). One night, after he'd just wriggled himself on top of me for about four minutes of awkward half-dressed fumbling, pumping, and groping, Mr. Duke was bemoaning how he wished he could take me to my senior prom. (I declined, feeling less embarrassed to take a penniless boy with Tourette's syndrome from the delinquents' high school than Duke. Never mind that my date broke his leg the week before and wore a cast from hip to ankle to the dance.) I remember lying there on Mr. Duke's makeshift couch/bench/bed, thinking two things: (1) "This hair on his back is kinda gross"; and (2) "Gee, he's immature." I should've known right then and there that my future love life would be doomed for quite a while. I was caught between two worlds: the little girl in me crying out for male attention and the woman in me whose intellect couldn't be satisfied. In Fantasy Phone Land, I was queen. But in the real world, I was a fucking misfit.

My boyfriendless lifestyle continued after high school graduation, when I decided to enroll in a private university by the sea. Pretty tan surfer boys dated even prettier blondes, and I was carless on a campus where a Cabriolet was slumming it. I wore Swatches when everyone else donned Rolexes, and the only other people of color were on athletic scholarships or minor celebrities or celebrity offspring (Tootie from *The Facts of Life* and Johnnie Cochran's daughter, namely). At first, I didn't realize how much I'd be the odd girl out. College marked my first venture out of my hometown, to the vanity-filled beaches of Los Angeles and, for the first time, the startling realization that I was actually a person of color. I had always joked that I'd gotten in on some Hispanic quota, but I didn't realize that folks were so intent on putting you in an ethnic box. And outside of the joke that was Menudo, no one knew what the hell a Puerto Rican was, including me. "Hmmmm, she doesn't look or act Mexican . . . ," I could hear them say behind my back. People asked, "What are you," and my sarcastic "a human being" didn't suffice. I got filed under the light-skinned black girl, a role that didn't bode well for me. I was intimidated by the forwardness of the black men who would proposition me. "Hey, sis. Come closer and show me soma dat sugah." Backing away, I would say defensively, "Um, I'm not your sister, mister."

In exchange for minority rejection, I still fought like crazy for Caucasian acceptance. I didn't want to be black. I didn't want to be brown. I just wanted to be me. But I didn't know who "me" was. Was I an exotic novelty act? A social aberration? A total freakazoid? As such, I became legendary for being able to hook up with some hot guy at a party. My gossip-hungry dorm mates would eat up my tales of the sexual antics fueled by my nocturnal alcohol-induced faux confidence. Take my spin with the pizza delivery boy, Jeff; our short-term affair consisted of me accompanying him on his route, where we'd bounce up and down in his Suzuki Samurai off the beaten paths of the winding Pacific Coast Highway. Or Phillip, who claimed he was in the Mafia and therefore had to keep a low profile, but in reality had a wife at home and spent his free time hopped up on heroin. Or the summer fling in Spain, where surely I thought I'd find some appreciation, but instead, Raul wouldn't take me to the public pool because he figured I was already "dark enough" without more sun. (Those cocky dwarfish Spaniards mocked my Mexican-kitchen Spanish and looked at me like I was a black Amazon from the planet Negronia.) Or relegating myself to being the other woman with an egotistical amateur bodybuilder, who assuaged his equally hard-bodied girlfriend (to throw off her scent) that he could never be attracted to my flabby ass; he was just getting me in shape. (Boy, was he! But the only weight I was pushing was his rippled 220-pound body on top of mine!) For a brainy chick who supposedly possessed more than a shred of common sense, I sure made a helluva lot of judgment errors. Yet, through it all, I put on a pretty resilient front, laughed 'em off, kept my heart ironclad—or so I thought. But with each failed attempt at romance, my armor was gradually cracking.

At age twenty-five, I finally allowed a man to unsheathe part of my jaded heart. And boy, did I regret it, because in one fell swoop, he filleted it open like a fish. It started off platonic enough: One of my sister's friends needed a place to crash temporarily for a new job opportunity in L.A. But within a few days and after a few intimate conversations, he gradually moved from the floor to sharing my bed . . . until one morning, I unexpectedly received a forty-eight-minute one-on-one tongue-tutoring session in between my legs, where he generously exposed the hidden pleasures of oral sex. And that's how I experienced my first full-fledged orgasm. Whoa. Body heaving . . . so intensely I was sure I was gonna need to peel myself off the ceiling . . . eyes fluttering into the back of my brain like a woman possessed . . . bottom lip quivering as if caught jacketless in the rain . . . a moment of sheer panic of losing all faculties, then . . . whoooosh! A release of a thousand nerve endings, from the tips of my toes to my fingernails . . . convinced I could die right at that moment, but simultaneously wishing for time to freeze, to suspend this fiery volcanic ride to heaven-or-hell-I-don't-care-where-I-go-anymore . . . ooooohhhhhh . . . ooooooooohhhhhh . . . coño. So that's what all the bochinche was about!

The afterglow is no joke: at that moment, I felt like the most beautiful woman in the world. I didn't care that he was already once-divorced, had bisexual tendencies, or used to fuck his stepmom in a nudie colony. I had muddled that momentary bliss with the initial feelings of love, making me completely vulnerable, shedding my cloak and dagger. Not only did he find my clit with such oral dexterity, he in turn taught me how to give the perfect blow job. He coerced me to talk about my deepest hopes and fears about falling in love. Just as I was willing to give my heart over and become his love slave, he ironically decided to move back in with his incestuous stepmommy.

His emotional about-face crushed me. Turns out I was just a

fuck and a temporary roof over his head. He had no qualms about boasting that I was essentially notch no. 55 on his bedpost, and in fact he gave himself extra props for sharing a gene pool (I discovered he had also slept with my sister years earlier). I promptly ripped the heart off my sleeve and tucked it under my arm like a briefcase.

"Carmen starts to bawl, bangs her head to the wall / Too much love is worse than none at all"

With heroin, they say addiction is immediate because you're always trying to recapture that first high. Similar theories could be registered when it comes to that first phenomenal sex trip. Throughout my foibles, I have become one of sex's most fervent aficionados, but a demanding one, jonesin' for that endorphin-charged feral Tasmanian devil–type sex that comes with more hard-hitting rallies and primal grunts than a Serena-Venus tennis match. Now that I'm in my thirties, I realize that dancing the intricate steps of the horizontal mambo can only improve with age. More important, once I can tap into that kind of human connection, my body discovers yet another new level of hypersensation, as if the pheromone gods are making it up to me for all that lost time with all that baaaaad sex in my teens and twenties. Maybe I think the fucking will become so intense I'll finally make that elusive love connection.

When it comes to the self-esteem part of the love equation, moving to New York City was a revelation. It's where I could finally settle in and find comfort inside my own café con leche skin. In the city my parents ran away from, I've discovered that my boricua beauty is an amalgam of soft curls and voluptuous curves. Ironically, all the ethnic traits I grew up fighting like a rabid raccoon are now coveted by blanquitas. (Tanning salons? White girls with weaves? Collagen injections? Butt implants? Estás hablando en serio?). I should've paid more attention to Sir Mix-A-Lot's lyrics way back when, to fully comprehend how grown men of color can't get enough handfuls of all that Rubenesque juiciness; I should've embraced that eager appreciation for my feminine form, rather than cower from it.

But instead of pulling out my rizos to fit into the white-girl size-four pancake-assed ideal, I am finally pretty secure with the guitar-shaped silhouette looking back at me in the mirror. Since embracing my royal Ricanness, I've been fortunate to have two additional good lovers, one fantastic one and one phenomenal one—the latter being someone I would like to consider my spirit's true mate, with whom the sex is so symbiotically and orgasmically intense it transcends all logic. (We most definitely have booted Aqua Porno Barbie and Ken out of the pool!) Moreover, it's out of the bedroom where he makes me feel more like una reina propia. Whenever his incredibly soulful eyes meet mine, or when I stop to admire his smooth sienna flesh enlaced with my caramel hide, it feels so second skin, so second nature. We talk in the future tense, not as giddy teenagers but as two old souls mapping this current life path together. And the biggest bonus? He loves me just as I am. Pero quién sabe? Not to be a pessimist, but just because you track down your better half, tackle him to the ground, and hog-tie him to your heart doesn't necessarily mean you'll wind up permanently conjoined. In the Spanish lexicon, the verb *esperar* not only means to wait, but also to hope. I can always hope.

And with that modicum of esperanza squeezed tightly in my sweaty man-fist, maybe one day soon I can make that leap, along with my fellow Nuyorican hermana J.Lo, and realize that enduring and fulfilling relationship in which in equal parts I can love, be loved, and make love—a romantic trifecta that has so far eluded both of us. The road to success is paved with a shitload of failures, right? So maybe I should cut Ms. Lopez a break, with her ill-fated, ill-advised, fly-by-night romances, 'cause I've been rowing fervently in a similar rickety love boat. But maybe, for the first time in my life, I feel like I'm actually steering my own course, instead of just letting some random Roman force me on a meaningless humpy-bumpy joyride. I don't fear eternal damnation for embracing my sexuality, nor do I believe that I've bypassed a chance at true love. Thirty years later, I might've just stumbled upon it. I'd like to think that ol' Josefina and Ezekiel might be smiling down on me, ultimately proud that her nieta is living honestly and—most important—following her heart.

III

"Am I or
Aren't I..."

AMERICAN GIRL

BY LORENZA MUÑOZ

I stood on the first-place podium, the Mexican flag waving in the highest place behind me. I glanced around this beautiful yet strange place—a swimming pool in the midst of a Mexican jungle, crickets singing in the trees, a cool tropical breeze blowing. In the United States I had never swum in such exotic places. The crowd at the Central American Games was watching. They clapped and beamed proudly at the thought that this fourteen-year-old girl had won a first-place medal for la patria.

I saw my mom in the crowd, crying with joy. I looked over to my teammates, some excited and happy for me. But others I could see were burning up with jealousy because I had won yet another swimming race. They thought, "Who the hell is that gringa to come here and take our medals?"

Then came the moment of truth: the Mexican anthem. I had never in my life heard it. I tried not to show my panic as it began playing. My secret would be revealed. I really wasn't Mexican. I was an American. I was sure everyone would notice I was just mouthing the words as they came along, trying to fake it. Suddenly I felt a stream of sadness. What was I doing here?

My parents moved to the United States from their native Mexico City in 1977 seeking a new lifestyle. They didn't have the typical immigrant story. They left, with my brother and me (ages three and six), out of choice, not necessity. Considering we would eventually end up in Los Angeles, it's funny to think my mother wanted to leave Mexico City to escape the pollution, traffic, and crime that plagued us daily.

A turning point came one day when my mother, my infant brother, and I got caught in one of those famous hours-long Mexico City traffic jams. The stoplights were not working. But rather than wait patiently and take turns, the cars lunged at each other in all directions. The result: a massive knot of traffic. My mother had had enough. She got out of the car and started directing the traffic herself. She stood in the middle of the road, placing her hand on the front end of cars to stop them and waving the opposite row of cars ahead. My brother and I were in a panic, screaming with fear that something would happen to her as men hollered "Mamacita, ay que buena estás" out their windows. After a while, she had succeeded in undoing the knot, got back in the car, and vowed to leave this "pinche ciudad de mierda."

A few months later, we left for Virginia for the summer. My mother thought she had arrived in Eden. Everything was green. There was no traffic. The cops were friendly and well uniformed. We picked peaches out of public orchards and swam in creeks. We listened to opera in an outdoor amphitheater while having picnic lunches. And, most important, my brother and I were running around with flushed cheeks, not smog, in our lungs.

To this day, my mother believes we were fated to come to this country. After Virginia, she told my father she wanted to move. He told her she was crazy. But within a few months of returning to Mexico, a mysterious phone call arrived.

Out of the blue, a longtime acquaintance of my father's wanted to know if he was interested in taking a job at the University of Southern California teaching Spanish literature. My mom sold everything, and within a few months we moved.

But finding a place to live proved harder than she thought. Every FOR RENT sign they saw in Los Angeles County stated: "No kids, no pets, no waterbeds." So they kept driving south and finally ended up in California's version of Eden: Orange County.

Orange County was a clean, conservative, homogenous place with absolutely no nightlife—the antithesis of cosmopolitan Mexico City. It was a rough transition for my parents. They were used to fineries—going out at night with their friends, eating at great restaurants, visiting art galleries, enjoying the political conversations that dominated their dinner parties.

Their lifestyle took a steep dive. My mom took the bus with us to the local Laundromat. A celebratory meal meant my mom could buy four giant shrimp—one for each of us. We shopped at Kmart.

In Huntington Beach at that time, a good restaurant was considered El Torito. (As a result of our immigrant ignorance, we visited this place once and were shocked to find that these chimichanga/burrito inventions were called Mexican food.) There were no art galleries. Nobody spoke Spanish. And while they were fortunate to find a group of adventurous and liberal Orange County friends, those folks were few and far between. But since it was all so new, my parents were more amused than annoyed.

Although my brother and I plunged into Orange County

life somewhat seamlessly, it was a harder adjustment for us. Neither of us spoke English fluently. At that time, bilingual education was true immersion. Hopefully, if you had patient, good teachers and parents, you could learn English really fast.

I remember my frustration one day in the second grade when we were asked to paint a birthday scene. I painted a piñata. Believe it or not, no one knew what it was. My face burned with embarrassment because I didn't know English well enough to explain how much fun it was to hit this paper cardboard thing that eventually broke apart and flooded the world with candy. I went home depressed, feeling like my tongue had been cut out.

Another time I got lost on the way to school. When a mom came out to inform us that the bus was not coming, I didn't understand, so I just followed everyone home like a good little duckling. Soon, all the other kids disappeared into their homes. When I was the last kid standing, the mom who came out to get us at the bus stop asked me where I lived. I had thought she was walking us to school. Again, I became mute. Eventually, she was able to locate my parents. As we were standing outside her home waiting for my dad to drive up, she asked me what kind of car he had. I proudly remembered and declared: "A Ford Fiesta!" But on that awful day, my dad came in another, unfamiliar car. My heart sank. I couldn't even get that right. (It turns out the Fiesta was in the shop, and my dad had rented another car for the day.)

As far as my family was concerned, we tried to blend in, but at times, our "Mexicanness" jumped out. When my mother screamed at us in Spanish, she demanded we answer in her language. Once, my dad decided to cook cows' brains in black butter and capers (a delicacy he learned to make from my grandmother) for dinner. He bought the brains, specially ordered from a local butcher, in front of a schoolmate of mine, of course. I never lived that one down. On the whole, though, we lived like normal Orange County kids. We enjoyed swimming, playing soccer, going to the beach, and eating double-doubles at In-n-Out Burger.

Of these activities, swimming competitively had always come first for me. I loved water as a baby and swam my first swim meet at age four in Mexico. During the fifty-meter freestyle, I got to the wall first, jumping on the first-place podium without asking anyone if I had won. As a kid, I swam competitively for Mexico and the United States, relishing every trophy as a step on the way to Olympic dreams. But something happened when I turned fifteen. I was bored and itched to find something else. I plunged into the adolescent's quest to find adventure, meaning, and love. So I decided to quit swimming my sophomore year, much to my parents' horror.

I longed for the fashion models' sophisticated, exciting lives I read about in *Vogue* and other magazines. And since I could not move to New York City alone, Mexico City was the closest attainable thing. I envied the life my relatives led in chic Mexico City. My grandmother, especially, embodied the model of classy living. She traveled all over the world and had a set of cultured girlfriends she would hang out with every week. She drank tequila with gusto and never seemed drunk. My aunt smelled beautiful, of a French cologne named Je Reviens. Even when she smoked, her perfumed scent lingered as she passed by in her silk blouse, designer pants, and heels. The women were always dressed up, wearing makeup and fashionable clothing—not the sweatpants and tennis shoes I saw on so many Orange County mothers.

So I went to Mexico for the summers of my sophomore and junior years. I made it my mission to learn Spanish with the perfect chilanga accent, as if I lived in Mexico City, a bourgeois lifestyle with las familias bien. I strived to become an entitled, upper-crust, young Mexican teen—my parents' worst nightmare: "Oh yeah, I know exactly where La Colonia Roma is. Meet you at a café at five and then at midnight we'll go to the Magic for all-night dancing."

In the morning the servants will wake me around noon with a generous serving of huevos rancheros, fresh-squeezed orange juice, newly baked black beans, and strong coffee. When I go take a shower, the maid can make my bed. I am so lucky to be beautiful and European-looking; I mean at the Magic the bouncer wouldn't let these two girls in behind me because they were such indias. Even though I want to learn how to salsa, I should never, ever ask a black man to dance because all of our friends think it is totally beneath us. Oh, there's Julio, my biggest crush! He is such a man, paying for everything, speaking French, slicking his hair back, drinking Cuba Libres and smoking Marlboro Lights as he scans the room, steadying his gaze at some girl with fake boobs. And here is my cousin, sitting next to me at the table with some dime-a-dozen floozy he found to play with while his girlfriend is in Europe. It's okay, that is what all Mexicans do. I'm such a naive little gringa, shocked so easily. Oh yeah, and those damned gringos. Such ignorant, uncultured beasts. I don't know how I could continue to live there.

I wanted to move back permanently. But my parents would hear none of it. My mother, who had many nightclub experiences when she was young, could somewhat understand my rebellion. But my father was less sympathetic. He had no tolerance for my quest to find vain and empty adventures. He wanted me to be serious and intellectual. There were some unsettling things about my desired homeland, but I pushed them to the back of my mind. (Why was my uncle's business partner—a man in his forties—playing footsie with a sixteen-year-old? Why did my own cousins call my brother a bolillo—a white bread?)

Still, I would come home after an entire summer in Mexico's nightclubs to the quiet, boring suburban life my parents had accidentally carved out for us. I hated strip malls and football captains. I dreamed of Mexico and the free lifestyle I could lead there. You could drink, smoke, drive, and date with total freedom, unlike the prison of America, where teenagers are forced to hide and are expected to reappear when they become sensible young adults.

In Mission Viejo, where my family had moved, my girlfriends and I would spend hours at the Little Caesars Pizza parking lot waiting for someone to say there was a "rager" at someone's house because their parents were on vacation. If we congregated in the parking lot too long, police helicopters would suddenly hover above, then aim a blinding spotlight at us, and a distant, omnipresent voice would declare, "You are in violation of section penal code 354499023. Disperse immediately. I repeat, disperse immediately." So, off we would go in search of someone's house to toilet paper or a girlfriend's bedroom to make crank calls from.

By my senior-year, panic brought me back to my senses. How was I going to get into a good college? Only a swimming scholarship would guarantee entry into a top school. So when a group of Mexican swimmers proposed to my mother that I compete for the Mexican National Team again, I was more than happy to oblige. Since I was a child, I had always dreamed of earning a gold medal at the Olympics, an international audience cheering my victory. The United States decided to ban foreigners from competing in the U.S. Nationals. Since I was a Mexican citizen, I only had one choice. I represented Mexico for several years, until my junior year in college. I traveled to Japan for the Pan Pacific Games, Australia for the world championships, and Cuba for the Pan American Games. I saw many regions of Mexico, swimming in all major national competitions. My rigorous U.S. training helped me nail many trophies, and the Olympics seemed closer and closer. But it was a baptism by lava; my years away from the country and back-and-forth lifestyle meant constantly having to prove that I was Mexican. My North American–bred impatience with chaos was tested on a daily basis.

We would rarely get our uniforms, swim caps, or swimsuits on time, if at all. One time, in Veracruz, the swimming pool was the color of mud. We had to work out in the shark-infested ocean until they "cleaned" the pool. While these incidents affected everyone on the team, there was an extraordinary amount of contempt reserved for me personally. I only showed up for major competitions in Mexico and abroad, yet I was beating all the other kids on the team and breaking all of the records. I was used to the extensive training and abundant resources in U.S. athletics, and the parents were starting to resent my achievements. I would get disqualified for alleged violations. We found out once that a parent had paid a referee to disqualify me to get me out of the way. My mother and I were stunned. How could this happen? I just blinked in confusion when my mother said to me, "I should have known better than to bring you back here." I would be given broken trophies. One time, there was no bed for me to sleep on. I made very few friends. Each negative experience chipped away at my love for the country I once wanted to embrace. Perhaps it was such a devastating experience because I was completely blindsided. The only side I had seen of Mexico was the love of my family. There was never a hint of what was to come. I soon became intimately familiar with the dark side of Mexico.

On the U.S. swim teams, we were taught to root each other on, to push each other. We congratulated one another and learned to play fair. In Mexico, cliques ruled, and individuals mostly tried to show each other up. It was rare for me to see teammates supporting one another. My career swimming for Mexico ended when I was twenty years old, competing at the Pan American Games in Cuba. My swim coach sheepishly called me over to him.

"Lorenza," he whispered. "Don't get mad. But the swimming officials forgot to enter you in your races. You are only swimming one event and one relay. I'm sorry."

I would only swim two races—a relay and the 400 individual medley—after having spent an entire summer swimming six hours a day, weight lifting and running with members of the U.S. Olympic Team at the University of Texas, where my old coach was now the head women's coach. I was stunned and fuming, and my old U.S. team were the first ones I went to. My Mission Viejo swim coach came over to tell me that he could not believe the incompetence. When I told my U.S. friends, including American record holder Amy Shaw, they tried their best to console me. But this had set me back too far. I wondered what to do as I sat in a corner of the natatorium one afternoon. The U.S. anthem began playing. In an epiphany, I suddenly found myself singing it out loud. I did swim that day, and I did it horribly. Our relay won a bronze medal, but it was a shallow moment for me to stand on the third-place podium, since the man who gave us the medal was the head of the Mexican Swimming Federation—my enemy.

There is something very pure about competition. It strips away weaknesses and excuses. It is also emotional and honest. How could I continue to represent a country that was so foreign to me? I would never represent Mexico again—and that meant missing the 1992 Barcelona Olympic Games. U.S. Olympic coach Mark Schubert tried to talk me out of it. But I told him that unless he was my coach, and I could wear the U.S. uniform, I wasn't interested. It was a decision based on principle as much as sheer exhaustion—I was just tired of having problems. I went home devastated.

To this day, during every opening ceremony for the Olympic Games I cry as I watch. I admit that I am still resentful and perhaps I have—unfairly—passed that resentment on to the entire country, not just a few brainless bureaucrats. Quitting the Mexican team is really the only act in my life that I regret.

I wrote a scathing letter to one of the nation's leading newspapers assailing the lack of professionalism, sportsmanship, and discipline that had prompted me to throw in the towel. This was not relevant to swimming only. The entire country was mired in mediocrity because of this, I wrote. Many journalists agreed with me, but these problems still persist. I became a U.S. citizen the same year I returned defeated from the Pan Am experience. I finished college at my dream school, UC Berkeley. I married a non-Mexican.

I would be lying if I said I don't resent Mexico. Like a "cafeteria Catholic," it has been a real struggle to figure out what to discard and what to retain of my Mexican heritage. I want to love it wholly. But I can't. This struggle has not been one of racial identity. Being Mexican is not a race, as Americans tend to see it. In America, you are expected to check off a little box. What are you? White, black, beige, yellow? As a dear friend of mine likes to say, "I always tell my American friends I am a Mexican, Basque, Jew. And then they ask, 'But what are you?' "

Being Mexican is a nationality, it's a culture and a state of mind. I hold dual Mexican and American citizenship. I love Mexican culture. But I can't seem to fully find that state of mind or feeling in my heart. Still, my little boy's name is Maximilian Lorenzo. He speaks more Spanish than English. I want him to travel the world and feel like his background is more complex than just "American." When I look at the old black-and-white photographs of my great-grandfather and grandfather receiving commendations from two Mexican presidents, I feel proud. When I hear the beautiful boleros of Tona La Negra, Los Tres Ases, and Agustín Lara, my mind floats back to the sunny gardens of Cuernavaca. I would much rather celebrate El Dia de Los Muertos than Halloween. My house is a deep terra-cotta color full of Mexican touches, from the bougainvillea vines throughout my garden to our paintings of Francisco Toledo and other Oaxacan artists hanging in our hallways. My lovely Catarina stands at the front entrance of our door and a silver framed image of the Virgin of Guadalupe adorns my nightstand.

Like all immigrants, I sometimes feel like I live in a netherworld. I am neither American nor am I Mexican. I want the best of both worlds—the relaxed way of life, the love of family, tradition, culture, and history that reigns in Mexico. I wish Americans had more of the que será, será attitude where accidents are allowed to happen and death is an accepted—even embraced—fact of life. Most of all, I wish I didn't live in a culture where everything, even death and tragedy, is consoled with money.

Perhaps I am bound to never find my place. I wonder if the perfect place is only in my mind. The day I learn to love one country unconditionally—just as I do my family—is the day I will know I have matured. When I reach that point, I will be at peace. Until then I will spend my days searching for something that is perhaps unattainable.

SE HABLA ESPAÑOL

BY TANYA BARRIENTOS

The man on the other end of the phone line is telling me the classes I've called about are first-rate: native speakers in charge, no more than six students per group.

"Conbersaychunal," he says, allowing the fat vowels of his accented English to collide with the sawed-off consonants.

I tell him that will be fine, that I'm familiar with the conversational setup, and yes, I've studied a bit of Spanish in the past. He asks for my name and I supply it, rolling the double r in Barrientos like a pro. That's when I hear the silent snag, the momentary hesitation I've come to expect at this part of the exchange. Should I go into it again? Should I explain, the way I have to half a dozen others, that I am Guatemalan by birth but pura gringa by circumstance? Do I add the humble little laugh I usually attach to the end of my sentence to let him know that of course I see the irony in the situation?

This will be the sixth time I've signed up to learn the language my parents speak to each other. It will be the sixth time I've bought workbooks and notebooks and textbooks listing 501 conjugated verbs in alphabetical order, with the hope that the subjunctive tense will finally take root in my mind.

In class, I will sit across a table from the "native speaker," who won't question why the Irish-American lawyer, or the ad executive of Polish descent, has enrolled but, with a telling glance, will wonder what to make of me.

Look, I'll want to say (but never do). Forget the dark skin. Ignore the obsidian eyes. Pretend I'm a pink-cheeked, blue-eyed blonde whose name tag says Shannon. Because that is what a person who doesn't innately know the difference between corre, corra, and corrí is supposed to look like, isn't it? She certainly isn't supposed to be earth-toned or be from my kind of background. If she happens to be named García or López, it's probably through marriage, or because an ancestor at the very root of her family trekked across the American line three or four generations ago.

I, on the other hand, came to the United States at age three, in 1963, with my family and stopped speaking Spanish immediately.

College-educated and seamlessly bilingual when they settled in West Texas, my parents (a psychology professor and an artist) embraced the notion of the American melting pot wholeheartedly. They declared that their two children would speak nothing but inglés. They'd read in English, write in English, and fit into Anglo society beautifully. If they could speak the red, white, and blue without a hint of an accent, my mother and father believed, people would be forced to look beyond the obvious and see the all-American kids hidden inside the ethnic wrapping.

It sounds politically incorrect now. But America was not a hyphenated nation back then. People who called themselves Mexican-Americans or Afro-Americans were considered dangerous radicals, while law-abiding citizens were expected to drop their cultural baggage at the border and erase any lingering ethnic traits. Role models like Vikki Carr, Linda Ronstadt, and Raquel Welch had done it and become stars. So why shouldn't we?

To be honest, for most of my childhood I liked being the brown girl who defied expectations. When I was seven, my mother returned my older brother and me to elementary school one week after the school year had already begun. We'd been on vacation in Washington, D.C., visiting the Smithsonian, the Capitol, and the home of Edgar Allan Poe. In the Volkswagen, on the way home, I'd memorized "The Raven," and I'd recite it with melodramatic flair to any poor soul duped into sitting through my performance. At the school's office, the registrar frowned when we arrived.

"You people. Your children are always behind, and you have the nerve to bring them in late?"

"My children," my mother answered in a clear, curt tone, "will be at the top of their classes in two weeks."

The registrar filed our cards, shaking her head.

I did not live in a neighborhood with other Latinos, and the public school I attended attracted very few. I saw the world through the clear, cruel vision of a child. To me, speaking Spanish translated into being poor. It meant waiting tables and cleaning hotel rooms. It meant being left off the cheerleading squad and receiving a condescending smile from the guidance counselor when you said you planned on becoming a lawyer or a doctor. My best friends' names were Heidi and Leslie and Kim. They told me I didn't seem "Mexican" to them, and I took it as a compliment. I enjoyed looking into the faces of

Latino store clerks and waitresses and, yes, even our maid, and saying "yo no hablo español." It made me feel superior. It made me feel American. It made me feel white.

It didn't matter that my parents spoke Spanish and were successful. They came from a different country, where everyone looked alike. In America, fitting in with the gringos was key. I didn't want to be a Latina anything. I thought that if I stayed away from Spanish, the label would stay away from me.

When I was sixteen, I told my father how much I hated being called Mexican—not only because I wasn't, but also because the word was hurled as an insult. He cringed and then he made a radical plan. That summer, instead of sending me to the dance camp in Aspen that I wanted to attend, he pointed me toward Mexico City and the Ballet Nacional.

"I want you to see how beautiful Mexico is," he said. "That way when anybody calls you Mexican, you will hold your head up."

I went, reluctantly, and found out he was right. I loved the music, the art, the architecture. He'd planted the seed of pride, but it would take years for me to figure out how to nurture it.

Back at home, my parents continued to speak only English to their kids while speaking Spanish to each other.

My father enjoyed listening to the nightly Mexican newscast on television, so I came to understand lots of the Spanish I heard. Not by design, but by osmosis. So, by the time I graduated from college, I'd become an odd Hispanic hybrid—an English-only Latina who could comprehend Spanish spoken at any speed but was reluctant to utter a word of it. Then came the backlash. In the two decades I'd worked hard to isolate myself from the stereotype I'd constructed in my own head, society shifted. The nation had changed its views on ethnic identity.

College professors had started teaching history through African-American and Native American eyes. Children were being told to forget about the melting pot and picture America as a multicolored quilt instead.

Hyphens suddenly had muscle, and I was left wondering where I fit in. The Spanish language was supposedly the glue that held the new Latino-American community together. But in my case it was what kept me apart. I felt awkward among groups whose conversations flowed in and out of Spanish. I'd be asked a question in Spanish and I'd have to answer in English, knowing that raised a mountain of questions. I wanted to call myself Latina, to finally take pride, but it felt like a lie. So I set out to learn the language that people assumed I already knew.

After my first set of lessons, which I took in a class provided by the newspaper where I worked in Dallas, I could function in the present tense. "Hola Paco, ¿qué tal? ¿Qué color es tu cuaderno? El mío es azul." My vocabulary built quickly, but when I spoke my tongue felt thick inside my mouth, and if I needed to deal with anything in the future or the past I was sunk. I suggested to my parents that when I telephoned we should converse only in Spanish, so I could practice. But that only lasted a few short weeks. Our relationship was built in English and the essence of it got lost in the translation.

By my mid-twenties I had finally come around to understanding that being a proud Latina meant showing the world how diverse the culture can be. As a newspaper reporter, I met

Cubans and Puerto Ricans and brown-skinned New Mexicans who could trace their families all the way back to the conquistadores. I interviewed writers and teachers and migrant workers, and I convinced editors to put their stories into print. Not just for the readers' sake, but for my own. I wanted to know what other Latinos had to say about their assimilation into American culture, and whether speaking Spanish somehow defined them. What I learned was that they considered Spanish their common denominator, linking them to one another as well as to their pasts. With that in mind, I traveled to Guatemala to see the place where I was born, and basked in the comfort of recognizing my own features in the faces of strangers. I felt connected, but I still wondered if without flawless Spanish I could ever fill the Latino bill.

I enrolled in a three-month submersion program in Mexico and emerged able to speak like a sixth-grader with a solid C average. I could read Gabriel García Márquez with a Spanish-English dictionary at my elbow, and I could follow ninety percent of the melodrama on any given telenovela.

But I still didn't feel genuine. My childhood experiences were different from most of the Latinos I met. I had no quinceañera, no abuelita teaching me to cook tamales, no radio in the house playing rancheras. I had ballet lessons, a high school trip to Europe, and a tight circle of Jewish friends. I'd never met another Latina like me, and I began to doubt that they existed.

Since then, I've hired tutors and bought tapes to improve my Spanish. Now I can recite Lorca. I can handle the past as well as the future tenses. But the irregular verbs and the subjunctive tense continue to elude me.

My Anglo friends call me bilingual because I can help them make hotel reservations over the telephone or pose a simple question to the women taking care of their children. But true speakers discover my limitations the moment I stumble over a difficult construction, and that is when I get the look. The one that raises the wall between us. The one that makes me think I'll never really belong. Spanish has become a pedigree, a litmus test showing how far from your roots you've strayed. Of course, the same people who would hold my bad Spanish grammar against me wouldn't blink at an Anglo tripping over a Spanish phrase. In fact, they'd probably be flattered that the white man or woman was giving their language a shot. They'd embrace the effort. But when I fumble, I immediately lose the privilege of calling myself a full-fledged Latina. Broken Spanish doesn't count, except to set me apart from "authentic" Latinas forever.

My bilingual friends say I make too much of it. They tell me that my Guatemalan heritage and unmistakable Mayan features are enough to legitimize my membership in the Latino-American club. After all, not all Poles speak Polish. Not all Italians speak Italian. And as this nation grows more and more Hispanic, not all Latinos will share one language. But I don't believe them. I think they say those things to spare my feelings.

There must be other Latinas like me. But I haven't met any. Or, I should say, I haven't met any who have fessed up. Maybe they are secretly struggling to fit in, the same way I am. Maybe they are hiring tutors and listening to tapes behind the locked doors of their living rooms, just like me. I wish we all had the courage to come out of our hiding places and claim our rightful spot in the broad Latino spectrum. Without being called hopeless gringas. Without having to offer apologies or show remorse.

If it will help, I will go first.

Aquí estoy.

Spanish-challenged and pura Latina.

ELIÁN: A LOVE STORY

BY GIGI ANDERS

It was a lazy Sunday in mid-April of 2000. My boyfriend Paul and I, both journalists, were eating bagels with cream cheese and drinking café con leche as we read the *New York Times*. Normally we'd be listening to American jazz or a Cachao son with the TV turned off. But this was not a normal day or a normal spring. Elián González, an adorable six-year-old Cuban refugee, was obsessing me and, so it seemed, the rest of the world. By now his story has entered into Myth Land, but at the time, it was a compelling myth in the making, a heartbreaking political and emotional saga, and a daily breaking news event with no clear-cut outcome that could ever satisfy anybody except, ultimately and as usual, El Caballo, Fidel Castro's nom de guerre.

To quickly recap the facts: Elián, whose parents were divorced, lived with his mother and stepfather in Cárdenas, a port city two hours east of Havana on Cuba's northern coast. On November 22, 1999, the three Cubans joined ten others in a sixteen-foot motorboat heading for the United States. The next day, the vessel capsized, drowning ten of its passengers, including Elián's mother and stepfather. After clinging to an inner tube by himself for some seventy-two hours in the Gulf

Stream in the Straits of Florida, Elián was rescued near Fort Lauderdale on Thanksgiving Day by two American fishermen, who delivered him to some distant relatives living in Little Havana, a conservative working-class Miami neighborhood of Cuban exiles. (The two other shipwreck survivors, both adults not related to Elián, separately got ashore, but nobody cared about them.) Elián enjoyed a tearful, joyful union with his extended family, who intended to keep him.

Then the proverbial mierda hit the fan.

Castro and Elián's father, Juan Miguel González, demanded Elián be returned. Predictably, the Miami relatives refused. Juan Miguel, a member of Castro's Communist Party, arrived in Washington, D.C., to reclaim his son and return with him to Cuba. Cuban Miami exploded in a collective frenzy, turning a tiny, innocent child into a political pawn in an international custodial tug-of-war, a Christlike symbol of the miraculous and the preordained, and a poster child for all Cubans.

"Is there any more coffee, Geeg?" Paul said.

I was too engrossed in the TV news show to hear him. Talking heads were butting heads over Elián.

"Geeg?" Paul repeated.

"What?"

"Is there more coffee?"

"Here," I told him. "You can finish mine. Sweetie, I really want to watch this."

Paul understood, and not just because he's a journalist. My gringo boyfriend of one year, looking mighty cute in his Romeo y Julieta–brand cigar T-shirt (I'd bought it for him many months before in a Little Havana tabaquería–cigar factory), had by now gotten a deep immersion in all things Cuban, thanks to me and my family. When my parents and I left Cuba in 1960, when I was a baby, we stayed in Miami for only six months. My folks found jobs in Washington, D.C., and that's where we remained. Of course, there were always trips to Miami, The Other Homeland, to visit friends and relatives and overeat at Versailles, my favorite Little Havana restaurant. Those vacations became increasingly less fun for me as time went by, however. The eternal, crushing heat. The political tunnel vision and dogma. The nonstop Castro-bashing mania over the airwaves, in restaurants, at people's houses. The clannish, provincial hysterics. All those things would have been my norm had my parents settled there instead of in our nation's capital. And yet, sometimes I've been sorry they didn't. After all, there's strength in numbers, a sense of belonging and acceptance and solidarity. In Miami, Cubans know who they are. They never have to feel ashamed to be it. That's one of the things I love most about going there, that instant unspoken understanding that nosotros somos Cubanos, just as Jews from anywhere feel when they go to Israel. When you're such a minority all the time, it's wonderful to be a part of a majority for a change. When I'm sitting in Versailles, the weirdos are the Americans who can't pronounce plátanos maduros.

And speaking of Spanish, I knew Paul was The Real Thing when, a couple of weeks into the relationship, he sent me an e-mail in perfect español. I wrote him back and asked him how in the world he knew how to do that. He sheepishly replied that a newsroom colleague was Hispanic, and Paul had told the guy, "Listen, I'm dating a Cuban woman and I want to impress her. How do you say, 'I love you and you make me so happy'? In Spanish?" I knew Paul was Really The Real Thing when, some-

time later, my family threw a huge bash for my father's seventi-
eth birthday and Paul, the sole non-Cuban present, didn't pass
out or go postal. Out-of-town guests arrived from all over, especially Miami. The restaurant was packed with more than a hundred screaming, insane Cubans (I guess describing Cubans that
way is redundant), and my man weathered El Huracán de la Familia Cubana with aplomo, not to mention several stiff mojitos.

So although I feel very Cuban most of the time, especially
in contrast to my New Yorker boyfriend and his North American family and most of the rest of the native English speakers
in my northeastern life, I will never feel as fanatically or defiantly Cuban, to the exclusion of all other things, as do my
friends and family who left in the early sixties, moved to Miami,
and haven't budged since. Still, when a crisis arises in the
community—and the fate of little Elián was certainly considered primo crisis material—we tend to close ranks and circle
the wagons.

Since Paul had polished off the remnants of my café con
leche and I needed more caffeination to couple with my freshly
lit Parliament and my Elián fixation, I unscrewed a fresh bottle
of Tab. Yes, bottle. Tab is available in most metro areas, but
usually only in cans. Canned Tab tastes metallic. In a pinch, I
can settle, but for some bizarre reason, only Tab in the fabulous
twenty-ounce plastic screw-top bottles works for me. Sometimes I have to drive over two hundred miles one way just to
get my hot-pink cases of those Tabs. All because I have an addiction. Paul said he knew I was Really In Love with him the
first time I willingly shared my Tab. It was the ultimate sacrifice. Well, what can I tell you? A girl goes puerco wild when
she's in love. Wild and blind. Just as my fellow Cubanos-
Americanos on TV were acting over Elián, a boy whom the

majority didn't personally know but with whom they were madly in love, madly to the point of blindness.

Watching the live footage of my fellow exiles in furious full-throttle right-wing mode on TV, ranting and raving, threatening to sue Attorney General Janet Reno and the U.S. government, and, weeks later, erupting onto the streets of Miami when Elián was finally returned to Cuba with his father, I was truly torn between cringing (Americana: God, these freaks are so embarrassing!) and empathy (Cubana: We may be short but we're fierce. You go, kids!). So. Which camp would I side with, which one should I side with? I had to ask myself whether Shakespeare was right in *A Midsummer Night's Dream* when he wrote:

> Lovers and madmen have such seething brains,
> Such shaping fantasies, that apprehend
> More than cool reason ever comprehends.

But then I thought of something equally important that another non-Latino had to say. It was a lesson I learned from Dr. Marvin Adland, my retired psychoanalyst and, like Shakespeare, a student of the human condition. It was one of the hardest lessons to get locked into place inside me. Namely, you don't have to raise your voice or use bad words to be effective and get your point across, which is, of course, the ultimate anti-Cuban attitude. As a matter of fact, acting "Cuban" in that way in certain milieus of this society actually weakens people's perceptions of you and makes them think you're just a typical, trivial, crazy, hot-blooded spic.

Maybe we exiles drink too much espresso and we're wired from the caffeine. Maybe we live in chronic sugar seizure mode from our ultrarich postres like flan de coco. Maybe we just have too much downtime. (Indeed, ask any Cuban old enough to have lived in pre-Castro Cuba about life in pre-Castro Cuba and you'll be incredibly sorry you ever brought it up. Ask about post-Castro Cuba and you'll be even sorrier.) I think what we really need isn't less caffeine and sugar and free time; it's better public relations. Because if the goal was to make mainstream America feel sympathy for the cause and understand that Castro's repressive, anachronistic regime was behind all of this from day one—dey totally blew eet, as my testy mama Cubana would say.

A few days earlier my mother and I had been on the phone, both of us watching the same CNN show in which famous Cuban-Americans had formed a human chain in front of the Little Havana house where Elián was. There was a well-known actor, a talk-show hostess, a singer, a musician, and, to my personal astonishment, a newspaper colleague whom I knew rather well. I could perfectly understand the celebs getting out there—all publicity is good publicity, after all—but a journalist?

"If I were her editor I'd fire her Cuban ass on the spot," I heard myself tell Mami. I was surprised to hear myself pop that out just like that. "She's entitled to her opinion—in print. But she's injecting herself into the news. That's not journalism. That's . . ."

"De newspaper might talk to her but dey won fire her," Mami said. "Chee has a consteetuahncee. De paper knows dat. Der would be an uproar. Dey have to take eet. Chee knows exactly how far chee can poosh her agenda."

On the Sam and Cokie show on TV, George Will was saying, without a trace of irony, that a communist cannot be a good parent.

"There's a howler," Paul said.

Was it a howler statement? Or was this situation a Cuban exile version of "It's a black thing, you wouldn't understand"?

"Jesus Christ," Paul continued. "Will's such an anal-retentive Tory."

"You think so?" I said, lighting a new Parliament and sipping my Tab.

"You know what the Justice Department should do? Reno should get a court order that the loony uncle [Lázaro González, at whose home Elián resided while in the United States] cough up the kid. And if he refuses, they should lock him up for contempt."

"You would *lock him up?*"

"Absolutely. 'Communists can't be good parents?' Christ."

"Maybe they can't," I ventured.

"Fidel is a hypocritical thug. But the Elián crowd, those people down there are loud, bombastic, right-wing, hard-liner assholes who are trying to use their political clout and campaign cash to put themselves above the law."

Paul picked up my bottle of Tab and took a long swallow. Now not only was he insulting my people but he had the audacity to drink my Tab right afterward, without so much as waiting for me to offer him some. This is my *life*, dammit. Don't you get that I saw myself in little Elián? It's the story of so many Cubans. Me cago en este cabrón jodedero! Shit! I was thinking very bad things about Paul, all because he insulted My Peoples and took my Tab. Would this discussion turn into one of those Civil War scenarios? You know, brother against brother? A house divided? And more important, could I continue to voluntarily sleep with a man who drinks my Tab and has an anti–Cuban exile attitude? I mean, it's one thing for *me* to criticize them, it's quite another for outsiders to do it.

"I know what you want me to say, dear," I said, trying my best to not repeatedly stab my gringo beloved with the now-empty Tab bottle. Empty! "Like in those multiple-choice quizzes in *Cosmo*, when you know what the 'right' answer is and you choose it just so you'll get a better score and not have to face the fact that your attitude's all wrong and you're all fucked up?"

"What does that mean?"

Where would I even begin? How to explain to an American, a non-Cuban, the passions behind this, the frustrations and hurt feelings of more than four pent-up decades? . . . Ay, Cuba. See, this is why I always wear waterproof mascara. You just never know when life will make you cry.

"Elián's mother died to get him here," I said, blinking and feeling my eyes brim. "What do you not understand? She wanted him *here*. You know how many other Cuban parents have made similar sacrifices? Hello, there's a *reason* for this. I realize no six-year-old gets to call the shots, but . . . ?

Coño. Elián was affecting me way more than I'd expected. I'd just mentally cursed out the man I love. At least I'd kept my volume in check. That's a real accomplishment for a Cuban. Here's the thing that clouded my judgment and got me so emotional: seeing that terminally cute (which is how Paul describes me, actually) Elián swinging on the swings in his Little Havana yard, playing with his five bazillion Toys "R" Us toys, drinking his little mamey nectar and enjoying all the fruits of los Estados Unidos. I was very moved. I identified with him. My parents didn't want me to live in Cuba under Castro either. They also took risks to get me from there to here when I was a tiny child. So to see all of Elián's mom's effort and risk and even death come to nothing for her son except a U-turn ticket back to Cuba after having lived it up here—it was just sadder than any words. Who knows what might have become of me had my parents been living apart, as Elián's were back in Cuba, and my mother had drowned trying to get me to America and my father had come here to reclaim me and return me to Castro's Cuba? I'd never have met Paul, that's for sure, or experienced the life-altering thrill that only Tab in the bottle can bring.

So Paul should be glad and Paul should agree!

Paul was glad—for me. But no, Paul didn't agree—about Elián. Hm. Maybe I should be involved with a Cuban, not a gringo. The machismo would turn me homicidal, true, but at least we'd agree on Elián and the importance of flan de coco and pastel de tres leches.

"Geeg?" the boyfriend asked.

"No sex for joo tonight, Mr. Señor Jahnkee imperialista."

"What? Why?!?"

"I'm too confused," I said. "I might be sleeping with the enemy."

"Come on."

"You should have seen this coming, dear," I said. "You know how I feel. You should have either agreed with me or just humored me and gone the hell along with it."

"Why? I don't patronize you. That's ridiculous. We can't disagree about a six-year-old Cuban and move on?"

It was a good question.

"You know what?" I said, lighting another Parliament, reaching for a new Tab, and pulling back in my chair in order to physically extend his proximity to my elixir. "My pussay is Cuban and your 'apprentice' is American."

"Oh my God."

"No more invasions for a while. Okay?"

Know how I was able to be so Cubanly ballsy with the boyfriend, who can be quite ballsy himself when the occasion calls for it? The same way I'm able to be that way with anybody who pushes me beyond my pathologically delightful Cuban limits. As Dr. Adland always says, "The only way to have a good relationship with anybody is to be prepared to lose it" (which is different than Mami's joos eet or loos eet). Cuban exiles are not prepared to lose their relationship with Cuba and are therefore doomed to go ballistic over Fidel over and over and over until they croak—or he does. I told Paul I needed to walk it off and he said that sounded like a pretty good idea. I took my cigarettes, lighter, Tab, and keys and went outside. It's a quiet residential neighborhood in a fancy 'burb, lots of old apartment buildings, grass, and trees. It had rained overnight and the sidewalks were still damp. As I walked down the tree-lined street, a few stray raindrops falling from the leaves touched my face.

Who do I want to be? I wondered, blinking a raindrop off my eyelashes. Do I want to be a person who dedicates her life to reacting to the arbitrary exhortations of one singularly sicko dictator named Fidel Castro? That's like being an abused wife, no? An abused wife who takes it and complains about it but who can never leave the abuser? My present psychiatrist, the Puerto Rican Manny Román, would call that the "Let me tell you what he did to me this week" school of victimized female patient-hood. What was my relationship with Castro, really? Was there a relationship, other than the one in my head and

in the foment of the Miami crowd? Well, maybe indirectly. Oh, please. Even I can't make myself believe that. The truth is that there is no relationship. Castro is a fact of life but I have no control over him. I can, however, control how I deal with me.
Oh.

To gain some perspective, I had to walk away from all the noise—the ever-buzzing TV set, the Internet, the newspaper, magazines—that had gotten me so riled up, caught up, and carried away every day from far away for months. Kind of like my family and me leaving Miami for points farther north. Kind of like turning off the news and going for a walk instead.

The street was calm. I saw the faint sun hovering behind a cluster of pale gray clouds, trying to come out. Cars went by, their open windows full of music. A passerby smiled. A woman jogged with a dog on a leash. A trio of kids laughed as some raindrops fell on them from the leaves. I had a relationship with Paul, not with Fidel, and I didn't want to lose it. I had wanted to make Paul understand me better as a Cubana, and to persuade him to respect and approve my exile-centric point of view. But now I just felt silly about it because—oh God, dare I say it—Paul was right. As long as the parents are good, their children belong with them. Period. Who are we as Cubans, or as anybody else, for that matter, to say what's best for Elián? It's outrageous and arrogant—two adjectives Castro hurls across the water at Miami exiles—to think otherwise.

I lit a Parliament and I thought and thought and thought. Watching that heartfelt but misguided human chain forming on TV had really disturbed me. It turned what was already a spectacle into an *Entertainment Tonight*-ready segment— which was probably the point of it.

I inhaled my cigarette and thought about Paul. I'd had

enough hours of expensive psychotherapy and watched too many *Dr. Phil* shows to know that if Paul and I had broken up over Elián, it wouldn't have really been about Elián, it couldn't have been. It's just as when couples divorce over "money issues": you know it's not really about money per se at all. There's something else going on and it's usually a power struggle. Once he's acknowledged and diagnosed that, Dr. Phil always goes, "So do y'all want to be right or do y'all want to be happy?" Mad, loving Cubans always want to be right. With Elián, Cuban Americans wanted to make Washington do their bidding against El Caballo. They lost. And how. I put out my cigarette, finished the Tab, and thought about how you can love people, feel tremendous empathy and affection for them, and still not be able or want to live with them. This wasn't good or bad, it was just the way it was for me vis-à-vis Miami Cubans.

I went home. Paul was napping on the sofa, his back turned outward. My cat Lilly was curled at his feet, as sweet as could be. I put down my stuff and noticed the *New York Times* haphazardly strewn across the dining room table, read and discarded. By tomorrow it would be yesterday's recycled news. The TV had been turned off and in its place a Cuban CD softly played an old mambo. My copy of *A Midsummer Night's Dream* was right where I'd left it, on the coffee table. I thought about what I'd like to have for dinner; there was still some fabulous puerco asado I'd made the night before that we hadn't finished off, and some white rice and black beans, Paul's adopted favorite foods.

I walked over to the sofa, knelt down, petted Lilly, and stroked Paul's hair.

"The course of true love never did run smooth," I whispered

into his ear. I meant my true love for Paul, and I meant the extreme love of Cuban exiles for Cuba.

"Hm?" Paul murmured, moving a little. He was very sleepy.

I traced a map of Cuba on his back with my fingertip, the bumpy brown mole where Havana, my birthplace, would be. There. Now the place and the person I loved most in the world—loved madly, seethingly, and without cool reason—were one.

"I love you," I said into his spine, laying my cheek on the Cuban capital. Paul turned toward me, half asleep.

"Love you too," he mumbled. "Still pissed?"

"Not really," I said.

We kissed.

"It's an old wound," I said, climbing on top of him and laying my body down across his. "It's the whole Cuban thing."

"You're quite a Cuban thing," he said, smiling. "My terminally cute Cubana princess."

I rested my head on his shoulder blade, matching his breathing, smelling the cotton of his cigar T-shirt. Unlike my lost island home, my vanished life, and one little shipwreck survivor heading back to that mythic home, Paul was here, warm and alive and real. He was what I could truly embrace.

So I did.

PILGRIM

BY CARINA CHOCANO

When I was a little kid, I used to fantasize about having a pilgrim friend. I think I got the idea from the episode of *Bewitched* in which Aunt Clara sends the Stephenses back to Plymouth Rock, and Darrin gets accused of being a witch for using a pencil. In my fantasy, my pilgrim friend would show up at my house, lonely, scared, and disoriented, and I would take her under my wing. I'd be very careful to introduce her to her new environment—the modern world, with all its crazy high-tech wonders—slowly and carefully. I'd do it in small doses and make sure not to overwhelm her.

I would begin with little things, easy things, like pencils (perhaps she would have already seen Darrin's) and breakfast cereal. I would make sure she was ready, that she had her bearings, before moving on to mind-blowing things like lamps and toasters. I would try to imagine what it might be like to be unable to fathom a toaster. I would break it down for her, teach her not to fear the toaster, assure her that the toaster was not, in fact, an instrument of the devil but an instrument of General Electric, which was a very large company that had offices and manufacturing plants and employees all over the world.

I would wait a reasonable amount of time before letting my pilgrim friend see a car, or a television, or anything else that might startle her into the kind of culture shock from which she might never recover. I didn't want my Pilgrim friend going into some state of catatonic stupor before I could show her off to my modern-day friends, who would be very impressed and forget for a moment that I was new.

By the time I was nine, about the age I was when I thought up my pilgrim friend, I had moved a total of five times. I had lived in four countries, three continents, and two states. I had learned three languages and forgotten one of them. I would have forgotten another if my parents had let me, but it was theirs, so they wouldn't. (There you have the difference between an immigrant and an expatriate.) I learned English, in what now seems like a few hours, with a New Jersey accent, which I promptly dropped within minutes of arriving in Illinois two years later. I identified, in a way that was totally incommensurate to the duration and timing of my previous sojourn there, with Chicago, the accidental city of my birth.

By the time I was nine, I was a world-weary jet traveler, the kind of kid who knew how to get on the good side of a stewardess, because getting on the good side of the stewardess means getting into the cockpit, a pair of plastic wings, and an extra dessert. I had spent a cumulative total of about one year living in hotels. (Room service held no mystery for me, though it never lost its charm.) On the day I turned nine, halfway through the third grade, I started at a new school. I was greeted at the door of the classroom with a rendition of "Happy Birthday." Most kids drew a blank after the word "dear."

If you grew up as a corporate nomad, particularly a non-American one, and your camel was the plodding conglomerate known as a "multinational corporation," then you understand what I'm talking about, and the geo-biographical rundown that follows won't strike you as romantic, exotic, exciting, or terribly interesting. If you didn't, and odds are you didn't, then you will likely find it to be all of those things. You will lament your own boring childhood in Shaker Heights, New Brunswick, or Fremont—the one you are constantly apologizing for—and I will envy you with a runny, inchoate, E.T.-like longing that no amount of phoning could curb.

I have told this story, in more or less detail, so many times I no longer know if it's even true. It's my story, but I have the distinct feeling that the most important parts happened without me. My parents were born and raised in Lima, Peru. Shortly after they got married, my father got accepted to graduate school in Chicago and the two of them went together. A year and a half later, I was born. We moved back to Lima six months later, and after that, thanks to a series of promotions and job changes timed almost exactly two years apart, we went from Brazil to New Jersey to Chicago to Spain. Beyond whatever house my family was living in at the time, which my mother was always careful to decorate almost exactly like the previous place to preserve a sense of continuity, like they do in the movies, any notion of home was completely abstract to me.

My family's first stay in Madrid lasted for six years. We went to the American School, which might as well have been a stray mother ship that had briefly alighted on a stretch of arid land just to try and get its bearings. Some of the American kids I went to school with were spending their first and only years away from home, but others seemed never to have actually lived in the United States, or had left when they were so young, they had no firsthand recollection of it. They might have had American passports, and they might have spent the bulk of their childhoods in Spain, Saudi Arabia, or Mexico, but they were really Firestonian, Exxonese, Merckan.

These were the kids that seemed frozen in a kind of cultural amber, still dressing, cutting their hair, and listening to the music that perhaps their older siblings or the cool neighbor kids had listened to "back home" when they still lived "back home." They referred to whatever town qualified, as if they'd gotten together on this, as "back home," a phrase that, for all its imperialist shucksiness, always struck a chord of deep longing in me. Even though these kids, with their ten-years-too-late southern rock records and their feathered hair, had a way of making their hometowns sound like a compound in Guyana; even though I knew deep down that "back home" was bound to disappoint one day, bound to fail to live up to its twangy, bucolic promise; as much as I just knew that their re-entry "back home" would be turbulent and alienating after all those years abroad, at least they were talking about places you could actually locate on a map.

After I'd lived in Madrid long enough to adopt the accent, I more or less adopted it as my home. Between my freshman year in high school and my junior year in college, my family moved back to Chicago, then back to Madrid, then back to New Jersey, then back to Madrid. I went away to college (back to Chicago) as they were moving back to New Jersey. I spent the year in Paris the year they moved back to Madrid. Then I returned to school, graduated, moved to California, and somehow, without really intending to, I never really went back home again.

When I go to Madrid now, which is infrequently, I am reminded of a movie I saw once when I was a kid, in which a city was hit by a bomb that killed all the life-forms but left all the buildings intact. I held on to the idea of Madrid as my home for as long as I could sustain it. When I was 25, my parents and siblings still lived there. About a year later, my parents had separated, my mom had moved back to Lima, my brother took a job in London, and my sister went to school in Texas. When my dad died about five years after that, all the buildings were officially empty.

I have lived in California for thirteen years, the longest I have ever lived anywhere. Even though it is, technically, my home, and I have all the documentation, it can't be home because I don't long for it. It can't be home because it's all around me. When you move a lot, you travel through space at the same rate you travel through time. Everything becomes relative. You pick things up along the way. You leave things behind and you miss them later. Some things you carry with you, even if they were never yours. You cling to things that weren't important in the first place. You hedge your bets. You are not one thing and you are not another. You are everything to all people. You are, as the American kids at school used to say when asked about their religion, "nothing." You find you can't listen to a national anthem sung with sloppy sentimentality without blushing or cringing or both. You are literally neither here nor there.

As a kid, on the last night of our annual Christmas visits to Lima, I would stand in the doorway of my grandfather's den, clutching a small bottle of salt water (my grandfather was fanatical about the Pacific Ocean and lamented most of all that we were being raised nearer to the subpar Atlantic), and will myself to commit everything in it to memory—his poker table, his coin collection, the low midcentury sofas upholstered in burnt orange tweed, the mirrored shelves that held his collection of amoeba-shaped crystal ashtrays and colored genie bottles, his ridiculous framed *Playboy* cartoons, in which stacked nurses in straining uniforms were humorously sexually harassed by doctors and patients alike, his extensive collection of *Playboy* magazines, which he had leather-bound by year. I would stand in this late '50s James Bond fantasy of a room, my favorite, naturally, in his old-fashioned house of the future, and think: Remember this. Remember this. This is where I am from. This is mine. This is me.

It was and it wasn't. Home is not a place I can find on a map. It's still undiscovered. It has mystical powers. It's the place I'm trying to get to when I set out, every day, to journey in a foreign land. I am my own pilgrim friend. I'm showing myself around.

YOU'RE HALF
SPANISH, RIGHT?

BY NANCY AYALA

In 1988, fresh out of my all-girls Catholic high school pleated skirt and my parents' house in the San Fernando Valley, I received a disturbing phone call at my college dorm.

"Your uncle José is coming to live with us," chirped my mother on the other end of the line.

"Who?" I asked, feigning disinterest. (I repeated to myself, It's not your problem. You've moved out of the house. This is not your problem . . .)

"Your dad's brother."

Now, just to get the story straight from the start, my dad has only one brother living in California, who's married with children and his name is not José. But my dad has more half-siblings than I can count on the hands of my family of five.

"Don't know who that is," I mumbled.

"Well, your dad's picking him up in San Diego right now. He's given him five hundred dollars to pay the coyote."

Back to my muddled senses, I began by asking the least important question: Who's *his* mother?

I knew that in Peru my pharmacist grandfather's many dalliances led to children, lots of them, including my father.

But then the real issues came up: Does Dad realize he's doing something illegal? Who is this guy, and what do we owe him? How long will he live in the house? Will he sleep in my bedroom? And, on a completely self-serving note, why me? Why can't my family be normal?

My naive mental image of what a non-Hispanic dysfunctional family was was always so . . . orderly. In my mind, it would be like all those repressed, well-dressed people in John Cheever short stories. On the outside civil and content, but scratch the surface and you've got more gunk under your fingernails than you would digging for seashells after a nasty rainstorm.

In Latino life, that gunk is usually pretty out in the open— no need to dig. I just couldn't get over the fact that our family had a virtually unknown relative dodging border police and coming to stay. Being first-generation, I certainly couldn't foresee something like this. That only happens to other Hispanic people, right?

So much for being asimalada, as my friend Javi would say.

My mom and dad arrived in the United States in the early 1960s, legally, from Nicaragua and Peru, respectively, when it seemed easier for immigrants to get ahead. Their accented English meant that growing up I would get condescending comments like "Oh, you don't have an accent." It was one step short of tapping me on the head and saying, "How cute." I would always hasten to say that I was born in L.A.

I guess that's why I wanted my family to speak English in public places to let people within earshot know that we *spoke the language*, that we hadn't just landed. At a young age I always had an unfortunate what-will-the-neighbors-think complex.

Instead of embracing the richness of my family, I just wanted to hunker down and be like everyone else. Our home life didn't match what the television informed me was a typical family, and I craved the same problems found in the Judy Blume novels I devoured.

I always felt like I was being dissected by my background, and I felt like I was having an internal fight with myself about who I was. I went so far as to pretend I didn't speak Spanish when I was addressed randomly by Latinos on the streets, in a retail store, wherever. Mine was a narrow-minded performance, one in which I was the sole audience member, and I was not applauding. Guilty as it made me feel—because I knew that there was a certain level of embarrassment—I still wanted to yell, "Don't label me!" I never fit the blonde mold alluded to in the Beach Boys refrain "I wish they all could be California girls," but who cared? I was heading to college, where I could be anyone I wanted to be.

So when I packed up for school, I subconsciously left my Latina genes tucked away safely at home with the rest of the baggage I thought I wouldn't need. I wanted to get by on my own merits as an individual, not a token anything. I even tossed any scholarship applications that were aimed at Hispanic students. If my parents had known about them, they surely would not have been pleased.

But my parents were always behind any decisions I made regarding school. They didn't ask too many questions. They were simply happy that I had decided to go to the same university as my middle sister and probably thought that our physical proximity would mean we'd see each other regularly. (Looking back, I hardly remember talking to my sister on the phone, let alone seeing her on campus.) The fact that home was a mere twenty-five miles away from school, and I was fully equipped with a car that could get me to and from without the burden of apartment costs, didn't matter to them. They trusted my judgment.

It was far enough away for me to wipe the slate clean and to try to reinvent myself. But my mother, being the perceptive person that she is and knowing some of the obstacles that might come up after such a sheltered life, said: "Don't ever let anyone make you feel like you're anything less than who you are." Those were jolting words that I would later find reassuring. She didn't have to point out that she was talking about cultural schisms that would inevitably come up.

My new domestic surroundings included sharing a "suite" with seven other women. I quickly realized that I wasn't the only one adapting to new surroundings. My private school was smack in the middle of a multiracial neighborhood. I had to endure potshots aimed at the "locals." After returning from a grocery shopping spree, one of my new friends used derogatory words to describe the mostly Latino crowd at Safeway. I was in a state of shock.

She finally turned to me and said, "You're only half Spanish, right?" as if my "white" side would override any quibbles that my Latina side would have. "No," I said. "I'm completely Hispanic. And I don't appreciate what you're saying."

I was flushed, angry, and confused. I was mad at myself for not saying anything until I was actually confronted. I knew my lackadaisical attitude was wrong. It was one of those awkward moments that involved an apology, and then everyone within earshot pretended to be distracted with something else. Maybe they thought I would start flinging things or yelling in Spanish. Or maybe they, like me, were not prepared to discuss race.

When a college friend who hailed from Texas innocently

asked me what my first language was a year later, I was taken aback. My first reaction was, "What's he implying?" But as soon as I choked back words of indignation, I realized that my prickly demeanor couldn't mask the truth: of course it was Spanish, and yet I'd never actually thought of it. His question made me feel like an outsider, which I know wasn't his intention. (This same friend would later be delighted to recite to my mortified mom the naughty words I'd taught him, nalgas and pisuñas—things you won't pick up in Spanish class.) In one of those smoky-framed mental images, I went back to Sunday dinners with my family: my non-English-speaking great-aunt (my "nana," to be precise) putting the finishing touches on some yummy Nicaraguan dish in the kitchen, my mother yelling Jor-ge! at the top of her lungs to warn him that dinner was ready if the scents hadn't yet clued him in, my dad typically ignoring her from their bedroom.

My culture would come up repeatedly during my college years. At one party, a Latino actually bristled when I introduced myself. I hadn't given the Spanish inflection that my last name warranted, he intimated, and he took me to task. A name's a name, right? Not always, I guess, if your attitude is more Raquel Welch than Charo (for the record, that's Jo Raquel Tejada). He asked me if that's the way my dad would say his last name. You're ashamed, he seemed to say. I felt there was no winning.

College was the kick start I needed. It's not as though I was completely blind to my background. I just wanted to be the person to bring it up and felt somewhat slighted when others did it for me. I found any reference to my background to sound prejudicial. How dare they! My attitude was I'll talk about it when I'm good and ready.

Getting over my self-imposed cultural hump was a work in progress. But I found that the longer I was on my own without the comfort of day-to-day family life, the more I wanted to cling to that part of me that I had snubbed. As a sophomore, I began taking Spanish classes for a second degree. I lived in Madrid for a semester to improve my Spanish and to get a taste of another world. Back in the United States, I worked as a mornings-only teacher's aide at a predominantly Hispanic elementary school, where the teacher I worked with didn't speak a lick of Spanish yet had twelve non-English-speaking kids in her class. How will these kids get ahead? I thought. As recent immigrants, they already had enough to contend with. But without a proper education, they're screwed. Everything that I had formerly shied away from started to take on new meaning.

Except, of course, I didn't give José a second thought, even though he was still living in my parents' house. He was shy, quiet, respectful. But I never made a real effort to get to know him. I tried to justify it to myself by saying that I was living away from home, I was in school, I didn't have the time. Outside of my family, no one even knew he existed. Going back home seemed foreign to me. Though sympathetic to the kids I taught, I didn't want to acknowledge similarities to my own family. It's hard enough to admit that today, but at the time, I couldn't even entertain that idea. My family *had* to be different. And it's not as though we knew who José was before he landed on this side of the Americas. I'd seen the cautionary yellow signs—images of an adult figure and child running across the heavily trafficked freeway—warning motorists near the Mexican border. They gave me chills—how horrible for *them*. I didn't want to recognize that that image had more to do with me than I was willing to admit. I removed myself from the situ-

ation altogether, so much so that I don't even remember when
José eventually moved out of the house.

It's only been in the last few years that I've heard "You've finally gotten in touch with your roots" from friends, both Hispanic and not. I must have been giving out a pretty strong vibe
about not feeling comfortable with my heritage. I probably
rolled my eyes once too often.

My friend Dawn has a funny anecdote that she likes to share
with friends. We'd planned on meeting to see an upcoming
movie, and I'd forewarned her that I'd probably be running
late. (If there's one stereotype that I'm a poster child for, it's living on Latin Time. It's rare when I'm ever early.) Little did I
know that she'd left explicit descriptions with the usher as to
how he would recognize me.

After jogging from the train station to the theater and making a mad dash through the lobby, I was stopped by an usher
who said, "Are you Latina?"

"What?!" I responded, stunned, while gasping for breath.

"Your friend is waiting for you. I'll take you to your seat."

My friend laughed when she heard this, since her exact description was "She's probably wearing all black, with red lipstick, and she's Latina." Makes perfect sense if you think about
it. Black clothing and red lipstick aren't going to set me apart,
but being Latina will.

I had one boyfriend who was fascinated by my background.
He liked the idea that his girlfriend had such a diverse family.
He loved me for who I was, and I loved him more for that. He
did struggle to understand why a year after we had been living
together I still told my parents that he was just my roommate.

But we were heading to Los Angeles for Christmas, so the truth had to come out. And when I told my mother on the phone, she, of course, wasn't surprised. Disappointed, but not surprised. And we were actually going to share a bedroom in the house, which was remarkable progress for my parents, even if I was twenty-seven years old.

He was looking forward to hearing stories about my upbringing and to have my mother share fanciful stories about the "old country." He also wanted to know about the hardships of coming to America. He wanted to ask her about our indigenous roots. I laughed, saying, "Don't bring up all that indigenous stuff if you want to stay on her good side. Most people in Latin America have Indian roots, but they don't like to talk about it." (It would have been the equivalent of asking my Peruvian father if he speaks Quechua. For the record, he doesn't.) I still don't believe there was any malicious intent, just immature notions of this different world he'd constructed in his head.

My father pulled aside the unsuspecting boyfriend at one point, specifically to the family room, behind a sliding glass door that had a Chuck Wagon refrigerator magnet Scotch-taped to the door so that my four-foot-eleven nana wouldn't keep running into it. I remember my middle sister saying, "Uh-oh. Wonder what Dad's saying to him." He wanted to discuss the thorny money topic. I'm not exactly sure what was said, but my English-only boyfriend later told me how awkward the conversation had been, how he felt that my father was trying to impress him with money—maybe he thought he was being offered a dowry or something. He missed the point that my heavily accented father was trying to make: in his traditional-minded way, my dad seemed to be saying that even though we're Latino, we have a lot to offer. And, just like me, my dad seemed to be saying, I just want to fit into your world.

There was a lot of turmoil in the last year of our relationship. Maybe because we'd already shed our tears, maybe because our conversation had nowhere else to go, or maybe because he wanted to make it clear that the relationship was over, but during one of our last excruciatingly civilized dinners, my boyfriend said, "What would our kids look like anyway?" All those deep-seated fears of feeling unworthy surfaced. As if trying to prove that we could have beautiful babies, I reminded him what my older sister's boys look like. They are a mixture of white and Hispanic blood, and they are beautiful. But I still couldn't believe what I was hearing. Who was this man? I knew then that for all his overtly progressive talk he didn't want a mixed-culture family. He didn't want to make his already shaky parents even more anxious that our children's skin might be too olive, that they might be too short, that God forbid they look too Latin. We obviously both got out of a losing situation in the nick of time.

It's funny how I can write about my confusion with almost a detached air. I don't even recognize who that person was, and she certainly wasn't someone I wanted to know—not then, not now. I wish I could say that there was a monumental episode that happened in my life that crystallized the person I wanted to be. But that's almost too easy. I've been on a lifelong journey of discovery, as hokey as that might sound. My expectations of a color-blind society have always been a bit suspect, but I don't agonize over it so much anymore. I am who I am, and one bad eye-opening breakup later, I've found worth in my family, my friends, and myself. And I'm much better for it.

Even though I've seen two shrinks for a few mental tune-ups in the last eight years, I have never broached my family life in sessions. Why do that when I can go on and on about relationships that are going nowhere? As I've joked with my sisters, the only way to open up about family stuff is to make sure that my therapist is Latino. Some nuances are just too difficult to explain. You have to live them in order to understand them. Most Latinos of differing backgrounds still have a unifying force. We can laugh about the things that make Latino life so incredibly unique, fulfilling, crazy, fun, and different. Things that I appreciate more and more every day.

I got choked up while reading Sonia Nazario's Pulitzer Prize–winning *Los Angeles Times* six-part series, "Enrique's Journey," chronicling the tale of a poor Honduran teen who overcame dangerous obstacles, including jumping from one moving freight train to another, to reach his mother in the United States.

Back in 1988, I was too bullheaded to acknowledge the perilous risk that a member of my extended family took to reach his dream. My parents had undergone their own trials to attain theirs, but at least they had the chance to realize it with Uncle Sam's passport-stamped blessing. Thinking about what José had to endure fifteen years ago fills me with a longing to know more. Thinking about my attitude at the time fills me with regret.

I found out not too long ago that José is doing spectacularly well. He's an American citizen and has adopted the American way of life, for better or for worse. He's divorced from his first wife, like half the first-timers in this country. But he's now happily remarried to his American-born wife and still lives in Southern California. Together, they have a boy and a girl, the perfect American family.

He recently asked my parents about me—where I was living, what I was doing—and he told them, "When she comes back out to Los Angeles, tell her to come visit."

I will. And this time, I'll make it a point to get to know him.

GETTING IT STRAIGHT

BY CARMEN R. WONG

S one of eh *beeetch!*" my mother spat as she slammed her palm down hard on the kitchen table. *Ding-ding-ding!* Round One had begun. Two of my four sisters, sitting in silent support—Lola, the youngest, and Nina, the firstborn after me—flinched upright in their seats. I barely twitched. I was on a long-overdue truth-finding mission. I demanded to hear from my mother Lupe's own lips who my real father was. And I was convinced the answer sat right in the middle of my face.

The four of us were sitting cramped together in the eat-in kitchen of my mother Lupe's new condo. She had finally sold the family home after her second divorce, resigning herself to the fact that not only was her former husband of twenty-three years not coming back, but neither were any of her grown children. The old furniture from the family house was too grand for her new compressed living space, and the formal high-backed chairs demanded too much of the tiny, casual kitchen. Despite being diagnosed with terminal cancer four months before, this domestic downsizing represented my mother's biggest defeat. Unfortunately, I was about to deliver another blow.

"Ma! I'm asking you a question!" I sputtered. "Where did I get this nose?!" I was using my I'm-the-real-authority-figure-in-this-family voice. It usually led me to victory, or at least the semblance thereof.

My nose had always bothered me. With a name like Carmen Wong, I felt I was owed a smaller nose, maybe a cute Asian button nose that would tone down my profile. But I had a strong bony nose. Protuberant even. When I was in grade school, I would press down on the slight bump in the middle, hoping that, in addition to creating a cleft chin with the force of my knuckles, I could be prettier in a more mainstream way.

It wasn't until my twenties that I started obsessing about my nose. In every mirror and at every passing reflection I would slip glances at my profile, tilting my head from side to side, left to right, doing a little head dance. At one of my just-getting-a-paycheck jobs, upon seeing my last name a Chinese coworker blurted incredulously, "Wong?! But your face is so"—she made a pulling gesture away from her own flatter face—"three-dimensional!"

"Yeah," I replied, smiling with resignation. "I look more like my mother."

Problem was, my Dominican mother, Lupe, had a small, long nose, consisting more of nostrils than bone. We didn't look much alike. Truth was, I didn't resemble anyone in my family. I didn't look anything like my tall, lanky, flat-faced brother who shared my last name. And I didn't look much like any of my four younger sisters either. My chest was fairly small compared to their C's and DD's. The running joke was that obviously I was Chinese from the neck down. They had half-Mediterranean olive fuzziness; I had thick, hairless, golden skin. They had unwieldy masses of curls; I had "good," fine hair.

It was as if I stood out on my own in the family, the recipient of a strange genetic roll of the dice.

Objectively speaking, however, there was no doubt that I looked more Latin than anything. Though when I blew my hair out straight, I often got "Persian?" "Greek?" "Pakistani?" Even "Hindi?" A few years ago I started whispering my nose's possible origins to myself: "Mediterranean? Maybe German?" If it were only that easy, to be able to pick a category. To check only one box. But wasn't being "mixed" what made me special? At least that is what my mother had led me to believe. But having discovered recently that I had been lied to for more than three decades about who my biological father really was, I decided it was time to get some answers.

Back in the interrogation kitchen, my mother sat frozen, staring at me with bulging, angered eyes. By asking about my nose, I seemed to have stumped her somehow. Either that, or she was stunned by my angry conviction. Knowing her, Lupe was just taking some time to churn up how to best frame the story (so as to blame her peccadillo on someone else), positioning herself as her most popular character—the martyr.

"Who told ju dees, eh?! He tell ju? What he tell ju?!" she yelled.

"Ma! I don't know who the hell you're talking about, but this is *not* a Chinese nose!" I jabbed at my face for dramatic emphasis. "And this is not your nose either. You know I'm not stupid! Every freakin' day I look at this face in the mirror . . . how long did you think it would take for me to figure it out?!"

In answer, my mother loosened her stare, threw up her hands filled with tissue, and began to bawl. "Ju know, I wanted us to tell ju togeder. He shood be here too! Jour fadder shood be here too, tellin' ju dis! No jus' me!" Her face reddened as flashes of rage, shame, and sorrow simultaneously made play on her face.

"Who are you talking about, Ma?!? Who?" I knew the answer, but I needed to hear it from the proverbial horse's mouth.

It was somehow satisfying watching my mother unravel before my eyes, her open wailing, her loud nose-blowing. She had knowingly and deliberately deceived me and our whole family (not to mention friends, colleagues, clergy, etc.) for over thirty years, and I was determined that she feel some of my pain in return. At the same time, it was heartbreaking to watch. Lupe was dying of cancer. And what she didn't know was that five months earlier I had discovered who my real father was and the betrayal was overwhelming. Hers was a sin of omission and deception, and this was my version of the Spanish Inquisition. The truth was long overdue. After all, she had had thirty-one years to get to me first.

At the table, my reinforcements were beginning to crack. Lola and Nina were looking at our mother with tinges of pity. Not to be dissuaded by tears, I kept up my resolve. It was time to get sympathy back on my side.

More stoically, I asked again, "Ma, who is my father?"

The Dominican-Chinese alliance in my family started in the early sixties. Shortly after landing on the shores of Manhattan by way of Santo Domingo, my mother, Lupe, her sister, and their half-brother each ended up marrying Chinese spouses. And since none of these newly acquired Far East family members knew anyone in the States, my older brother, cousins, and I grew up surrounded by our freshly American, Dominican-Chinese family. We were a gaggle of mixed children of all shades: café con leche, eggshell, burnt sienna, ecru, dulce de leche, and ebony. We jabbered in Spanglish, played under the hydrants in the summer, sucked on sugarcane, and shook our backsides to merengue music before we even knew what messages our bodies were conveying.

The man on my birth certificate, Papi-Wong, was a high-strung, fast-talking, batty man originally from Taiwan. He came over the apartment once a week or so, peeling twenty- and hundred-dollar bills off a roll from his pocket for me as he trilled, "How much yu wan'? Wun hundre' dolla'? Tu hundre' dolla'? You buy los' o' Barbie, no? See! Yo' Papi good to yuuuu! Papi luuf yuuu!"

Actually, Papi-Wong scared me a little. But that didn't stop me from taking his money and looking forward to his very "green" visits. Everyone told me that this boisterous older man was my father and I had no reason to question them—he was my older brother's father too. On Saturdays he would pick us up for dim sum in Chinatown, ordering my favorite dish whole steamed bass—always trying unsuccessfully to get me to eat the eyeballs. The restaurant hosts greeted Papi-Wong like an old friend, bowing their heads, grinning, seating us at the best tables, doting on us throughout the meal. The restaurants we went to were swathed in silky red fabric, accented in gold and porcelain figurines. I thought it all to be very glamorous and was glad to be a part of it.

Papi-Wong had good hair and bad teeth. He used Brylcreem to hold down his lush black hair and a toothpick held a semipermanent spot between his lips. He spoke fast, no matter what language or dialect he was speaking, and waved his hands around like any Latino or Mediterranean. Actually, he was the most Latino Chinese man I had ever seen: arms flailing, temper flaring, wads of cash in the pockets, Dominican-lingo flowing, unbuttoned shirts, shiny loafers without socks, full of machismo. He fit in with our family very well. I enjoyed my extended access into his downtown world and considered it my world too.

What was not to love about being China-Latina? When I was young I considered it a precious bit of luck to have "smart" and "hardworking" layered on top of other bittersweet stereotypes like "temperamental" and "fiery." As I got older, my exotic mix, combined with my tendency toward social activism, led me to join every minority affinity group available. I was a member of groups for Hispanics, Asians, and African-Americans (my mother hated to admit it, but we all knew her kinky hair did not come from our German-Jewish great-grandfather, as she insisted, Dominican-denial-style), along with other multicultural groups that believed the future of America would look, and have names, a lot like me. Racists and purists be damned. As a powerful former boss bellowed at me one day in his southern drawl: "Cahr-man Wawng, yeew are the feewture of America!" I felt privileged to hear it and believed wholeheartedly in what my existence represented—love and success between people of all colors, a multiculturalism that allowed me access to several worlds, with understanding and fondness for all.

Despite the racial mezcla in my family, our Latin identity was never questioned. That is, until my mother divorced Papi-Wong and married Charlie, a self-designated "gringo-hippie" Italian-American from Detroit. Soon after their marriage, our new dad got a job transfer out of Manhattan and relocated us to the "wilds" of New Hampshire. I don't think my mother, my brother, or I had any idea what a different world this was going to be from the merengue-singing streets of uptown Manhattan. Or how often we would be questioned about our racial origins—virtually every day, everywhere we went. Were we black? "Oreos?" Were we adopted? Where is the Dominican Republic? And why was our mother suddenly telling everyone we were Spanish instead of Dominican?

Chimps in a zoo. Freaks in a freak show. My brother, Alex, wasn't allowed on the junior high football team because the coach considered him a "nigger." At the bus stop in the mornings, high school girls in their rolled-short plaid uniforms would beg me to count in Spanish, reacting at my oration with variations of "Oh! Isn't she wicked cute?!" They'd marvel at my ringlets—not once asking my permission to fondle and pull them as they did. "Look at her hair! Is that natural? My mom pays a shitload to get her hair permed that way."

They would lean down and talk at me loudly, as if I were deaf. I'd flutter my lashes, looking down, embarrassed at all the attention, at the same time thinking, "Damn, these people are easy to impress." I caught on quick. I figured out how to capitalize on my aberrant shade, my curls, my name. I was different. I was special. Such bloated, defensive thinking took out some of the sting when I often heard "spic" or "chink."

But as I got older, the constant you-don't-look-Chinese's were infecting me under the skin, like mites laying eggs one by one, itching and waiting to hatch.

There are many obvious reasons why no one would want to question her own paternity. Mine was mostly because my Chinese side was given credit for my good qualities. At the annual open house at school, the nuns would patronize my mother with stories of how smart I was, punctuating their praise with "It's the Chinese in her." My mother, disappointingly, would pat my head, smile, and proudly agree. "Jes, da's right." After our northern migration, Lupe made it very clear that my brother and I were to emphasize our "other" half. And my new younger sisters were not to learn how to speak Spanish or to get too much of a tan in the summer. It was a strange adaptation.

I missed my multicolored, multicultured family in New York. I missed the smell of Abuela's chicken, the shedding tiles in the railroad apartment, clothes hanging to dry out the kitchen window, chasing cucarachas with a slipper, the beat of salsa thumping from the apartment upstairs. I missed speaking Spanglish and peeling my sweaty thighs off the plastic-covered furniture. I missed bumpy taxi rides to Chinatown for mooncake, firecrackers, and deep-fried bean curd. I missed eating mofongo under Abuela's oil-splattered kitchen calendar of pretty Chinese ladies with demure smiles and tight silk dresses. My existence there felt more alive, more real. Here, I was buried, stifled. My skin felt heavy. My identity became hidden and I became easily ashamed, defensive, and prickly.

It wasn't until after college in Connecticut, when I returned full-time to Manhattan at twenty-three years old, that I felt an unshackling, a door opening, and familiar air to breathe. I met Dennis, a young Latino professional, and warmed to the possibilities. In this tall, educated, handsome Ecuadorian-American from Dyckman Street, I thought I could surely reconnect with my roots and quell the pain felt from my much-missed Latin upbringing. He too thought he had found a solution to his need: a Latina who was as American as he was and, most important, as educated and more worldly. A wife he could proudly tout on his arm at his all-white investment banker cocktail parties. After all, when we met I was working at the bastion of Anglo-hood, Christie's fine-art auction house on Park Avenue. You'd have to cross the Atlantic to get more "establishment" than that.

Our mish-mosh love was frantic. Its skewed trajectory only accelerated when he first took me to his parents' home, a cramped one-bedroom railroad apartment he grew up in with his brother and grandmother. I climbed those short linoleum stairs to the fifth-floor walk-up, inhaling the sweet smells of Latin cooking. I paused around the fourth floor, closed my eyes briefly, sighing privately, "Home."

Unfortunately, the marriage began to dissolve even before the day we eloped downtown at city hall. The man who had presented himself as an educated American Latino peeled away to reveal a simple, self-indulgent mama's boy and machista, with all the distasteful qualities that the stereotype has to offer.

One summer Saturday post-elopement, Dennis fumbled in through the apartment door loaded down with shopping bags. My mouth hung open and slack. We were in no financial shape to be spending any money that wasn't necessary. I had my own debts from struggling to support myself in creative fields while living alone for four years. He was close to six figures in debt from two graduate degrees combined with ridiculous spending habits he learned on the streets, where success was trumpeted prematurely with D&G shoes and Armani sunglasses.

"Oh my god, Dennis. What is all that?!" I did my best to not start screaming right away. My heart pounded in my ears at the thought of what he had done. The bags were from Barney's on Madison Avenue.

"What? Nothing! My father went with me to get some new suits." He dropped the elegant black bags in the middle of our tiny apartment on the parquet floor—where they looked glaringly out of place—and plopped himself down on the couch in shopping exhaustion.

"New suits? From Barney's? You have so many suits! How

much was all this??" I already felt defeated. I heard a voice in my head whisper, "I told you so . . ."

"What?! It's nothing . . . I dunno . . . they were like two thousand dollars each." He smacked his lips on his gum, challenging me.

"Dennis! You know you can't afford that! I just spent a week's pay on our phone bill from when you were in Mexico because you said that you couldn't afford to help me with that!"

"Look, I need these suits!" He stood up, angered. "Anyway, we picked up something for you too. Here." He pulled out a plain crumpled plastic bag from the Barney's pile and handed me two stained, obviously worn, badly folded sweaters. My God, was this what I was worth? Tears stung my eyes as the significance of this "gift" sunk in. As his esposa, my needs and wants would always be second fiddle to his—the man of the house. He honestly expected me to go from receiving Hermes scarves from him while we were dating to used sweaters from a street vendor postmarriage.

"What is this?" I rasped, my eyes not able to leave a particularly gross crunchy white stain on the top turtleneck. "These are dirty sweaters. From a street vendor. Probably stolen from someone's apartment. They haven't even been washed . . . are you serious?!"

"Hey! We take the time out of our day to get something for you and you're not even grateful?! We could have gotten you nothing at all! My dad would be so upset if he heard you right now."

My ears rang, incredulous. What could I say? There was no arguing with the absurdness of that. Stunned, I picked up my purse, straightened out my ponytail, wiped my eyes, and left him in the apartment surrounded by his loot. I needed to treat myself to a three-dollar latte.

Soon after what I now call "The Barney's Incident," I decided I needed to take a risk to advance myself professionally, so I applied to graduate school. Education was my answer to many things in life. Few things made me happier than getting an A. The complaints from Dennis's parents began to grow louder. Why did I need to do that? Didn't I already have a good job? And a husband? Why can't I just be happy and give them grandchildren? Over that year, my "Latin" marriage sickly rotted. So it was true. I wasn't "Latin" enough for any of them. The buzz had started decades earlier with my cousins' taunts of "Ju talk white!" to more recently living in South America, getting tsk-tsked for my feminist forward thinking. The various attempts I made at keeping truthful to "me" kept colliding with the reality around me, and the veils I had built up to fit in and be accepted were slipping off, one by one.

A bright afternoon during my separation and pending divorce, I sat alone in what used to be our marital apartment, watching the Dominican Day parade on television through a glaze of self-pity, shock, and sorrow. Suddenly, I was struck with fear and panic as I wondered if losing this man was akin to losing a chunk of my Latin identity. I started a heaving crying jag that lasted five minutes. Then I stopped abruptly as I realized: "Wait! He can't take that away from me. He can't take away my memories, my family. He can't take my identity! I can't give him that too." And to squelch any further self-doubt that day and reward myself for my quick recovery, I stumbled off the couch, sniffing and wiping my face, and poured myself a hearty screwdriver.

Any happiness and stability I had at that time came from going to graduate school at Columbia University, right down the street from where mi abuela used to make her wonderful maduros. There I found a confidant in Tina, a biracial transplant from Bermuda with her own sad story of growing up brown and curly-haired in a moneyed white world with a parent who didn't share her last name. We were ambling down the stairs from an afternoon class in our psychology program when I asked her about my nose.

"Yeah, you know, your nose does look very European. Have you thought about asking Papi-Wong to take a paternity test?" she asked, very matter-of-factly.

"Oh geez. I could never do that," I replied. And as Tina knew, there was no asking my mother. I had stopped speaking to her months before, as she became vitriolic and unbearable when I split from my husband. Her successful, young, educated daughter, a divorcée? She was horrified. Actually, Lupe was normally unbearable, only now it was magnified as she finalized her own nasty second divorce from her American dream man, my stepdad Charlie, after twenty-three long years.

My mother had set up our toxic relationship from the start, giving me no choice but to play the role of the second mami in the house. I took care of the babies, cooked, cleaned, and worked, at a ridiculously young age. These days, Lupe would be arrested for some of her antics, like leaving me alone in the car at twelve years old with four tired, hungry babies, in ninety-degree heat, while she shopped for two hours. By handing over the reins of responsibility my mother had unwittingly made me an authority, and since I showed myself (even at twelve) to be a better, kinder, more patient, affirming parent than she, we battled like dictators over a small country.

If there was anything my divorce was telling me, it was that in order to take care of myself for once, I needed to get rid of people that would stand in my way of again being happy, accomplished, and independent. Considering I had married a male version of my mother (a volatile, needy vortex), cutting both of them out of my life at the same time seemed like a survival tactic. It was dump 'em both or get dragged down along with their miserable selves.

Thankfully, as two years of fresh single-hood went by, I became more and more confident that everything was going to not only be okay, but better. My foundations were settling. But it was to be a calm before the next family storm.

Six months into my mother-moratorium, Lupe decided to hold a quasi-confessional in our nearly empty family home with one of my sisters and our older brother. These two siblings were chosen as they were the only ones able to tolerate her bitter, now Pentecostal state of mind. Lupe's "cleansing confession of forgiveness" consisted of letting her captured audience know that she had had abortions when she was young. One abortion between my older brother and me, two right after I was born. I was debriefed on this confessional through the sisterly telephone-support web and a bulb went off. Long, quiet suspicions surfaced. Wacky, obnoxious, wrong-side-of-the-law Papi-Wong may not be my biological father. Why have those abortions during their marriage if the children were his? And before and after I was born?

In retrospect, the seeds of paternal doubt were most likely planted when I was sixteen years old—the year Papi-Wong "disappeared." One afternoon that summer my mother came to my bedroom door, looking very serious, telling me that I wouldn't be seeing or hearing from him for a while. He had gotten into some trouble with the police, and when he was released, he ended up on the run (utilizing his Spanish skills in Venezuela, no less). Huh. Maybe I didn't want to be his half-Chinese daughter anymore—not if being his daughter meant having a con-man as a father. Though it lent further authenticity to my rough-and-tumble urban-girl persona, I couldn't understand how I could be the product of a man who didn't embody any of what I thought were the good parts of being Chinese, but instead seemed like a gangster, who happened to be Chinese.

Early in the fall of last year, my phone rang late and I figured it would probably be my stepdad, Charlie. Ever since his divorce from Lupe, my family role with him had changed. Charlie began dating again, and I was now taking his late-night calls as he agonized over how to deal with his new girlfriend and her commitment phobia. We became mutual dating coaches—though I had the upper hand, having had more recent experience.

I tried not to sound exasperated, even though my dinner was getting cold. "Dad, what's wrong?" I asked. He sounded strained and anxious.

"Um, I need you to come visit. I really need to talk to you in person about something."

"What? What is it that you can't tell me over the phone?" I honestly had no clue about what could be so important that I had to drive north three and a half hours to hear it in person.

After several pleadings for delivery of this information via the phone line, I started throwing out guesses. "Is it your will, Dad? You want to talk about your will?"

He had started getting his affairs in order recently, even

though his health had never been better. It seems that his younger girlfriend had started questioning him about his daughters and how prepared things were for us should something happen to him.

"Yeah . . . that's it. My will." He sounded resigned and started breathing easier.

"Ok, Dad. I'll come this weekend, all right? But I can only stay one night, okay?" Who was the parent here?

"Yeah, sure. That's fine. As soon as you can," he replied. A beaten man couldn't have sounded more defeated.

Seventy-two hours later I was crumpled and sobbing at his kitchen table. Charlie sat across from me with his head down. He had started this loaded conversation with a tone-setting statement: "Peter is not your father."

As soon as I registered that he was referring to Papi-Wong, using his American name, I knew what was so important that he needed to see me in person.

After a few moments of shock-filled silence, I asked tentatively, "Then who is, Dad? . . . You?"

"Yeah," he whispered.

My heart tore.

Now that he was divorced from my mother, he felt the need to come clean after thirty-one years. His girlfriend at the time was the first one to hear the truth. When he told her, she was horrified that he hadn't told me yet and demanded that he come clean as soon as possible. I owe her many thanks for that.

I was even more shocked and hurt that even after my brief, failed marriage and her own terminal cancer diagnosis, my mother hadn't been able to tell me herself. If it wasn't for my dad's girlfriend, would the truth have gone to the grave with them both? I was going to find out the full story from my mother before she got too sick to have the time and energy to tell her side of the "truth."

"Are you talking about Charlie, Ma?"

Lupe sniffed and blew her nose loudly. "Jes," she hiccupped. "I'm talkin' about jour fadder."

I was furious beyond words and the surge of adrenaline was making my chest tight.

"Why didn't you tell me?!" I screamed at her. "For God's sake, Ma! I was married! Why didn't you at least tell me when I was getting married?! What if we had had kids? What were you waiting for!!" I wanted all these questions answered and my voice, though scolding, took on a pleading tone.

"I don' know . . . I wanted us to tell ju togeder. He put me t'rough so much, dat man! An I didn' luf him! I didn'! He made me luf him." I made an undetected eye-roll.

"He would'en leaf me alone! I try an' try to get away from heem, but he would'en leaf me alone!" Her sobs now were making it hard to understand her. It was going to take some tactical manipulation to get the story I was looking for.

"Ma, you guys didn't marry for a long time after I was born. When did you meet him? You were still married to Papi?" My switch into detached-therapist mode would be more productive at this point.

"Jes. I was still marry to Peter. Jor godmoder introduce me to heem and he jus' would'en leaf me alone!"

"Who knows about this, Ma? Did Grandma and Grandpa know? Did Mama or Abuelo know?" I asked. All our sets of grandparents had passed away and it killed me to think that they all died without knowing whom I really belonged to. Especially Grandma and Grandpa on the Italian side. They were Charlie's parents and they took me in as if I were their own. Seems like they may have known best.

Over the next hour, a quarter century of drama-according-to-Lupe unfolded. But I had one more very important matter to clear up. Why didn't Charlie adopt me once they finally did get married? Why keep up the charade then? It seemed like the easiest and most legitimate time to come clean. Why not then?

My sinuses throbbed as I fiddled with the half box of wet tissue piled on my lap. I had to continue, "Ma, why did you make me keep the name 'Wong'? Why were you always so vehement about Peter being my father when he wasn't? He wasn't even around to be a real one anyway! Didn't he know?"

The other shoe was about to drop and it was a disclosure that my dad had left out of his bombshell months before. It made a lot of sense why he had.

"Charlie didn' want ju! He gafe me money for an abortion. Peter was da one who make me keep ju. He say: 'Lupe, I luf ju! I be da fader of dis baby. Keep dis baby! I be da fader!'

"I had de money en my han' for de abortion. Peter was de one who es responsible for ju bein' alife now. *He* es jor fader!"

I had heard this "father" correction many times before. This time the meaning of those words was dramatically different. I never thought I would hear them in any other way. It was my turn to be stunned silent.

"An' when ju came out, Peter was at de hospital an' he say: 'Lupe! Dis girl haf light eyes an red hair—dis a white baby!'"

"But Ma, you said he knew. You said he knew that I wasn't his."

"Jes, but in hees mind already, ju were hees, because he wan'ned ju. Charlie didn'."

My head hurt even more. For thirty-one years I had seen my dad, my stepfather, Charlie, as the savior of the family. An educated American man who brought us to the right side of the tracks, if you will. Built us a big house; taught us how to chop wood; helped us with our homework. I had been a daddy's girl, and to think that he had never wanted me to be born. What a metric ton of guilt that must be.

This was going to take years to digest. Years to get the full story and years to forgive. In two defining moments, all within six months, I had gone from being a China-Latina Manhattan mezcla, an embodiment of the new "multiculti" America, to being half European-American. Half white. My stepfather, my real father all along.

The rest of my mother's revelations were an exhausting and exhilarating three hours. There was screaming and hand flailing, accusations thrown, names called, judgments made. Nina and Lola refereed as best they could. Only with their intervention were my mother and I able to stop short of coming to blows. In the end instead we collapsed into each other's arms. Lupe crying for forgiveness, me crying in pain for the deceived little girl who so desperately wanted to share a last name with her mother and sisters. The little girl who wanted so badly to fully belong.

Back in my apartment the next day, I contemplated tearing down my Chinese silk screens and throwing away my antique Chinese snuff bottle collection. It all felt terribly false, every piece a reminder of a very long, very deep, and painful lie. Thankfully, I stopped myself. Yes, I had found out the truth of my genetics, but that hadn't changed my memories of eating dim sum with Papi-Wong every weekend in Chinatown, or meeting his gangster buddies in gaudy restaurants on Canal

Street while he proudly showed me off—his daughter. It didn't change Charlie's smiling face when I showed him a particularly good school paper or his laughter when he let me beat him at badminton. In many ways, nothing had changed. In many ways, everything had. I was going to take my time with this one. It was my truth now. A truth to be told when I was good and ready.

I'm not a tricked-up car with one make and model stamped in chrome on the outside, a different engine under the hood. Over my life, my name had become more than a label. I was my name and my name was me. A brand. I wouldn't change it, because like my curly hair and round backside, people's reactions to it had shaped me. I am all the complicated things and stories my name conveys and more. And to the naysayers and I-told-you-so's I say fuck it: I know who I am. I am an American. I am Latina. With a splash of Chinese and a dash of Italian. A city girl with a little New England. A mish-mosh and hodgepodge of conundrums and contradictions. Like it. Accept it. Deal with it.

I have. And I'm still trying.

IV

"When I Grow Up . . ."

CONVERSATIONS
WITH JESUS

BY CAROLINA BUIA

I t's hard enough launching a new product, but it's tougher dusting off an old one to attract consumers' attention—and their dollars. Take deodorant, for example: with new brands like Dove and Tom's of Maine popping up, how can the Dry Ideas, Arrids, and Secrets of the shelf compete? They must reinvent themselves with far-fetched scents like Ambition, Icy Surge, and Tropical Satin. They must promise to deliver more, like "no white residue" and enough odor protection to skip a day. And some, like Secret's latest solid, suggest miracles, vowing to rejuvenate your underarm skin through a "revolutionary blend of skin conditioners and vitamins."

When you're the oldest of three, you reach a point in your life where you feel a little like that old deodorant stick. You're constantly reminding your parents that you were their number one choice—before they even had a choice, before the competitors started squatting on your shelf. And while you're vying for your parents' attention, you're also trying to be the most popular brand in school—a rather competitive market environment. In the fourth grade, it became all too evident that I needed to turn branding into a religious experience. I needed to find a way to stand out on the shelf.

My six-year-old brother, Chris, was chronically on my parents' radar due to his inability to sit still in class. He started food fights and suffered memory lapses when homework assignments came due. When they were handed in, they were crumpled up and clumped with dirt. His teacher had our home number on speed dial; she and my father were on a first-name basis.

I, on the other hand, trusted brand that I was, inexhaustibly skipped home with "Super!" branded on the tops of my hands, delivering neatly folded report cards lined with straight A's and syrupy-sweet comments. I always brushed my teeth, washed my face, and prayed before meals. I never forgot to say "please" and "thank you."

Then there was my sister, Melissa. She was two at the time, that age when children start walking, talking, and acting so damn cute it makes you nauseous. Don't get me wrong, I adored Melissa. I didn't mind her saliva and sputtered milk solids all over my uniform shirts, playing patty-cake over and over again, and changing the occasional dirty diaper. But I did mind when her first somersault overshadowed my first flip on the monkey bars. And it was beyond me how just when Mom and I were going over my lines for the school play—for which I had the lead—Melissa cut into my rehearsal time by peeing all over the Persian rug.

So, as I maneuvered through the fourth grade, a little soul-searching was in order.

One night . . . it all fell into place. It came to me in the form of a dream. An angel appeared dressed in a purple, flowing robe with long, windblown hair. It wasn't quite the angel Gabriel, more of an androgynous apparition. In a cotton-soft voice, a powerful message was delivered: "One day soon you will become a disciple of Jesus and perform miracles all over the world. Prepare for that day, for it is at hand."

Immediately, I woke up sweating, the dream dancing in my mind. It was the middle of the night, but I was unable to fall back asleep. I was spooked. I was nervous. I couldn't wait to brag.

At breakfast the following morning, I broke the good news to my family.

"Are you listening to me?"

"Yes," said my mother, her mind drifting. "How is it that you always remember your dreams? I don't remember mine."

"I don't remember mine," Chris echoed.

"This isn't *just* a dream," I said, exasperated. "This was a holy vision!"

The profound implications of my calling clearly eluded her. We were an ordinary family. Extraordinary things weren't supposed to happen to us. Perhaps she didn't believe me? Sure, science might refute my claim, discard it as nothing more than the vivid imagination of a ten-year-old disseminating bits of her waking life, and dropping them into the kaleidoscopic petri dish of her slumbering brain. But I'm telling you, that angel was real. And no, the *Highway to Heaven* episodes, reruns of Sally Field in *The Flying Nun*, and the austere religious program at my new school had nothing to do with it.

"Did you hear about Carolina's dream?" Mother giggled as my father walked into the kitchen.

It was no use.

Just wait till I perform a miracle, I said to myself. Just you wait.

My first miracle happened on a bus. A yellow school bus, to be exact. The driver was Mr. Fernández, a middle-aged Cuban immigrant with a tobacco-cured voice and a hairy stomach visible through thinned white T-shirts. He drove kids to and from three different schools.

On board there was a girl from public school who sat alone. She wore different hats, obscuring chemotherapy sessions under the broad-rimmed coverings. Other kids teased her and refused to sit next to her. I made it a point to sit beside her. It was the Christian thing to do. As I was opening my colorful King James Bible and proselytizing from the Gospels, I told her about the time Jesus turned water into wine, about the time he cured a leper, and about . . . my vision with the angel.

"You must ask Jesus into your heart," I pressured her. "He'll cure you."

"But I'm Jewish," she replied.

"It's okay, Jesus was Jewish too."

The two of us carried a heavy cross that year as we were the daily target practice for an overweight sixth-grade bully. As the butt of his jokes, he nicknamed us Bald Girl and Bible Freak. I tried to be patient, drawing strength from scriptures I knew by heart yet barely understood. But the day came to teach this Doritos-chomping, Milky Way–inhaling oaf that he was messing with divine power. When I couldn't bear his assaults any longer, I channeled the Lord, prayed three Our Fathers, and stood up in the middle of the moving bus—holding my Bible in front of me.

"God is watching you—and there is a special place in hell for people like you!" I seethed. My brother slinked in his seat.

"Fuck you," the bully replied, standing a foot taller than me, taking a couple of unsteady steps in my direction. The other kids whispered under their breath.

"I'm not afraid of you," I continued. "The Word of the Lord is my shield and It will keep me safe."

Dozens of eyes were upon us. Idle chatter halted.

"*Fuck* you," he repeated, louder.

"Hey, no es-standing up," yelled Mr. Fernández from his perch. No one paid him any attention.

I edged in closer. "I dare you to say that vulgarity again. In front of the Bible." My eyes were rabid, I hissed like a dragon. "Say it! Say it! Come on, I'm not afraid of you," I goaded, knowing that if he touched me the bus would stop and he would fall to the ground, writhing in pain. I was David to his Goliath. *Jesus, I hope you're watching. Teach this boy a lesson!*

I saw a glint of fear in his eyes. His knees began to wobble. His face turned white. "Whatever, Bible Freak," he said with a dismissive hand gesture. He turned his back, sat down, and never once bothered us again.

Since that day, everyone on the bus—except for my brother, who began to suspect we were unrelated—treated me with respect. The girl with the hat revered me as her protector and asked Jesus into her heart. At home, Mom seemed blown away by my bravery. That night, she crawled into bed with me, and I nuzzled my head against her soft satin gown, retelling my story. I felt like a moving constellation, positioning myself in the center of her universe. I had found not only salvation in Jesus, but a way to make my mom proud of me. I told her about dreams where Jesus made cameo appearances and the two of us would take long walks, break bread, and even play tennis.

I imagined how, once we were all tucked away in our beds, my parents would whisper behind closed doors, discussing my fate:

"Cesar," Mom would say. "Our daughter is a chosen one."

"Mother Teresa will be calling soon. She'll take Carolina to India," my father would add. "We'll lose a daughter, but Jesus will gain a disciple."

My path of righteousness also made me a star in the eyes of Miss Arliss, my fourth-grade teacher. She was a tall woman with long, auburn ringlets and flowing skirts. She had an etherealness about her, mismatched with a steely resolve. Childless, she looked on her six fourth-grade students as her brood. In the first week, she asked us what we wanted to be when we grew up. I looked her straight in the eyes and said: "A nun. A disciple of Jesus. A miracle worker." The token actress, president, fireman, and Olympic gymnast did not stand a chance alongside my ramblings of holy visitations. My sycophantic eagerness became a benchmark for the rest of the class.

Religion was my favorite subject. Bible stories were always set in exotic locales featuring big families and oozing with dramatic tension. There were more plot twists to be found than on *Dynasty*, my mom's favorite soap. Sometimes, for effect, I'd break down in the middle of a story, like when Lot's wife looked back and turned into salt. Miss Arliss would stop her lecture, slide from her high chair, and hug me as I caught my breath between gulping sobs. I felt safe in her doughy, Oil of Olay–scented arms. The others were green with envy.

"How was school today?" my mother would ask.

"Great. I got an A plus on my math test, and Miss Arliss gave me this four-color pen," I bragged, hoping to spark some jealousy over my close relationship with my teacher. "I'm Miss Arliss's favorite student." But Mom was too busy cooking up one of her elaborate meals to capture my Machiavellian subtext.

There was only one thing that kept me up at night: a dirty secret that for months I had managed to keep hidden from both Mom and Miss Arliss. I dreaded the day that it would be exposed: since starting School of Our Savior I hadn't been eating my school lunches. I had begged my mom to make me a bagged lunch, but she'd have none of it. "It's already paid for," she'd say. "They're not feeding you rat poison."

That was debatable. My family had moved from Venezuela, where we'd never encountered American "preserves": canned greens overcooked within seconds of discoloration and bologna sandwiches slathered in Hellmann's Mayonnaise. To this day, anything with mayonnaise on it, in it, or beside it sends me into panic. See, Mom spoiled us at home. She made everything—even the mayo, which we called aioli—from scratch. And though I didn't really care for her exotic creations like Indian curry and Polish borscht, I loved it when she made Venezuelan dishes like crispy arepas, moist carne mechada, and red snapper ceviche.

But no amount of home cooking seemed to stave off my worrisome weight loss. Mom would ask about lunch at school. I'd lie, knowing full well I had spent the hours of twelve to one sitting in front of a cold plate, trying to feng shui its contents with my plastic spork. The quicker other kids ate, the more nervous I became that Miss Arliss would walk in from her break and demand to know why my food hadn't been touched. My Little Miss Perfect reputation would crumble.

Usually, I got away with throwing a paper napkin over my lunch and tossing it in the trash. But Miss Arliss had been coming in from her break, snooping around the cafeteria. When she'd ask why I wasn't eating, I'd explain my food allergies.

One afternoon, she gave me an accusatory look and said,

"Let me get this straight, you're telling me you can't eat *anything* on that plate? You're allergic to macaroni and cheese *and* green beans?" She raised her perfectly penciled brow.

I nodded.

"You're not lying, are you?"

As the days wore on and my list of gastronomic aggressors grew, she began to question my alibi.

Weeks later, over dinner, the telephone rang.

"No, no," my father assured the caller on the other end. "My daughter has *no* known allergies . . . we're sure, my wife's a doctor."

The Inquisition began.

"You've not been eating your lunch?!" yelled my mother. "That's why you're underweight!"

"Can't I bring a sandwich or leftovers from home?"

"We pay for that food!" continued my mother. "We work hard so that you can get a good education and be fed. Why do I work so hard? Every day I ask you if you eat your lunch . . . and you say yes . . . I knew it! That's why you're so skinny!"

"Montse," my father tried to calm her.

"You look like a skeleton! Do you think that's pretty?" My mother's red face was starting to tear up. This, over food?

"Montse! Enough!" my father yelled. "From now on, Miss Arliss will eat lunch with Carolina and make sure she finishes everything on her plate."

I was mortified.

My mother looked crestfallen. How could Miss Arliss betray me? Why had she told my parents? I was her favorite student. I could do no wrong.

I would never forgive her, I thought. Never.

Not even Jesus could save me for what was to come. I was

forced to resort to guerilla tactics like stacking green beans in between cheek and molar, squishing Hamburger Helper into my tight jean pockets, using water to slide whole pieces of food down my esophagus, and even the lame napkin trick. But Miss Arliss was onto me. She went from nurturing to militant, watching me like a hawk. One time she made me unfurl my napkin in front of my giggling peers to display the remains of a lacerated egg sandwich. Another time, she held on to my glass of water (with tiny bits of chicken-rib meat floating like plankton) while making me demonstrate how to chew and swallow a Post-It-size Chef Boyardee ravioli. Again and again, she'd remind me of the thousands of starving children in Ethiopia, thinking that it would bring me one bite closer to finishing a corn dog. I offered to vacuum-seal my food and send it abroad.

"I want that entire corn dog finished," snapped Miss Arliss.

"Can I eat the dog and leave the corn bread?" I bargained.

"I give up," she said, as I began dismembering the corn dog.

Most fourth-graders will tell you that lunch is their favorite subject. For me, I'd have rather carried a crucifix around the playground while reciting Psalms in Coptic. I usually missed recess because I was stranded in the cafeteria: half-nibbled fish sticks in front of me, Miss Arliss behind me. I'd console myself by imagining what good training this was for when I would be starved in a windowless cell for believing in Christ. Oh, the apocalypse was at hand. Jesus would return, and the CEO of Hellmann's would be nailed to the cross.

When the school year came to a close, I gave Miss Arliss a cold, reluctant good-bye hug. She had caused me to go from being a model student to a recalcitrant introvert. She'd let another girl take my place as teacher's pet and even gave her the lead in the school play. I'd done everything I could that year to become a saint, and yet other than the miracle on Mr. Fernández's bus, Jesus had dropped me from his roster of saints-in-training. Had I made Him angry? Why was He punishing me? Leaving me to become just another unremarkable girl, too skinny, too quiet, too directionless. Sitting alone in her pink bedroom, hopelessly daydreaming.

That summer, as my whole family watched the Miss Universe pageant (a devout tradition), my mother turned to me during a commercial break and said, "Carolina, you're pretty enough to be a Miss Venezuela."

"I'm going to be a nun," I replied halfheartedly.

"When are we going to drop this phase?" she snapped back. "Last year was the year of the spy, the year before that you wanted to be a ballerina, and now this nun-sense. What's next?"

"Mom, it's not a phase. When I get the stigmata—"

"For God's sake, if you don't cut this out," she threatened, "I'm going to personally give you the stigmata."

I began to cry. She was right, I had tried on a number of different roles, but none seemed to fit. I was like an actor having a hard time reciting her lines, because they were in a foreign language.

"Montse, relax," said my father. The pageant was back. On TV, perfectly proportioned Barbies—by nature or scalpel—flashed their Vaseline-coated teeth and strutted the tacky stage with their country's banners displayed over immodest bathing suits. Did my mom really think I'd exploit my body like a hussy in front of millions of people when I was destined to an ascetic future? I wasn't interested in wearing mascara and hairspray. I wanted to don burlap smocks and walk barefoot over burning asphalt.

They were awfully pretty, though. They had poise, elegance, and femininity. Did Mom think I was pretty enough to be in a beauty pageant?

That night, Barbara Palacios Teyde, Miss Venezuela, won the crown, looking resplendent in her blue ruched dress and matching heels. As the new Miss Universe glided to canned music, waving her hand like royalty, I grew teary-eyed again. She was the most beautiful woman in the universe, and she seemed so happy. Could I one day be her, on television, shocked when the announcers call out my name . . .

"And this year's Miss Universe crown goes to . . ."

Would I one day look like Barbara Palacios Teyde? Imagine, my parents sitting in the front row, beaming with pride. Outside, the UN Airbus plane revs up its engine, ready to whisk me away to the jungles of Peru, where I am to teach indigenous children how to read and write.

". . . Carolina Buia, Miss Venezuela."

What a silly thought! As if.

That night I overheard Mom tell my father, "We're taking her out of that school. It's filled with religious fanatics, and it's turning our daughter into a religious *narcissist*. No more food fights, no more conversations with Jesus."

In a way I was relieved. I felt that no one there liked me anymore. I was ready for a new beginning; hopefully, somewhere where food was not included in the tuition. I spent that whole summer fantasizing on what my new school would be like, how I would dress, how I would act. Maybe I would try and join the volleyball team? Maybe I would make the cheerleading squad?

I started fifth grade in a public school. Again the new product on the shelf, among forty other students who had all journeyed together through the lower grades. Immediately, I learned that praying before a test with eyes closed and lips moving did nothing but solicit ridicule. And showing off my pink crystal rosary from the Vatican was about as cool as wearing orthopedic shoes. All that mattered in this school was joining the Pink Ladies: a cultish cabal that admitted only popular girls. They traveled in packs, crimp-fried their hair, wore pink Guess jean jackets, and were every prepubescent boy's fantasy. But first, I had to pass The Test.

How many guys have you French-kissed? (I put down a safe five, having no idea what a French kiss was.)

What is a blow job? (A what? Surely nothing to do with a Blow Pop. I left that one blank.)

Are you allowed to see R-rated movies? Which ones have you seen? (I'd never seen an R-rated movie. I penciled in yes. And I'd seen . . . uh? . . . *Ruthless People* with Bette Midler and Danny DeVito?)

Who would you rather have sex with: David Lee Roth or Kirk Cameron? (Sex?)

Up until this point, I had longed to meet the Pope, not hook up with Kirk Cameron. These Pink Ladies lived off big allowances and lived in big houses, but they had little interest in learning new vocabulary words or bringing home aced report cards. Something felt wrong in asking Jesus to help me become a Pink Lady—none of these girls even prayed before their meals. And I was too embarrassed to pray in front of them. God forbid they call me a religious freak behind my back. Did I really want to join this crowd? *Dear Jesus, please let me be a Pink Lady, please, please let them pick me.* Before I knew it I was dressing like Madonna (the singer, not the Virgin), applying my first coat of Maybelline lipstick at my mother's vanity table, pouting my lips like a beauty queen, and playing my first game of spin the bottle. I became a bona fide Pink Lady. And some-where between my first French kiss and my first AA bra, I stopped calling on or searching for Him. He became more like the friends you meet in summer camp. You promise to write, but then you never do. And sometimes you catch yourself thinking about them, but too much time has passed that you wouldn't know where to start. You'd have to start anew.

I'm in my late twenties, and some days I think I've figured life out. Other days I'm as confused as I was in grade school. I never seem to stay in one place more than three years—whether it's school or a job. I'm always changing and reinvent-ing myself, sometimes in Spanish, sometimes in English. Occasionally I abbreviate my first name so that it sounds more American. I've analyzed investments on Wall Street, appeared in TV commercials, taught New York couples how to dance fox-trot and salsa, written about Venezuelan politics for a news magazine, and covered the Martha Stewart trial on television. I've given up the notion of becoming a saint or Miss Universe, but I'm still trying to be all the things in between. Compla-cency terrifies me. My family and I left Venezuela in the early eighties. We left behind a common language, friends and fam-ily, Mom and Dad's respected university posts, social nights at the Club Internacional. We also left behind a crippled econ-omy, express kidnappings, and the nameless faces of poverty, stopping your car with rope and begging you to drop a Bolivar into their dirty Styrofoam cup. In America, we started anew, trying to not lose ourselves in the land of wide supermarket aisles, colossal cars, and supersized dreams.

About a year ago I was working as a television reporter for Telemundo. I received a call from a woman in Queens. She'd been bounced around to different telephone extensions, until finally reaching me. Excitedly, she told me that her name was Lulu and that the Virgin Mary had appeared in her oven window twice this month. I had to see it to believe it. How soon could I come? Did I have pen in hand?

Now, in the Latin world the Virgin Mary makes as many appearances as Elvis does in the South, but something about Lulu's story compelled me to visit her. I jotted down the address.

In her cramped, well-worn kitchen, Lulu showed me the oven window. With trembling finger, she traced the sketch of a woman formed from caked-on grease splatters. It certainly looked like the image of the Virgin Mary—or somebody's profile.

"Esta es la imagen de La Virgen," she began. "This was never here. And then, the other day she appears. Moves her head, smiles at me. Two days later, does same thing. I told the Virgin that I want to go with my husband. She no answer. There must be a reason for me staying here. I don't know what it is. She hasn't told me yet. I'm waiting."

Lulu looked into my eyes to try and gauge my reaction. She seemed disappointed that I had come alone—without a cameraman. She had dressed up for the occasion: salt-and-pepper hair tied back in a chignon, lips painted crimson, and her bony frame wrapped in a red and black dress redolent of mothballs. And even though it was eighty degrees outside, she had on black opaque panty hose.

"You believe me, right?" she asked, her cloudy gray eyes squinting.

I normally dismiss these types of stories on Latin television, but I believed Lulu. Or at least, I believed that *she* believed it.

She asked if I was going to come back tomorrow with my cameraman, interview her, and film the oven image. I'll see what I can do, I said. Then, she offered me a codfish sofrito she had in the refrigerator and an orange soda. I wasn't hungry, but I felt bad saying no. Tenderly, she heated up the fish in a frying pan and with great care placed it on old, fancy china. Before picking up our forks, we said a blessing together.

"I pray before every meal," she said. "You have to give thanks for what you have." I smiled and nodded in agreement, as if to say: I do this all the time. The truth is, I couldn't remember the last time.

Lulu explained to me that her husband had passed away in his sleep less than a year ago, two days after his seventy-fourth birthday. Except for distant relatives in the Dominican Republic, Lulu had no family left. Alongside her, I toured her warmly lit hallway. It was filled with Kodak-paper ghosts: photographs of her youth in Santo Domingo, of her wedding in Puerto Plata, of her teenage son who drowned in the Caribbean, of her first visit to the Statue of Liberty. Lulu seemed so pitifully frail standing among her memories and clinging to her faith. She took my hand and squeezed it.

"You tell me when you come again," she said. "I get all pretty for the camera. Me pongo más bonita. Do you think you can come this week?"

I never produced Lulu's story. Her religious encounter was an intimate one. Telemundo might have run her story, but I didn't want to reduce it to sappy sound bites and bright lights. The truth is, most people, from the comfort of their sofas, would think she was nuts. I know I would. I could just imagine the tease in the beginning of my show: "Y en Jackson Heights, una Dominicana dice que ha sido visitada por La Virgen—y esta ha dejado su rostro en la ventana del horno [insert soundbite]. No se lo pierdan!"

Still, Lulu's story stayed with me. I thought about all things I had to be thankful for: my husband, my family, my health, a career that I loved.

It had been at least a year since I'd been inside a church, but that Sunday I went. After mass was over, I lingered a while. The limestone womb's coolness echoed silence, and fragrance of frankincense soothed me. I bowed my head and began a conversation with Jesus. The first one in a long time.

J.'S TRUE

HOLLYWOOD STORY

BY JACKIE GUERRA

As a child I never dreamed of being an actress or winning an Academy Award; instead I was inspired by my sixth grade visit to the capitol in Sacramento. I remember feeling so small in the capitol building and looking at the historic documents and pictures thinking, "Big things happen here." I became obsessed with history and government. I read every book I could get my hands on about our government, the Constitution and the Bill of Rights.

I remember when my dad received his U.S. citizenship. We all helped him study for the test; American trivia became our dinnertime entertainment. When the day came, the whole family went to the federal building downtown in new matching outfits and watched my dad stand up with the hundreds of other immigrants who were realizing the American Dream by becoming naturalized citizens. Afterward, my mother walked over to him and gave him a passionate kiss and said, "Now you can vote, mi vida."

My first foray into public service was as an organizer for the

Hotel Employees and Restaurant Employees Union, Local 11. It was there that I learned everything I needed to know about being in show business. If you can learn to be an organizer, you are prepared for anything.

I worked with great people who had been involved during the civil rights movement and had worked for the UFW side by side with César Chavez. One of the best lessons I learned working for the union was how Latinos in general, and Mexican-Americans in particular, are perceived by people in power in Los Angeles. It's here that the images people see every day in their homes and in theaters are created. It is these images that tell us who we are and how we are perceived.

I made the transition from organizer to entertainer on a dare. I was working as an organizer on a boycott against a major hotel chain. I was in charge of gathering signatures on the boycott petition and running a picket line every Friday in front of the downtown hotel. One night after the picket line some coworkers "kidnapped" me and took me to Rage, a very lively gay club, in West Hollywood, California. I don't drink, so it seemed like a waste of time, and I was irritated because I hadn't gotten as many signatures that day on the picket line as I would have liked to. Bored and frustrated, I found out there was a talent show. So I signed up, thinking that I would solicit support from everyone at the bar for our boycott.

Everyone in the club was there to have fun, and I felt a little uneasy about using their good time for my cause. The show started, and I was number five. I waited through two sisters who sang the theme song to *Beauty and the Beast*, a fabulous drag queen who did the conga in a way that would have made Gloria Estefán proud, a comic who made disgusting noises, and a woman who could "sing" the national anthem through her nose. By the time it was my turn the three hundred or so people in the audience were well into their second or third drink of the night and I was terrified. I got onstage and just started talking about my day. Looking out at all of these expectant faces, then hearing the laughter and the applause, I was hooked. The best part of the whole experience was that after ten minutes onstage, I got more signatures for my boycott petition than I had gotten the entire month on the picket line. At that moment I thought, This is how I'm going to make a difference. I left my job at the union six months later and started doing stand-up comedy.

Most comics have war stories about their early days of comedy and the humiliation they had to endure to get ten minutes onstage. But to me it was exciting and a lot of fun. I started doing open mikes in Los Angeles. I made a few comedy buddies and every night we'd try to do at least two to three sets at different places. Most of my fellow comics were guys. I was pretty shocked at how segregated the world of stand-up comedy is; most clubs have a "girls night," a "Latino night," a "gay night," and of course an "urban night." I don't know how it happened that in the art form made popular by Lenny Bruce, George Carlin, Richard Pryor, and Roseanne, people who seem to me to be vanguards, there is so much segregation. I was surprised at how few women were working in comedy, let alone Latinos. As a fledgling comic, in order to get stage time at the big clubs, you have to audition for the club owners. I was told over and over that I should write more "Mexican" jokes. One club owner even suggested that I just focus on writing material about growing up in the barrio and crossing the border. I was born in San

Diego, California, and have lived most of my life in the Valley. What the hell do I know about crossing the border—except in a plane—or living in the barrio?

Within five months of doing stand-up for the first time, an agent approached me. She helped me put together an act and began booking me in colleges and universities around the country. I hit the road with my act, a tape recorder, a notebook, a camera, and a whole lot of enthusiasm. I was so happy to travel around the country, especially to learn that there are places outside of Los Angeles where there is conversation beyond the latest diet, gym, colonic, or workout craze. I was shocked that in many of the towns I visited, there were people who had never met a Mexican.

Exactly one year after I did stand-up for the first time, I was offered a deal by Columbia/Tristar Television and the WB Network to star in my own sitcom. I felt like I had hit the lottery because I was going to be playing myself on television in a show that was based on my life. Little did I know I was in for one of the most eye-opening experiences of my life.

We shot our pilot, called "Jackie G." The script was great, and after network approval, we began the casting process. This is when I realized that I wasn't just starring in a network sitcom; I had to educate people about who Latinos are. I sat in a room with network and studio executives during a casting session for the actress who would play my best friend. My roommates had already been cast—both Anglo. I was determined to cast a Latina. A black Nuyorican actress named Tracy Vilar came in to audition for the role and was phenomenal. Everyone agreed that the role was hers. But then someone in the room said "She isn't Latina." I said she is, she's Puerto Rican. I was met with a room filled with silence, broken by, "But she's black." For the next twenty minutes I did my best impression of Mr. Mercado, my seventh-grade social studies teacher, to explain the ethnic and racial migration of Puerto Ricans. The same person then told me she thought I wanted the role of my best friend to be played by a Latina and weren't Latinas from Mexico? I was shocked. This was a room full of successful, educated adults who wield a lot of power in the entertainment industry. And all this happened in a place that used to be Mexico. After my insistence, Tracy got the role.

The day we taped the pilot was one of the most thrilling days of my life. Everyone I loved was there. A few weeks later I was at home when I got a call from the president of the WB Network to tell me that our pilot was being picked up for a series. The next day, I flew first class to New York. When I arrived at my hotel room, which was bigger than my entire apartment, was filled with flowers from the network, my business manager, and my attorney. I felt like royalty. I had arrived!

Three weeks before we began preproduction on *First Time Out*, I met with the new network executives to discuss hiring Latino writers. In order to get into this competitive field, you need experience; to get experience you need to write; but to get a chance to write, you need to have experience. It's a vicious cycle, and I was told that because there hadn't been many Latino shows, there weren't any experienced Latino writers. I asked why couldn't Latino writers write on shows that don't feature Latino casts? No one had an answer.

First Time Out ran on the WB Network in 1996. If you looked at the Nielsen ratings backward, we were the number two show. It wasn't a blockbuster, but it was an incredible experience. I got paid to learn about television production and I met some incredible people who became lifelong friends. And I worked with my childhood crush, Scott Baio, who directed our show. That's the good news. The bad news was that I found my-self constantly putting out fires—I played the role of Jackie on a show that was supposed to be based on my life, but I was forced to play a person that I didn't even know. Jackie was the execu-tive producer's idea of who a young Latina is. Each day I desper-ately tried to keep a piece of myself in the show. I thought of what my mother said to me approximately seven hundred thou-sand times, "Mi'ja, do your best because you never know who is watching." And every day I told myself, "Do nothing that offends your soul." Whether I liked it or not, as the first Latina to star in a network sitcom, I was a role model for my commu-nity. I was an actress, activist, organizer, and I was scared.

In the meantime, my personal life was in total chaos: my brother was getting married, my mother was sick, and I even had my own stalker. One of the network people that I loved had to go back to another show because of a contractual obli-gation (the new executive producer called me a "fat fucking cunt"). I also was falling madly in love with one of the writers (who is now my fiancé).

People say that politics is dirty, but, believe me, it's nothing compared to show business. A Hispanic media watchdog group picketed *First Time Out* on tape night because, according to them, we didn't have enough Latinos working on the show. This was the ultimate irony, since our show employed more Latinos at every level than any other show at that time. We had two Latina leads—neither of whom were playing maids, hookers, drug addicts, or gangbangers. And we had more Latino writers on staff than any other show. Every week we cast brilliant Latino actors as guest stars, including Rita Moreno, who played my grandmother. And we had Latinos on our production staff. It wasn't perfect, but it was a lot more than had been done in a long time on prime time. I was devastated that a group that claimed to be a civil rights group turned their organizing efforts on our show.

I knew the end was near one Tuesday night when I read my script for the next day's table reading and saw that that week's episode was one where my character had a toothache but no dental insurance. The writer wrote a story about my best friend and I taking a road trip to Tijuana to get my tooth fixed. I was literally paralyzed with shock when I read the script. I called a network executive and pleaded with her to step in. I was crying on the phone and told her that neither I, nor anyone I knew, had ever driven from Los Angeles to Tijuana for cheap dental work. I'll never forget what she said to me: "Jackie, you're a first-time sitcom gal. Go with the program. Keep your mouth shut, and cash your check, and buy yourself a present. One day all of this will be a page in your book." So, I found myself one night on a soundstage in Culver City, California, sandwiched between The Nanny and Mad About You in front of about 175 studio audience members. I was sitting in a dentist chair on the set doing a scene where I'm waiting to be seen by the dentist in Tijuana, and he walks in wearing a charro sombrero and a sarape. It was the most surreal moment of my life. I prayed for an earthquake to make it stop. First Time Out was canceled three weeks later.

While I was shooting the show, Selena had been murdered. And even though I didn't know her, I felt like the wind was knocked out of me. I'd seen her in concert just a few months earlier and thought she was such an amazing live performer. I really felt like I'd lost a friend. But I had no idea how intimately her death would affect my life.

After my show was canceled, I began working on a movie called *Eat Your Heart Out*, and one of the extras mentioned that a movie was being made about Selena's life. During my break, I called my agent and said, "I don't care what I have to do, I have to be in this movie. I'll sweep floors, I'll work as a production assistant, but I have to be involved in this film." I couldn't even explain it, not even to myself, why this meant so much to me, but I just felt that I had to be involved in this movie. My agent called me the next day and told me that the director of the movie wasn't interested in seeing me because my background is in comedy and *Selena* was to be a drama. He also mentioned to her that Selena and her family had very indigenous features and were very dark-skinned, and he felt that I wasn't physically right for the part. I was particularly irritated and motivated by that comment. When I saw Selena in concert, I also saw her sister, Suzette, and was shocked at how much we looked alike. We were just about the same height, same weight, same body shape; we were wearing the same color lipstick and had on the exact same shoes. So, I told my agent to call back and say that all I wanted was an opportunity to read. In a way that only agents can speak, she explained to me that it was impossible and that "the door was closed."

I called my friend who had worked with the director of *Selena* and asked her if she had his home phone number. She told me I was crazy but gave me his fax number. I wrote a letter to Gregory Nava explaining to him how much it meant to me to be a part of this movie and what I thought I could bring to the character. Before I had a chance to fax the letter, I got a call from my agent telling me that they would see me, but the only time was July 25—my birthday. I showed up on the lot in full stage makeup and a long-sleeve black dress; it was about 105 degrees. As I made my way across the lot, I ran into an old friend named Bobby who was working as the editor on the film. He took me right into the casting director's office.

I walked in knowing that this was my part to lose, and I gave the best audition of my life. I walked out, got in my car, called my agent, and said, "I nailed it. Let me know what my call time is." I went back to work on *Eat Your Heart Out* and told everyone that I was going to be playing Selena's sister, Suzette, on the movie *Selena*. The next day I called Bobby and he told me that they had hired another actress for the role. Never say no to someone whose last name is Guerra. I was disappointed, but somehow I knew that I was going to play that role. Even after Jennifer Lopez had been cast as *Selena*, and the entire cast was already in Texas rehearsing, I kept telling people I was going to be in the movie. I was possessed. About three weeks later on a Sunday afternoon, I came home from brunch with my parents and I had seventeen messages on my voice mail and nine faxes in my machine. Everyone was trying to reach me—my agent, my lawyer, the casting director from *Selena*. I called my agent at one forty-five, and she told me I needed to be on a plane at four o'clock to go to Texas. The actress who'd been hired wasn't working out, and Greg wanted me to come to Texas to read with Jennifer and meet the family. They told me that if all went well, I would come home the next day to get my things and go back to shoot the film, and if not, I would be home on Monday. When I landed at the airport in San Antonio, Texas, I was greeted by my old friend Nancy, who was working on the movie. She took me to a hotel in downtown San Antonio where immediately I went to my room, took a shower, and got prepared to meet Selena's family that night. She explained to me the family had casting approval and this was an important meeting. They had to like me. I waited for the call from the lobby that they were there, and I nervously got into the elevator. The door opened up and I saw Suzette. Once again, a year and a half later, we were wearing the exact same shoes, lipstick, and earrings. It was eerie. The meeting that was supposed to last for an hour went on for five hours, and at two in the morning I went back to my room to prepare for my audition the next day. They liked me. And I loved them.

The next morning a car picked me up for the audition. When we got to the stage, I was whisked into a small room and saw Jennifer. She looked at me with her back to Greg and mouthed, "This is yours." We read a scene together that was very physical and I picked Jennifer up, threw her onto the couch, and pounced on top of her; she once again mouthed to me, this time saying "You got it." As I finished the scene, Greg said, "Do you play drums?" and I answered that of course I did. He told me that he wanted me to stay in Texas and play the role of Suzette, Selena's sister and drummer in the band. I didn't go back home for six months. After that audition, Nancy drove me back to my hotel and explained that my schedule for the next week would include rehearsals, fittings, getting my hair cut and colored, acrylic fingernails, and daily visits to the tanning salon. That took care of my lack of indigenous features. Back in my room, I immediately picked up the phone and called Suzette in a panic. I said, "Suzette, I've never picked up a drumstick in my life, except on Thanksgiving." In typical Suzette fashion, she took care of it. She brought a practice pad to my hotel and sent her personal music teacher to give me lessons every night for three weeks straight from 11:00 PM to 1:00 AM. Nobody knew.

Filming the movie *Selena* was one of the most exciting things that has ever happened in my life. I met people who I will forever call my friends, and it also reconnected me to my roots in a way I could've never predicted. It was written, directed, and produced by and starred Latinos. There were Latinos behind and in front of cameras, and it was the first time in my professional career where I heard Spanish on the set and it wasn't craft services.

When *Selena* came out, there were offers and parties and interviews and invitations for personal appearances all over the world. All of us got offers to do other movies, television shows, development deals. I knew this film had changed the way that Hollywood would see Latinos. *Selena* was a movie about a dynamic family and an incredible young woman who happened to be Mexican-American. None of us were asked to do fake Mexican accents; it was amazing. Gone were the days when we were only maids, hookers, or ex-cholas. Or so I thought. Until one afternoon when I found myself in a beautiful office across from some television executives who offered me the opportunity to play Cybill Shepherd's maid in her sitcom. What? What the hell about me, my life, my acting, my anything said "maid"? They explained that there was a guarantee of a certain number of episodes at an obscene amount of money. I did the math in my head and realized that they were offering me the chance to make $1 million in the next year. Even so, I didn't hesitate. I was so pissed. The final straw was when they asked me if I could do a "Spanish" accent. I got up and walked out of the room and never looked back. It was a wake-up call that it was going to take much more than one movie about a successful family who happened to be Latino to change many years of stereotypes. I am proud to be a full-figured Latina. And I like myself and my family and my community way too much to perpetuate an overused stereotype just for the money.

Shortly after that I was offered an opportunity with Dick Clark and Buena Vista Television to develop *The Jackie Guerra Show*, a daytime talk show. Other members of the *Selena* cast were finding their own success. Jennifer (Lopez) was set to star in a movie with George Clooney, Constance Marie was starring in a sitcom on NBC, Jacob Vargas was acting in movie after movie, Edward James Olmos was working nonstop, Jon Seda was starring in a one-hour drama on NBC, and Greg Nava was fielding directing and development offers. The show didn't pan out for me, but the movie had succeeded, and it created amazing opportunities for all of us. Every day was superexciting and wonderful. And then on July 21, 1997, my mother died unexpectedly.

My mother, who had been the one person in my life that I could *always* depend on, was suddenly and permanently gone. My world stopped. For the first time in my life, I was scared, and I couldn't think of a reason to smile. Suddenly, the business that I had come to love and be lucky enough to thrive in seemed really silly. The pain of losing my mother so abruptly overcame me, and I quit show business.

I stayed in my house and watched as many of my friends and people I had worked with became more and more successful. I watched, with the rest of the world, as my friend Jennifer became J.Lo. It was incredible. I was very happy for her and everyone else, but I was so wrapped up in my own grief. I was, for all intents and purposes, out of show business. I left my agency and my manager and I decided to go back to my first love, politics. My mother's death left me feeling so empty. I wanted my life to have meaning, I wanted to make a difference.

I decided to work full-time for the 2000 Gore campaign. I was home with my nephew, Aryton, one afternoon and he was flipping through the channels. *Selena* was on.

I hadn't seen the movie since the premiere. I sat there and, as I watched, I realized that I was crying. I remembered all of the fun that we had making that movie. And I thought about Selena. I thought about how much her life and her passion affected people. I thought about the strength it took for her husband and her family and her friends to go on after her death. I looked at myself on screen and thought about how I had no idea when I was making that movie that one year later my mother would be dead. I looked in the mirror and saw someone I didn't even recognize. All of the reasons that I got into this business in the first place still mattered, and I wanted to make my mark. My mother and my father worked very hard so that my brother and I could pursue our passions and dreams. My mother always said, "Do what you love and the rest will take care of itself."

I heard about a movie being directed by the brilliant director Alfonso Arau and starring Woody Allen. I went in for a meeting with Alfonso and came out with a part in his film, called *Picking Up the Pieces*. I got a new agent at the William Morris Agency and worked like I'd never worked before. I learned a hard lesson: it's much harder to "come back" than to be "discovered." I did about five pilots that didn't go anywhere. One afternoon I got a call from Barbara Jitner Martinez, who had been a director on *Selena*. She and Greg Nava were in the process of developing a one-hour drama for PBS about an American family who were Latino. They offered me the role of

Gordie. A few months later I met with some executives from the Style Network and came out of that meeting as the host of a new show called *You're Invited*. This was truly a turning point for me. My personal hobby has always been crafts. I am a jewelry designer, I love to decorate and, much to my fiancé's dismay, I also love to entertain. Because both *You're Invited* and *American Family* were being shot in Los Angeles, both shows gave me the opportunity to work on other projects and pursue other passions: I began writing a monthly column for *Grace* magazine and went back to doing stand-up. I was living.

In the fall of 2003 I signed a deal with CBS to star along with fellow (Latino) comic Freddy Soto in a sitcom about a brother-sister "odd couple" in the fall of 2004. And, I signed a deal with Homerun Entertainment to host a show for the DIY Network about jewelry making.

People have an amazing capacity to learn and grow and evolve in a short time. I've learned that hard work does not always ensure success, but not working hard almost always ensures failure. Latinos will truly gain power in the entertainment industry when we are in positions of power, and that's at the studio and network level, where we can develop and greenlight projects. In my career and in my life, I've realized I am much stronger than I'd ever imagined. My life as an actor is not so different than my life as an activist. Every day is a struggle, but I wouldn't trade it for anything, except, of course, a seat in the U.S. Senate.

I GET UP TO WORK

BY CECILIA BALLÍ

I woke up sensing my mother's body at the foot of the twin bed where I sleep when I visit her house. When I opened my eyes she was staring at me, her face anxious and sad, a thin line of worry splitting her forehead. The book I had given her the day before sat on her lap.

"You're not going to print this in the magazine, are you?" she asked. There was no good morning.

The previous day my mother had turned fifty-four and she had received what I was sure was the best birthday present I would ever be able to give her: an anthology that included my essay about her life. It was the first piece of writing that I had ever published in a book, a collection of young women's writings on feminism. Surely, by some stroke of fate, I thought, the publisher had released the book early, just a few days before her birthday. I'd wrapped it in elegant beige paper and slipped a pink rose under the ribbon.

"I don't want them to put this in the magazine," she said as I lifted my head and stretched my legs, brushing her side lightly with my toes. The sun was burning already.

"To put what?"

"The things you said about your father. You're disrespecting him." Her voice seemed to crack.

I dropped onto my pillow and exhaled. My mother doesn't speak or read much English, but she can skim my stories and grasp little bits of what they say.

"But you saw me taking notes," I protested, blinking at the ceiling as my throat tightened. "You knew that I was asking you about your life so that I could write your story."

I felt sick, and I wanted the rules of journalism to save me: Say something on the record, and it's on the record. Many months before I had sat my mother down as I would have sat any other source and had talked with her about her life, taking notes in my skinny reporter's notepad. Our "interview" had gone on like this for hours, and sometime during our talk she had told me about that day when she and my father had been working the fields in California, and he had hit her when they got home because he'd seen her chatting with a male field-worker. She says she was simply asking the young man if he and his girlfriend liked their classes at the local community college. In the essay, I wrote that he busted her eye the way he would have busted the eye of any drunk at the bar.

I had shared the piece with the editor at the magazine I write for, and he had immediately asked me if he could reprint it. I told him that I first wanted to see what my mother thought of the idea, since the magazine's audience would be much larger than the book's, and closer to home.

"If the women from work see the magazine and they read what you wrote, they're going to laugh at me. Tell your editor I said no," my mother said with the firmness of marching orders, and she got up with her broken eyes and left the room.

My face burned. I spent most of the day sniffling in the bedroom, but she never came back to ask what was wrong.

My mother is a cook at a school cafeteria in Brownsville. Every morning she wakes up at 5:00 AM, hits the snooze button once, then finally drags herself out of bed and runs the coffeemaker while she takes a ten-minute shower. She slips on one of the school district's maroon uniform shirts, a pair of the blue cotton pants she sews for herself, and the cushioned work shoes she buys with the gift certificates that we give her for Christmas. She pulls her short, thick black curls into a tiny ponytail and makes sure that she has a good hairnet in her purse. She scrambles a quick egg-and-something breakfast, setting some aside for my sister, then pours her coffee into a thermal mug. She yanks up the grumbling garage door and heats up her silver Nissan Frontier in the foggy dark of south Texas. By the time the cafeteria manager pulls up to unlock the gates of Hudson Elementary School at 6:00 AM, my mother is already waiting in her truck, which is spewing out its morning yawn.

She got the job seventeen years ago, after my father died of cancer, and she says she still enjoys it. Though some days she counts her years until retirement because her feet are tired and her hands and arms fall asleep frequently now, most days she tells me rambling stories about the fluffy biscuits she baked, the new Chinese entrée the kids refuse to eat, and the thin-thin teachers who order salads for lunch. She talks, endlessly, about Rodrigo, the first-grader who loves her, and about each of the internecine fights that are waged daily among the kitchen staff. There are several women who are jealous of her, she says, because she has three attractive daughters with college degrees and theirs are living at home with their babies, divorced after two years of marriage. Pure jealousy, she says.

When I visit Brownsville and am preparing to leave, my mother will ask me to stop by the school during her lunch break so that I can eat with her, but I know that what she really wants is for her coworkers to see me. She tries her best to explain my complicated situation to them: I'm in graduate school earning a doctorate in anthropology, but I also write for a magazine and I travel to report my stories. She tells them that the magazine is sold in all of the grocery stores in Texas and that my name appears on the cover. She tells them that it's called *Texas Monthly*, and they nod and promise her that they'll look for it when they go shopping. She invites her two friends over to her house and lends them her own copies, which she keeps in a growing stack on her living room bookshelf. The glossy pages are curled at the edges where she flips them, searching for meaning in my long stories.

The truth is that I have only recently begun calling myself a writer, and only hesitantly. As a child I was more of a quick reader than an avid reader, and by the fifth grade I was sitting in a corner of the classroom, doing the sixth-grade reading book on my own. In Brownsville I attended schools in which we read textbooks instead of novels. In junior high I joined the newspaper, writing features on the band drum major, and by high school I was writing real stories about high school talent shows and beauty pageants for my hometown daily. I decided that I would be a journalist.

When I moved to California for college I fell in love with history, and, missing Texas, I wrote meticulously researched papers about race relations and culture in my state. I also began to formally study Spanish, the language I spoke at home, and became fascinated by its quirky grammar—the strangely conjugated verbs, the million exceptions to the accent rules. I traveled to Mexico for a semester to study with "real" Mexican college students, and while they waxed philosophical during our international relations class, smoking with the professor, I jotted down the vocabulary words they used in the margins of my notebook. My mentors decided that I would be a college professor.

It was during those years that I first began to notice the vast gulf that had begun to form between the amount of language and ideas that my mother and I each knew. In the little notes she sent me with care packages of antibiotics and homemade pajamas and IRS forms, I noticed her tentative print and the funny spellings of her words in Spanish. It had never occurred to me that the seven years of Mexican public education that she had received as a child had not been enough to master even her own language. Not only had school given me a tongue she didn't understand, but I also now spoke hers better than she could. It was as if I were beating her at a game she had never agreed to play.

The thought made me a little bit sad, but in the big picture the concern was secondary. In the large scheme of things it was not one of the more serious deprivations in life. Who cared if my friend's mother edited her papers? Who cared if my roommate faxed physics problems home to her father, who worked them out for her and faxed them back? When I wrote my 120-page honors thesis, which won the university's highest prize, it was enough that I could show the bound copy to my mother and flip through the pages, making the endless litany of words tumble across at a dizzying speed. "Can you believe I wrote all this?" I asked her, with a little grin. I think I was the one who was more amazed.

My older sister, Cristina, came into the bedroom to find out what had happened. She knew something was wrong because my mother was going about her chores without saying a word and I refused to get out of bed, where I lay reading. She sat down by my feet and I recounted the conversation our mom and I had had that morning.

"She's so focused on herself, she can't appreciate what I do for her," I whimpered, detecting the thick resentment in my own voice.

My sister nodded, acknowledging my feelings. She's a social worker by training.

"She doesn't even care that I was trying to honor her, she doesn't care what it means to me. All she cares about is what people are going to say, that's the only thing she ever worries about. She's so closed-minded and self-centered."

It hurt to hear myself say those words about someone I considered my best friend. I know that my mother is extremely private and proud, that she has worked very hard to make everything in her family's life look in order. I could imagine that she felt betrayed. I could imagine her horror at having her coworkers see her as a defenseless or weak woman.

But my mother's rejection hurt so much more: I felt that in one morning she had invalidated everything that I do. If my words couldn't reveal something deeper about her life—if they couldn't make it clearer or more significant—what good was my work?

"But Cecilia," my sister coaxed, "she can't read the poetry.

She can't read between the lines, the way that you do justice to her experiences with words. She can only grasp the events."

I stayed quiet. That was true—perhaps I should have thought of it myself. Yet this explanation was also more painful. It meant that my mother would never understand how I make sense of the world, how I try in some tiny way to change it through my writing. She might grasp the enormity of my assignments by flipping through the magazine pages and seeing how many of them I fill up with my words, but the person who I work to make proud would never be able to judge or appreciate the depth of my messages.

The thought made me feel even more empty and dejected. I called my twin sister, Celia, a lawyer in Houston, and told her what had happened. She was only partly sympathetic.

"Cecilia," she said, "that's the reality for all of us who don't have college-educated parents. Our mom doesn't exactly understand the work that I do, either. All we can do is try to explain a little bit of what we do."

"Yeah," I said, "I guess so."

She was right, but she wasn't. I wanted to respond with the things a writer would say, to tell her that my writing isn't just my job—it is my reading of the world, my notion of truth, my vision for a different kind of place. But all of this seemed somewhat presumptuous.

The next afternoon I tried to make peace with my mother. I walked into her bedroom and told her that I wanted us to get past this, that I didn't want to cry anymore. I just had one condition, I said: I wanted her to give me back the book I had given her. To forget it ever existed.

It was a dramatic declaration, the kind of thing you tell your lover when you're pretending to leave so that he'll take you back and remind you of all that you mean to him. But she said nothing, and she reached into her closet and placed the book in my hands.

My romance with writing didn't flourish in some bohemian café in New York or Bogotá, as the most romantic of writer's stories go. In fact, it was less a romance than a studied, labored relationship. When I left my first newspaper job in San Antonio at the age of twenty-four to work on the PhD that my professors had wanted me to get, a senior reporter who worked at the paper and had once written for *Texas Monthly* pulled me aside and said I was not a reporter—I was a writer. He sent one of my pieces to the magazine's editor, who decided to give me a break by asking me to write a six-thousand-word story. Shortly after I moved to Houston to enroll in school, he offered me a contract as a writer at large.

This meant that I became twice a student. At night I read social theory and anthropology, but by day, when I was having lunch or dinner, I always ate with a highlighter in hand and a magazine by my side—*Harper's*, *The New Yorker*, *The New York Times Magazine*. I diagrammed good magazine stories. I marked words I would never have thought of using. I looked for original sentence constructions and paid attention to how writers described people's physical appearance in words, something I'd never had to do in my newspaper writing. I divided a small journal into parts and recorded my finds under three sections: "Words," "Pretty Sentences," and "People Descriptions."

My mother, who had come up from Brownsville because of my recent foot surgery and driven me to that first meeting with the magazine's editor in Austin, was curious about my new project. I explained to her that most journalists considered this the best writing gig in Texas, and that people from New York moved here just to work for the magazine and then went on to write for prestigious national publications. She wondered whether I would get to meet important people. My mother knows that I've always been more inclined to write about regular folk, about the "working class," as I learned to say in college. For my honors thesis research I had hung out in dance halls and bars with more than a few drunks and ex-convicts. I gave my mom long-winded lectures about how writers like me were celebrating the ordinary and how people at the bottom of the social ladder often have more insights about the way the world works. But she wasn't sold. "When that's been your life, you don't find it very amusing to read," she used to say. And that was that, because I never came up with a good comeback.

It wasn't until we were in college that my sisters and I learned that my mother liked to read. Growing up, the only reading materials around the house were the Bible, the racy Mexican novelas she got at the supermarkets across the border, and a two-volume set of medical encyclopedias she had bought in Spanish. When she visited me in college I took her to the library and walked her to the floor where there were rows and rows of Latin American literature. I checked out a few books by Mexico's literary greats—Rulfo, Paz, Fuentes—and was surprised to find her devouring them in my dorm room as I read for class. She wasn't too impressed, however. "Mexican writers are so vulgar," she complained. She said she preferred reading about people with glamorous lives, something different from what she already knew. She read about Frida Kahlo and about Jackie Kennedy Onassis. She liked "stories about inspirational women," she said.

I began talking to her about my work. I tried explaining

vague concepts such as "literary journalism" and "cultural anthropology." I wanted so much to share my new life with someone, with the single person who most cared about what I did. It required translations and simplifications, references and examples. Really we were both trying to understand these things together, across languages and some eleven years of schooling. I explained the idea of a magazine that is both writerly and informative. She said she wished there were something like that in Spanish that she could read.

One time I was invited to present a research paper at a bilingual conference in Mexico, and I took her with me so that she could travel. I had not figured out what I would have her do to pass the time once the conference began. I decided to register her so that she could sit in on a few panels and get a taste of these academic gatherings to which I constantly traveled. We attended a few of the talks together. Then, I taught her how to read the program and we went our separate ways, agreeing to meet for lunch. Throughout the bus ride to the restaurant, she rattled on an endless stream of information she had learned about Mexican migration to the United States. On her program, she had printed the names of professors she thought I should look up for my own research.

The following year I had a series of oral surgeries that left me dazed and in excruciating pain. On one of those occasions my mother offered to make the five-hour trip to Houston to drive me from the doctor's office to my apartment and be sure that I ate. In my living room I had a stack of Mexican anthropology journals that one of my professors had passed on to me and that I had not read, since they were filled with tiresome, old-school studies of indigenous religious rituals and patterns of social organization. I slept the entire day. But when I stumbled out of the bedroom for a glass of water, I saw that my mother had slipped on her reading glasses and planted herself on a wicker chair I had by my stack of books. She was absorbed in the journals. Hours later, when the day had been blanketed in darkness and a single lamp burned in the living room, I got up for another drink and found her still reading. She mumbled, without looking up, "This is really interesting."

I thought the essay I had written about my mother was the best inspirational woman story I could ever write. But she could not see it that way—in her eyes, my words were strange and ridiculing. For days I moped. We had never felt so distant. At night I cried because I knew that no matter how much I explained to her, it would always be this way: my mom would not understand what I did with language, how I understood life and reconstructed it on the page. It was as if I were standing on my little literary podium screaming out to the world, yet my biggest fan, my mother, would never be able to hear me.

I wanted to accept this and to move on. I wanted to stop feeling sorry for myself, to be like my sister and suck things up and be grateful for my lot in life.

One night, after my mother had turned off her lights, I opened her door and slid onto her bed in the darkness.

I lay quietly for a moment. Softly, I said, "I'm sorry."

And she began to cry.

It was then I knew the depth of her wounds. My mother is an abnormally resilient woman—a woman who, I was sure, had come to terms with her past. It was only then that I realized that the physical blows that I thought had dignified her on paper because she had survived them were still crippling her. It was only then that I saw that the damage had not, that it might never, go away.

I cried—deep, angry sobs. I had misunderstood her, too.

"I don't *ever* want to get married," I sputtered. My words took us both by surprise. Everyone knows that I'm a romantic.

"Don't say that," my mother chided gently. Her tears had subsided.

"Why would I want to get married if it brings this kind of pain? I'm fine on my own, thank you. I have a pretty good life."

"But look what marriage gave me," she said.

"A bunch of pain," I taunted.

"It gave me you three."

I didn't say anything. It was a rhetorical strategy, I told myself. I wasn't convinced.

In anthropology we concern ourselves with ethics, and we worry obsessively about the risky seduction of wielding our power and our writing over people who cannot "talk back." In writing, on the contrary, words and stories are held to be sacred, little fragments of truth that must be spoken and liberated from the dangers of silence. Who should I believe? I am teetering on a borderline between so many things: between honoring the people I write about and disrespecting them, between healing through truth and revealing dirty secrets, between writing as necessity and writing as privilege. Between a world that I live through words and a world that my mother just lives.

There is a memory that lingers lucidly for my mom, of the time my father died. When the funeral was over, my twin sister returned to school cheerfully but I lay in bed for days, unable to face my fifth-grade class. I said nothing. I retched with everything I ate. And a terrifying thought struck my mother: What if she lost me, too? How could she possibly survive?

Mom, I'm sorry—sorry about my words and about the memories they couldn't heal. I will not write your pains again.

I'm twenty-seven now. It's been eighteen months since our fallout. Eventually my mother and I struck a compromise and her story ran in the magazine without the anecdote about my father's blows. It was on every grocery store shelf in Texas. The editors hired an artist to do an illustration of her, and the image now hangs framed on her living room wall—my present to her on her fifty-fifth birthday. I guess one figures these things out as they come.

On a brisk January afternoon she is helping me pack up my apartment, marking boxes with a green pen so that we can figure out what's going and what's staying. She sneaked out several dozen flattened cardboard boxes from work, labeled with the brands of tortillas and taco shells. I leave for El Paso in a week, to research and write my first book, an account of hundreds of women and girls who are being murdered in Ciudad Juárez, on the Texas-Mexico border. I had offers from two major publishers, which culminated in a trip to New York and meetings with the company president and with a couple of national magazine editors who have taken interest in my writing.

I asked my mother if I could leave my desktop computer at her house while I'm gone, and a few days later she asked me about e-mail, if it was something I thought she could learn. So that she could write to me. "Of course you can," I told her, "I'll show you." She has already called the phone company and knows who offers the cheapest dial-up service, a bargain compared to what I was paying for mine.

"El Paso with an *s* or with a *z*?" she asks me, disrupting my thoughts. "With an *s*," I say. I look down at the floor so that she won't catch me grinning. She marks the box, and we stack my books inside of it and seal it with tape.

CHESSIN'

BY NELLY ROSARIO

> *Life is a kind of chess, with struggle,*
> *competition, good and ill events.*
> — BENJAMIN FRANKLIN

You know how to play chess, Jet Set?" my cousin Albertín[1] asked me in the summer of 1986. We were loafing around on our grandparents' porch in Villa Altagracia, a small roadside town in the Dominican Republic. I was a flat-chested fourteen-year-old, still pronouncing the game "chest."

"You're smart, Jet Set, so I'll teach you."

I thought his nickname for me came from the logo on the seat of my new jeans: a tiny jet puffing smoke from its tail. But to Albertín, my siblings and I were spoiled American kids who automatically got quarters from our parents to buy cold maví across the road. All together, my father, mother, three siblings, and I had packed twelve suitcases for a month in the Dominican Republic; it was a long-due vacation from the daily grind of New York City. That summer is my most sustained memory of my mama country.

---

[1] Name not changed in order not to protect the not-so-innocent.

There were folks to visit in Villa Altagracia, Santo Domingo, San Cristóbal, Santiago, and up north in Puerto Plata, where we enthusiastically swam in virgin beaches, peed in latrines, and drank water from jugs teeming with larvae. Toward the end of our trip, my parents had spoiled us with one luxurious night at Casa de Campo, so we could "see the full breadth of what our country has to offer" (must have taken months of sweat to eke out that money back in New York). By the time we made it to Villa Altagracia, we were all cheeky and glowy and chatty and just plain *happy*.

Albertín taught this jet-setting girl all the wrong moves on his portable magnetic chess set. According to him, pawns could arbitrarily move one or two squares forward and could pillage and plunder just the same.[2] He played likewise off the chessboard: it was Albertín who offered to take my twelve-year-old brother to a brothel; and he tried to steal a sloppy kiss from my sixteen-year-old sister in a movie theater, while next to them I fought off his friend's advances. Much later in his life, after countless family scandals, he finagled his way to the United States and subsequently served time for his real-life portrayal of Peoples from the movie *Shaft*.

"This is the horse. He can move two-by-four squares,[3] like the letter *L*," he told me, making the white knight look like a colt in his thick fingers.

"Unlike the others, Jet Set, he can jump over other pieces to make his moves."[4]

---

[2] Pawns capture diagonally. They may move either one or two squares straight ahead on their starting squares, and only one square forward thereafter.

[3] The knight moves from one corner to the other of a two-by-three rectangle of squares.

[4] I'll cut him some slack on this one.

When I reached for the white knight, Albertín shooed away my hand and said that the black knight suited me best because my hair was kinky, my nose like a chancleta, and my bemba kissable if only I'd put on some lip gloss.[5]

And once you capture an opposing piece, according to that son of a mother, you don't have to remain on the square the attacked piece occupied.[6]

"Always gotta keep things movin', Jet Set."

But Jet Set found it hard to generally keep herself moving at DR speed. I couldn't roll out as quick-fire a Spanish, complete with metaphors and double entendres. Couldn't beat my cousins in our wheelbarrow races from one end of the porch to the other. Couldn't avoid being swindled into giving away money for which I had to ask my parents. Didn't dare tell that pervert who snapped the straps of my double-A's que se lo haga a la maldita que lo parió. In the mornings, the air already felt as if I had walked into a mouth. Food was tastier, and my sweetened American blood incensed the mosquitoes. My hair found even more renegade roots. Dominican Republic: languid country, fast-thinking folks, coup d'etats, self-preservation, tactical threats, chest-thumping kings, strong-ass queens, black versus white, expendable pawns, crooked rooks, diagonal bishops, stealthy stallions, guerilla tactics, hot damn, jaque mate . . .

In chess, one wins by killing the father-king; the word "checkmate" comes from the Persian for "the king is dead." Though I had no conscious desire to commit patricide—ay Dios, no!—I did subconsciously grasp that the piece most capable of killing the almighty father-king is the versatile mother-

[5] Not too far off. In both chess and in DR, White plays first.

[6] . . . not.

queen; that the lowly pawns find strength by working together; that this game, in Jungian terms, is rich with symbols of fundamental dualities, such as conscious/subconscious, male/female, light/dark, life/death. I was smitten.

Back home in New York, I dragged my own father to Toys "R" Us. When I read the rule booklet inside my shiny new chess set, I realized that I would have to relearn the game I had spent weeks trying to master with Albertín in Santo Domingo (sentimental analogy about my father as agent to rectify rogue rules already in my head is another essay for another time). As I read up on the correct rules, I wondered who the hell taught Albertín (whose father I've never met) how to play. And more important, who taught him how to live?

Over my years I've seen Rooks get tooken by the Knight
Lose they Crown by tryna defend a Queen
Checkmate, in four moves the Bobby Fischer[7] of rap

—JAY Z

FROM "THIS LIFE FOREVER"

In the Jewish section of Williamsburg, Brooklyn (also known as Kings County), there was a bazaar owned by a Hasidic elder. On Saturdays, I loved to stroll from the south side with my mother to the old factory in what we kids called "Jewtown"; once you crossed under the el on Broadway, the concrete would burst open with columns of muscular trees accompanied by chirping birds. Suddenly, there would be quiet and very little litter, and brownstone after brownstone. Once inside the

[7] American Bobby Fischer won the 1972 world championship against the pride of the Soviets, Boris Spassky. The victory set off a wave of chess interest still referred to as the "Fischer boom."

bazaar, Mami and I would find rows and rows of bric-a-brac, which made our hands tingle. We'd take our time looking through the merchandise haphazardly thrown into wooden boxes. One day, while she looked through a pile of girdles and socks, I found my own treasure: a cylindrical box containing a chessboard in the shape of a cross, complete with four plastic armies. Quadra-Chess was a five-dollar find that promised fun for the whole family. It was indeed to bring me and my siblings hours of fun . . . and battles and tears. Finally, a safe gladiator arena on which to mercilessly duke out domestic politics.

Usually, the two younger boys played against the two older girls. Sometimes it was the youngest and the oldest versus the middle siblings—or everyone against the victim of the day. While we massacred each other, our parents would smile at their four beautiful children playing what Goethe called "the touchstone of the intellect." They never imagined our cruelties, the pain we inflicted with those little blue, orange, yellow, and green men—and women.

At the start of a game, there would be a fervent laying down of rules, with the trusty rule booklet as Bible. We knew any one of us was bound to break them, depending on our mood. We played with mistrust, our allegiances temporary, foul play on the board bound to spill over into an argument later, and vice versa. During a game, aspects of the players' personalities emerge; a game can expose faults we'd like to think are folded quietly in the corners of our minds. The Jungian school of thought speculates that dreaming of chess can represent the dreamer's higher moral integrity contending with baser motives. Well, teamed up with my little brother, my baser motives would gain supremacy: I would wait until I had enough of his pieces near me, then turn on him when our chances of winning slimmed. It didn't matter that he had learned the game with amazing speed to keep up with his older siblings. They would join in on my feeding frenzy. I remember how outrage and betrayal would moisten his eyes as I assimilated his unsuspecting army into mine, complete with evil cackle.

It was the power, man, that magnificent rush of voltage that made me feel like the baddest bitch in the whole, whole land. Too bad, l'il bro. Life's a ghetto. Just remember the times you sat playing ColecoVision while sis and I had to slave away cleaning up after you. Not everyone played by the rules. Not even me. Because I got tired of playing by the rules all the time, of getting good grades, of keeping my mouth shut around the elders, around men, of being the Goody Two-shoes of the household. My little brother—with his sensitive nature, his hesitant speech, his chubby cheeks, his little-brotherness— was always an easy target . . . but target he was. How expressively oppressive we the oppressed can be . . .

And then there was the day I violated my other brother's sacred comic book collection by taking them—ay Dios, no!— out of their plastic covers. He got a hold of my precious magnetic chess set, and in *that* war, the metal landscape peeled away from its wooden base (whose board, by the way, folded up to store the adorable little pieces for easy toting). I tore one of his comic books; no way was I going to tackle the armor of his body. I didn't know what to do with all that sour foam that gurgled from the guts of my soul. Because my rage wasn't about that stupid chess set. My anger spewed forth from the fact that J. M. from down the block had ignored my three-year crush, and that my father had omnipotent eyes, and that my mother made me and my sister hand-wash everybody's socks on Fridays because the Laundromat couldn't do the job right, and that I had small tits, which guys loved to rank on, and damn it, Carl Jung, probably from a subconscious, unacknowledged, meta-physical rage toward El Generalissimo Doctor Rafael Trujillo Molina, Benefactor de la Patria y Padre de la Patria Nueva, who once lorded over all the pieces of a chessboard with an iron fist, once upon a time.

"*I hate yoooou!*" I screamed at the top of my lungs. My brother laughed.[8]

♜

Castling is a special defensive maneuver invented in the 1500s to speed up the game and to balance offense and defense: the rook switches places with the king. Castling, roles switched, exchanged, and switched back again: this has defined my life.

Growing up, I nursed a competitive disposition toward everything, from sports and academics to understanding politics. If my uncles didn't give five shits about my views on politics, I would join in their debates anyway. I worked with my hands or, worse, got them dirty. I was a do-it-yourself chick, who turned down offers for her books to be carried, the chick in the flicks who "could be so much more attractive if only she'd be more ladylike": not curse so much or be so outspoken, not laugh with such abandon, not be so buddy-buddy with the guys, not talk so freely about sex, maybe spend more time on hair and fashion instead of trying to conjure up a formula that would articulate the deeper workings of the world. And many times, it fell upon me to be my parents' ambassador to the court of the white king.

[8] Canute was an eleventh-century king of Denmark and England. During a game with a Danish earl, the king made a bad move and tried to take it back. The earl over-turned the chess table. The king had him killed.

So, at eighteen, despite my parents' horror at their youngest daughter going off by herself to a city more than three hours away, I went off to study environmental engineering at a predominately white male school (where trying to find a women's bathroom was like being inside a Borges novel). During my junior year, I went even farther away to spend a semester abroad in Belize. It was three months of rugged existence in bush country, studying natural and cultural ecology. With months of studying, hiking, swimming, and camping behind me, I then returned to New York City that summer for an internship at a public utilities company as an engineering aide. I had just gotten my driver's license and was excited about the privilege of driving the company's "Blue Bird" to all five boroughs of New York City inspecting facilities. Still, for me the job was an abrupt transition from study in a natural environment abroad to work in the industrial sprawl of the city.

Imagine a brown-skinned college girl, wearing a hard hat and holding a clipboard, telling the grizzled white manager of a facility that he should not be smoking a cigar as per the NO SMOKING sign behind him. No amount of camping, cave explorations, or deep-sea snorkeling had prepared me for the many insolent and veteran managers I dealt with out in the field. According to some chess masters, it's best to castle early during a game; this way, you can safely tuck your king behind a fortress of three pawns and the rook. That summer, I soon developed my own defensive maneuvers, my own castling. Inspection days were drag-king days: I would make sure to wear the muddied hiking boots that had served me well a few months prior; I chewed more gum than usual; I made sure to camouflage my body in loose pants and big shirts, which I borrowed from my brothers; my voice went down an octave; I wore my hair in a ponytail, no makeup; and, come to think of it, I would arrive late to the sites because I refused to ask for directions.

Did my castling work? No. The problem was that under my costume, I was still unsure of my abilities. I anticipated negative reactions to my youth and my gender—and many times, I bought into them. I manifested the same insecurities in school, often the only Latina and black female in the hydrology course. I pulled less than good grades because of my fear of asking a question during lecture, and pride kept me from going to the TA when a problem set stumped me. After all, I wanted to believe that I was there on the merit of all the high school A's I had raked in, and not as an affirmative action quota.

Eventually, I got a wonderful evaluation at the job. I had learned the ropes throughout the summer, and with that, many of my anxieties disappeared. My semester in Belize had come into play after all: I lost all my urban terror of sleeping outdoors and deep-sea snorkeling. Beginnings can be difficult, but with each new start, you learn to rely on abilities you've inadvertently discovered in yourself through previous experiences. Glass ceilings aside, the internship also taught me that in male-dominated fields, the point is not so much to prove anything to men, but to learn the job well, then put out your best.

Another concept in chess is "developing your pieces": It's important to get your stronger pieces into play as quickly as possible, before you begin advancing and setting up battles. When I finally applied this concept to my chess games, I left a lot of opponents muttering stuff about my mother—but more on that later. It takes the development of the many pieces of our selves in order to truly confront our battles. In turn, as females, our own development as whole individuals is what contributes to the development of all women.

"What's the quickest way to become a chess master?" Hector Perez, director of El Centro Latino in Florida, asked some elementary and middle school chess students.

"Is it 'A: Eat a lot of candy,' 'B: Eat at Kentucky Fried Chicken,' or 'C: Move all your pieces off the back line?' "

"Move all your pieces off the back line!" the children shouted.[9]

You certainly don't win with the queen hiding in the back line.

♟

A few years ago, I went to Martha's Vineyard with Then-Fiancé. While we were window-shopping one day, we came across a thirty-five-dollar onyx chess set. It was a sweet deal, with an orange-and-black marbleized board and heavy pieces that clacked down on every move. I was deliriously pregnant at the time, already imagining myself teaching my child how to make a three-move checkmate in a three-thousand-plus-year-old game by the age of three.

As magical as pregnancy was for me, it was also a very confusing time, in which I felt as if I were losing the essential thread of myself: now I was suddenly being asked to fulfill an assortment of traditional female roles in a relationship that had previously sought to debunk many of those conventions. I had no idea that a man could break out in hives at the mention of doing dishes or that in public it was my duty to wobble over and serve him his steaming plate of food before I even got to eat mine. And I complied against my own intuition. A pregnant woman should rest: I hobbled about working on a variety of

[9] Isaac Groves, "Students Learn More Than Chess," *Herald-Sun*, February 17, 2003.

freelance jobs, then stayed up late nights trying to finish a novel. A pregnant woman should nest: I had trouble keeping up with housework, laundry, groceries. A pregnant woman should glow with the new life inside of her: the skin on my cheeks broke out in eczema rashes. A pregnant woman should be the bestest wifey she could possibly be: I slammed doors and yelled like a scorned opera singer.

This time, I did not become a drag king, but morphed into Supreme Earth Goddess, trying to balance the world on swollen feet. I was now reacting to the hallowed image of my supermother, who after a long day at the sweatshop would come home and serve up the Dominican flag (meat, white rice, a vegetable, fresh salad, and beans, which she had had the foresight to soak the night before—not from a can) in less than forty-five minutes flat.

A good chess player knows when she is following the "thread" of the game. Sensing what's important, she can play intuitive moves and see her way through all kinds of tactical complexities with surprising accuracy. That's one way humans can beat computers at the game. On the other hand, when she hesitates and seems confused, she has usually lost the thread and will have to rely on pure calculation—the computer's specialty. That's when humans lose to computers . . . as well as to themselves.

This time, I wore the camouflage of my anxiety *inside* my body. Emergency signals came on. I attributed my exhaustion, rashes, bouts of melancholy, lack of appetite, and colds to pregnancy. And by the time labor came around, I literally exploded under the pressure. It was as if the threads of my body had coiled into a vise grip. Labor was long and arduous for Supreme Earth Mother, who was supposed to squat and spit out radiant baby without need for drugs or surgery. But you take life as it comes. The baby couldn't get out of my womb's grip even with three doses of Pitocin, uterine massage, and all the hokey New Age visualization techniques suggested by the birthing center. The world would have to wait for this new queen: forty-eight hours, an epidural, and a cesarean later, I finally had a baby girl.

My worst tries, I've learned, can be when I *am* trying. I can't help but think about the chess player at a Hastings tournament who was clenching his teeth with such concentration that he broke his false teeth and had to forfeit his game to go to a dentist. Or about the boy who gave British Army General Rahl a spy report that George Washington was crossing the Delaware to attack, and the general, being so immersed in a chess game, put the note in his pocket unopened; it was found when he died in battle. My "unopened note" was my body's emergency signals. I ignored the messages and continued to try being all that I *could not* be, even as I felt the threads of my body unraveling. And as I adjusted to the new demands of motherhood, a persistent ache under my shoulder blade would flare up after many arguments with my partner.

Among a myriad other issues, our most intense arguments centered on roles. We buckled under all the role negotiation as our tallying of tasks made the "gender ledger" grow longer. Who's supposed to wash the dishes? Who takes the car to the mechanic? In public, a woman should stand beside her man no matter what. A man is supposed to know how to fix the boiler when it breaks down. Who addresses the crying in the middle of the night? I paid the bills last month. No, I did. Nice hour to come home. Why should you drive? Who throws out the dead mouse? Who cleans if we both work? Six loads of laundry, three turtledoves, four hummingbirds, five golden rings. The baby's crying. What's for dinner? Fuck you. A woman shouldn't talk like that. Fuck you. A man shouldn't talk like that. Fuck me. Who goes on top? Who goes on the bottom? The store is this way. Which way is north? Which way is south?

About two years later, I decided that I had had enough of the shoulder pain.

The consequences of our parting are many, good and bad. Yes, I no longer answer to a man, have one set of rules in my household and a renewed sense of personal freedom. But as the sole head of my household, there is also the danger of falling into the trap of once again trying to do everything and be everything—to my child, this time.

She is four now. When she was a baby, she would knock over the onyx chess pieces, and eventually, the queen and the rest of 'em all lost their heads. Though the pieces and Then-Fiancé are no longer with me, I am still in the company of my daughter, the chessboard, and the thread of myself. Mothering, writing, and teaching have retrained me to be still enough to listen to myself again in order to tie up any loose thread. Silence. This means feeling content with simply doing *nothing* for at least one entire day out of the week. This means not being afraid to say no to opportunities that may seem exciting but are not in line with personal obligations. This means writing from an honest part of myself, instead of trying to write blockbuster narratives. It means listening to my students so that I may learn from them, too. In silence, you shed all camouflage and embrace the core part of yourself outside of what the world demands. You stop kicking and screaming. You put away the work. You play.

Now that I've set new pieces on my old chessboard, I try to show my daughter how to play—but all she wants to do is line up her pieces in a circle on the squares and let them play Ring around the Rosie. At least she can identify both the king and the queen on the chessboard.

"Mami, why chest got no princesses or princes?"

And she calls the rook a "princess castle" and the knight a "horsie."

"We'll win together, Mami, you and me, okay?" and with a smile, I wonder who's teaching who how to play, and think harder about who's teaching who how to live.

♟

Confession: My name is pluma72 and I am addicted to online chess. Sometimes I'm a twenty-four-year-old white female with long brown hair and electric-blue eyeshadow. Or I can be a white seventy-two-year-old New Yorker with a scraggly bun and glasses. Other times, I'm a black professor with a receding hairline. Unfortunately, the server doesn't offer cartoon faces of black females. A thirty-one-year-old Dominicana is left to choose from icons that include a yellowish girl in pigtails, an orange tiger, and an androgynous face with a green mohawk. Thank God for choices, though. You can do some serious damage when playing as the blue demon with the goatee.

Gerald Abrahams (1907–1980) once said, "Chess is a good mistress but a bad master." I'm admitting an affair here, aberrant behavior. After my daughter's asleep, I stay up playing into the night, with the specter of unwritten novels and a good night's rest gnawing at my conscience. Still, I want to tighten my opening moves and learn more strategies; many believe that the mastery of chess can somehow lead to the mastery of one's self.[10]

[10] Terry Anderson, one of the hostages held by terrorists during the Iran crisis, credits chess with helping him survive the ordeal.

To date, I've battled in over a thousand games online. It's, um, nobody's business how many I've won or lost. As a beginner/intermediate, my rating fluctuates between 1,100 and 1,370. I try to play with those ranked higher than myself; when my self-esteem is way below sea level, I play against "provisionals" and the 1,000 crowd. There have been some intense exchanges with players from around the world, our misspelled dialogues confined to the text box at the bottom of the screen. But sometimes, things get sticky . . .

His name was peaceart, Aquarius, a forty-five-year-old restaurateur, a Canadian of Italian descent. I was the old white lady with the scraggly bun from Queens, New York. Of course, peaceart asked me if the 72 in pluma72 stood for my age or my birth year. "Age," I wrote. As we played, he went on about how my Alzheimer's was going to raise his rank. He kept kicking my ass, while I hid behind my "age" as an excuse. He was intimidating, a full thousand ahead of me in rank. And I was frustrated with how easily I gave up pieces with hasty decisions and botched attacks. Still, I kept coming back for more, determined to beat him, maybe represent the senior citizens of America.

> **peaceart:** The problem with women is that you think too locally. Don't see the big picture, don't see the patterns, you can't strategize.
>
> **pluma72:** Or maybe deep down we just don't believe in the premise of war.
>
> **peaceart:** Don't gimme that, ol' lady. Women ain't saints, they're the most warring, conniving species. Spent a year in jail cause of a woman.
>
> **pluma72:** . . . and you say we can't strategize. Can we just play now?

He liked my playing/chatting style: more defense than offense, nice openings, virtually no blood spilling. I told him my real age; he told me he liked art and peace. He seemed sensitive, astute, and frankly, I was aroused by his sharpness on the board, how he claimed my pieces with stealth, always a few moves ahead of mine. The flirting started, tentatively at first, then plunged into full-throttle dirty talk in English, Spanish, and Italian. Of course, he mentioned his trip to the Dominican Republic, how he loved it out there, the beaches, the music, and yeah, the women, how an Italian stallion coupled with a Dominican hottie would be explosive, and he played on the word "checkmate," blah, blah, blah. Soon he asked for my pic. We e-mailed each other. I sent him a vague JPEG of myself. I opened his e-mail, eagerly expecting a face with soft, dark eyes, maybe a goatee. Instead, I was dismayed to find a blonde all over a black man.

I hadn't bothered to write the scathing e-mail I probably would have in my twenties: *You sonofadog patriarchal fathafuckin' racist bastard . . . How could you?* He'd probably e-mail back a paragraph of equal slurs in caps—and more porn. I sighed. I had dealt with toddlers before. Life goes on after tantrums. Instead of being pissed off, how do I advocate for myself now?

He had forgotten our previous exchange a few weeks later, when he popped up on my table. Only after I mowed down his king did I call him out on his rudeness.

peaceart: You're really taking this bad, aren't you.
pluma72: No. Just thought you were a little above
    that.
peaceart: I'll send you some more . . .

pluma72: Can we just play now so I can kick your ass?
Another game. I win. Another. I win.
pluma72: Hurts, don't it. I can hear your cock
shrinking.
peaceart: You're a stupid fucking bitch . . .
pluma72: Yawn.

A remarkably stupid exchange, but after a series of losses, I
started to feel that familiar twinge . . . the power, man, that
magnificent rush of voltage that made me feel like the baddest
bitch in the whole, whole land. I hoped that even off the
board, he would be able to appreciate the power of the dama,
who became the most powerful piece in tribute to Queen Is-
abella in the late 1400s; for whom, up until the late nineteenth
century, it was mandatory to say "check to the queen" or
"gardez" when she was attacked.

Me, I was on mad offensive during the game. That familiar
sour foam gurgled, but by now I had learned: rage makes me
move without thinking; it makes me rush ahead with too many
plots; it makes me make empty threats. Instead of trash "talking" à la Fire Breather George Golden,[11] I silently flooded
peaceart's king with my army. I held my tongue and just focused
on the thread of the game. I knew my enemy, knew his patterns.
He always used the same knight openings. It was easy to lay out
bait for him, because he was greedy, often sacrificing strategy for
a capture in order to scare his opponent. He was good at distrac-
tions, such as chatting you up about spirituality and the state of
the Middle East while his bishops zigzagged across the board.

---

[11] A notoriously trash-talking player in the Black Bear School of Chess, which was
started in the mid-1970s by a group of black men who met around the chess tables
in Brooklyn's Prospect Park.

But I have my mojo, too. My pawns are not expendable. I play them as if they are queens or rooks. They're good for building up a solid front, and from the onset of the game, I sent them out to dam up the middle of the board. A pawn is like a caterpillar in that it advances slowly, silently, but can eventually be "promoted" to a queen if it reaches the other end of the board.[12] Again, my best tries can be when I am *not* trying, when I play the steady, ordinary, unassuming, unremarkable, persevering pawn. And when my black pawn metamorphosed into a queen, peaceart found himself with two women on the board;[13] sho 'nuff, I heard the little computer beep as peaceart abandoned the game.

I sat there, Alice in wonder:

"But how *can* it have got there without my knowing it?" she said to herself, as she lifted it off, and set it on her lap to make out what it could possibly be.

It was a golden crown.

— FROM LEWIS CARROLL,
THROUGH THE LOOKING-GLASS,
AND WHAT ALICE FOUND THERE[14]

---

[12] When a pawn reaches the last row of the chessboard, it may become any piece the player chooses. A queen is usually chosen because she is the most powerful chess piece, with the power to move an unlimited distance in any direction across the board.

[13] Early chess rules in some countries did not allow a promotion of a pawn to a second queen on the board; that was thought of as promoting bigamy.

[14] In *Through the Looking-Glass, and What Alice Found There* (MacMillan, 1871)—the sequel to *Alice's Adventures in Wonderland*—Lewis Carroll bases the adventure's narrative on a chess problem, with Alice navigating through the looking-glass world (chessboard) as a pawn who wins in eleven moves.

♜

In Sir William Jones's seventeenth-century poetry, there is a wood nymph named Caissa, the muse-goddess of chess. She personifies my pure love for the game, my pure love for life. In chess, as in life, I have eons to go on my learning curve. Chess forces me to have a conversation with myself and, like dreams, brings out my subconscious, allows me to hold my mind in my hands.

> It's a concentration game. . . . It's about thinking, it's about plotting, planning and observing, that's knowledge. . . . That's how life is in general, you have to plan ahead of time.
>
> — WU-TANG CLAN'S GZA

Legendary genius of soul Ray Charles learned chess in 1965 after being busted for heroin addiction. He went cold turkey and learned chess in the hospital, using a peg set made for the blind.[15] Mind over matter. It's through the mind that we attempt to perceive and understand the fundamental laws of life's truth.

"People aren't free until they've achieved mind, body, and soul. We've accomplished much with our bodies . . . also . . . our soul, but we have yet to show . . . all we can do with our minds," said Maurice Ashley, the world's first and only black grand master, at a Harlem Chess Day event in 2000. This was the very message my parents conveyed to me and my siblings

---

[15] Buzecca, a Muslim player, played two games blindfolded in Florence in 1265. It took another 518 years before three games were played blindfolded, by Philidor in 1783; and seventy-four years after that, Louis Paulsen played four games blindfolded . . . simultaneously.

throughout our childhoods. And I smile at the fact that two great blessings first introduced me to life and to the game: family and the Dominican Republic. Sure, there are still remnants of the drag-king and Supreme Earth Goddess in me, but I tote all these pieces inside of my magnetic "chest" set, alchemize their strengths and their weaknesses in playing the game of life.

When Napoleon died, he willed that his heart be cut out and placed inside a chess table. Life, death, chess, love, body, mind, soul. Everything's connected.

CONTRIBUTORS

Gigi Anders, a special correspondent for the *Washington Post*, has written for, among others, *Glamour, Allure, American Health for Women, USA Today's USA Weekend, American Journalism Review, Hispanic, Latina,* and *First for Women*. She is also the author of the upcoming novel *Jubana!* to be published by HarperCollins. The author and her cat, Lilly "Sweet Pea" Anders, live in a Hackensack, New Jersey, high-rise apartment overlooking Manhattan and the semi-bustling Teterboro Airport.

Nancy Ayala is a freelance writer/editor. She was an editor at *USA Today* for ten years, where she was part of a group that started a Latino initiative program for the national newspaper. She was a Fulbright journalism Scholar. She also taught Saturday English classes for the Latin American Youth Center's Upward Bound program in Washington, D.C. She lives in New York City with her dog, Frida.

Cecilia Ballí is a writer at large for *Texas Monthly* and a doctoral student in cultural anthropology. A graduate of Stanford University, she has written for the *San Antonio Express-News,* the *Brownsville Herald,* and *Latina* magazine. She is currently working on a book about the murder of young girls and women in Juarez, Mexico, to be published by Metropolitan Books.

Tanya Barrientos, a journalist for more than twenty years, is a staff writer at the *Philadelphia Inquirer*. Born in Guatemala, she grew up in a Texas border town but now lives outside of Philadelphia with her husband. She's published two novels to date, *Family Resemblance* (Penguin, 2002) and *Frontera Street* (Penguin, 2003), and is currently working on her third.

Carolina Buia, is the New York correspondent for *Celebrity Justice*, a nationally syndicated television show. She has written for *Time*, the *Washington Post*, and the *Miami Herald*. Her entertaining book, *Latin Chic: Style, Sass, and Salsa* (Rayo, 2004) is due out later this year. She lives in Manhattan and was born in Valencia, Venezuela.

Carina Chocano is the television critic for the *Los Angeles Times* and the author of *Do You Love Me, or Am I Just Paranoid: The Serial Monogamist's Guide to Love* (Villard, 2003), a satirical relationship guide. She lives in Los Angeles.

Angie Cruz, a New York born Dominicana, is the author of *Soledad* (Simon & Schuster, 2001). Her fiction and activist work have earned her numerous awards including the NYFA, Van Lier Literary Fellowship, and Barbara Deming Memorial Fund Award. She wrote this essay while in residence at the Camargo Foundation in Cassis, France, where she is at work on her second novel, tentatively titled

Let It Rain Coffee, forthcoming in spring 2005 (Simon & Schuster).

Jackie Guerra is the host of *Jewelry Making*, a new show on the DIY Network. The actress and comedienne also stars in PBS's Latino drama, *American Family*. Born in California, Jackie was one of the first Latinas to ever have her own sitcom. She has starred in numerous films, including *Selena* with Jennifer Lopez and *Picking Up the Pieces* with Woody Allen. She lives in Los Angeles.

Daisy Hernández is the coeditor of *Colonize This! Young Women of Color on Today's Feminism* (Seal Press, 2002). She has written a column for *Ms.* magazine, reported for the *New York Times*, and edited op-eds for the online magazine inthefray.com She's written for *Newsday*, the *National Catholic Reporter*, and *Bitch* magazine. She lives in San Francisco with Zami. Daisy is a Gemini.

Maria Hinojosa is CNN's urban affairs correspondent. Based in the network's New York bureau, Hinojosa joined CNN in 1997. Hinojosa has garnered numerous awards and honors, including the 2002 Latino Heritage Award from Columbia University and the Ruben Salazar Award from the National Council of La Raza, which recognizes a journalist's outstanding body of work. Hinojosa has written two books, the critically acclaimed memoir *Raising Raul: Adventures Raising Myself and My Son* and a book that grew from an award-winning story about gang members, *Crews— Gang Members Talk with Maria Hinojosa*.

Adriana López is the editor of *Críticas* magazine, published by *Publishers Weekly*. Formerly, she was the arts and culture editor at soloella.com. Her features, essays, and arts reviews have appeared in the *New York Times*, the *Washington Post*, and the *Los Angeles Times*, among many others. Her most recent essay, "Difficult Chicas," appeared in *Colonize This! Young Women of Color on Today's Feminism* (Seal Press, 2002). She is currently finishing her master's in journalism at Columbia University.

Letisha Marrero is a talented and versatile writer of many genres. Raised in San Diego, she currently resides in New York City. Her celebrity profiles, service pieces, and music reviews have been featured in *Latina*, *The Source*, and *Oneworld*, among others. She is also the author of *The Unauthorized Biography of Ricky Martin: Livin' La Vida Loca* (HarperCollins, 1999). Most recently, Marrero has been developing a fiction series for Hispanic teens.

Robyn Moreno is a writer/editor based in New York City. A native Texan, she is a former editor at *InStyle* and *Latina* magazines. She coauthored a fashion book, *Suave: The Latin Male* (Universe, 2001), and has written for *Woman's Day* and *Glamour*, among other national publications.

Michelle Herrera Mulligan is a writer originally from Chicago, Illinois. She's published articles in *Time*, *Publishers Weekly*, and *Teen People* magazines, among many others. She was an associate articles editor at *Latina* and coordinated a special issue of *Time Latin America* focusing on young Mexican leaders. She is currently working on her first novel.

Lorenza Muñoz was born in Mexico City. At the age of six she moved to California in 1977 with her family. After a brief stint working on the Kathleen Brown gubernatorial campaign, she began working at the *Los Angeles Times*. She has been at the paper since 1994 and has covered a range of topics, including politics, breaking news, and now the entertainment industry. She lives in Santa Monica with her husband and infant son.

Nelly Rosario was born in the Dominican Republic and raised in Brooklyn, where she now lives. She received a BA in engineering from MIT and an MFA in fiction writing from Columbia University. She is the author of the novel *Song of the Water Saints* (Pantheon Books, 2002), which won the 2002 Pen Open Book Award. She was named a "Writer on the Verge" by the *Village Voice Literary Supplement* in 2001. She's working on her second novel.

Lynda Sandoval is a former police officer-turned-novelist with fourteen books and numerous short stories and articles to her credit. She's the author of *Unsettling*, forthcoming from Rayo in May 2004, and also writes young-adult novels for Simon & Schuster and romance novels for Harlequin Books. She still doesn't speak Spanish . . . but she regrets that particular act of rebelliousness and she definitely wants to learn. She's based in Denver, Colorado.

Laura Trujillo has been an editor and reporter for newspapers across the country for over ten years, including the *Albuquerque Tribune* and the *Oregonian* (Portland). Currently, she edits *Yes* magazine, the *Arizona Republic's* fashion magazine. She resides in Phoenix, Arizona, with her husband and her three sons.

Shirley Velásquez is a freelance writer living in New York City. She was an associate editor at *Ms.* magazine, and her articles have appeared in various publications, ranging from the *South China Morning Post*, to *Críticas*, and *Complex* magazine.

Carmen R. Wong is currently an editor at *Money* magazine. She has a master's degree in psychology from Columbia University and an undergraduate degree in art history and psychology from Fairfield University. She formerly worked in public relations and spent several years in the art business, primarily at Christie's auction house, where her last post was as business manager of the Latin and South American offices. She currently resides in Brooklyn with her fiancé.

ACKNOWLEDGMENTS

From Robyn Moreno: I would like to thank my beautiful mother, Yvonne, for encouraging my independence, inspiring me to be a lady, and instilling in me the virtues of compassion and persistence. A triple thank-you to my lovely sisters: Nevia, Yvette, and Bianca. Your love and support have allowed me to succeed in the world, while your humor and fierce honesty have kept me real. I would be lost without you.

To all the inspiring women in my family: My grandmothers, Ruth Vela and Natalia Moreno, who are my beacons of grace and style; and my numerous aunts and cousins whose sass and sexiness embodied what it was to be a Latina, long before I knew the word.

To the tough hombres in the family who had to put up with us feisty Latinas, especially: Mac, JJ, VJ, Zach, and the "Godfather," Julio Vela.

A special thanks to my fellow Tejana friends, who are too numerous to mention.

I owe a very special thanks to mon amour, David Stephan, for your constant encouragement, and for being a sweetheart while I worked during our vacations. And finally to El Rey, my father Rudy Moreno, for everything I do is in your honor.

From Michelle Herrera Mulligan:

My eternal thanks go to my brothers: Dan, for his endless strength and optimism and Rick, for lifelong guidance. You both taught me how to be bull-headed and giving at the same time. Thanks, Mom, for always accepting me and encouraging me to rely on myself.

Thanks, Dad, for turning off the TV for two years and for suggesting I could make a living at writing. I would like to thank my love, Bryan Vargas, whose daily, unfailing support sustains me. Thanks for putting food on the table, making me laugh, and being my live-in sounding board.

Thanks to all the friends and family whose lives exemplify Latino cool, especially Andy and Alicia Perez, and Ed Morales, for putting it all on the page. Thanks to Avelina, Roberto, Felipe, Fernándo, Gerardo, Alma, Mario, Tamara, Alan, Uriel, Elijah, Omar, and my abuelitas, Alma and Shirley. Your unconditional love for each other defines Latino for me.

From both of us:

First of all, we must bestow our deepest gratitude to our sweet chicken, Tamara Ikenberg, for giving a name to our labor of love. To our agent, Joy Tutela: thanks for believing in our project and for having a ridiculous amount of patience. You're the best! To Rene Alegria, our editor, thank you for the incredible opportunity: you're a legend in the making. Un abrazo to the brilliant Andrea Montejo, for your amazing edits and vision. Our deepest thanks go to the phenomenal contributors whose essays appear in this collection. Thanks for your patience through exhausting rewrites, your bravery through the sharing of painful truths, and your generous time for two long years, as well as the invaluable advice. We're forever grateful.

A profound gracias del fondo de nuestro corazón to Julia
Álvarez and her agent, Susan Bergholz, for hearing us out and
sharing inspirational wisdom in the foreword. Thanks for letting us stand on your shoulders.

A special thanks to La Maestra Sandra Cisneros, for giving
such a beautiful voice to our experience. You have set the standard very high and we are so much better for it. Thanks to
Cathi Hanauer for editing *The Bitch in the House*, and inadvertently moving us in the right direction.

We are profoundly grateful to Carolina Garcia-Aguilera,
Raquel Rivera, Luz Maria Castellanos, Juleyka Lantigua, Fabi-
ola Santiago, Carmen Armillas, Celia San Miguel, Betty
Cortina, Ivette Manners, Suzan Colon, Sandy Fernández, Car-
olina González, Alisa Valdes-Rodriguez, Macarena Hernández,
Veronica Chambers, Michelle Serros, Marta Lucia Vargas,
Cristina Ibarra, Erica González, Dawn Valadez, Elizabeth
Aguilera, and all the women who shared their wonderful sto-
ries with us. Your words and conversation inspired this process,
and helped us define the Latina experience.

Our sincerest gratitude to Kevin Nance, August Darnell,
and Joseph Greenburg for granting the permission to run the
lyrics of their beautiful song, "There but for the Grace of God
Go I."

We'd also like to thank the friends who've encouraged us
and helped us in innumerable ways, enduring endless neurosis
and long talks about this book, including Carmen and Brian
Letscher, Deborah Moss, Victor Gallo, Lisa Martin, Irasema
Rivera, Laura Warrell, Jennifer Ortega and the irrepressible
Bianca Moreno. We couldn't have done this without your be-
hind-the-scenes help.